THE HOLY SPIRIT
AND
THE PRAYER BOOK

THE TRINITY SEASON
BEING VIEWED AS A LONG
WHITSUNTIDE

BY
JAMES HAUGHTON, A.M.

WITH A FOREWORD
BY
THE BISHOP OF ALBANY

PHILADELPHIA
THE JOHN C. WINSTON COMPANY
1911

TO THOSE
CHILDREN OF THE CHURCH,
STILL IN THIS LIFE, OR ALIVE IN CHRIST FOR EVERMORE,
WHO WERE MY
PARISHIONERS AND FRIENDS
IN A
PERIOD OF FORTY-THREE YEARS,
IN THE DIOCESES OF
NEW HAMPSHIRE, ALBANY, NEW YORK
AND
PENNSYLVANIA,
THIS BOOK
IS AFFECTIONATELY INSCRIBED

FOREWORD

I have a sense of safety in recommending this book for two reasons:
First, because of the subject with which it deals, and because of what
I know in outline of the method of the deal, and still more because I
know the writer. The subject is certainly one of large and deep importance, and it concerns every one of us, in the very most essential and fundamental parts and phases of our Christian life.

W. C. DOANE.

Bishop's House, Albany
Lent, 1911

The grace of our Lord Jesus Christ, and the love of God, and the communion of the Holy Ghost be with you all.—2 Cor. 13: 14.

The love of the three Persons formed the covenant of grace from everlasting, in which they were equally and individually concerned. It is an error to suppose that we are indebted to one more than another of the divine Persons; for their love is but one and the same love, as their essential nature is one and the same.—Ambrose Serle.

PREFACE

Great themes call for great writers; call the louder if they are in any sense new; and it is certain that the present work would not have been taken in hand, had not such a work long appeared to me most desirable, while no writer was forthcoming to satisfy the desire. It is hoped that, in making the attempt, it has not been a fault to imagine an "audience" of very different ages and classes. As the Bishop of Albany has said in his necessarily brief, but very kind, Foreword, "the subject dealt with concerns every one of us." Somehow, and to my great pleasure, the privilege enjoyed, not many years since, of coming in weekly contact with the students of the Philadelphia Divinity School, has in this book seemed to repeat itself. Their faces and voices have often come to me; but with them have appeared other seminarians, and some of the younger clergy. Sunday School and Bible Class teachers, a layman, a thoughtful child, would "drop in" and listen for a while; and it was for the subject's sake. The Prayer Book concerned "every one."

So ran my dream, and the point of chief interest was the Trinity Season regarded as a long Pentecost. Careful readers of the Bible, seminarians, deacons, priests, and bishops, may find little that is new to them in the first Chapter. Chapter II,—on the Prayer Book and the Christian Year,—offers little that is not familiar to many.   Chapter III contains a question, and the attempted answer to it, to which thoughtful attention is invited.   It is in Chapter IV that the main thought of this book is developed; and the remaining portions are substantially the expansion and the application of it.

The question which suggests itself in connection with that chapter and to which "every one" is most urgently invited to give serious consideration, is not whether or no we are all making enough in the American Church to-day,—indeed in the Anglican Church as a whole,—of that study of the Person and Work of the Holy Spirit which Dr. Arthur Cleveland Downer says has been "strangely neglected by the Church throughout her history,"—making enough of the Blessed Spirit's part in the entire work of redemption from the moment of sin's entrance into the world on till the Second Advent of our Lord; of His essential and vital relation to the life of the individual Christian and the Church's life, to the unity of the Church, and its extension to the uttermost part of the earth. We shall all as one man reply, We are not: we speak, and especially think and act,—at least the greater number do,—as though we had scarcely heard whether there be a Holy Ghost.   If we do believe, and at times reflect upon, the first words of the third section of the Nicene Creed,—think of the Third Person as a person, and the Lord, and Giver of all life, and worship and glorify Him as we worship the Father and our Blessed Saviour Himself,—in what practical relationship to ourselves and to the Church corporately do we contemplate Him, and for what cause worship and glorify Him?

For example; we read in Romans 5 : 5, that "Hope maketh not ashamed because the love of God is shed abroad in our hearts by the Holy Ghost which is given unto us"; believe the assertion, in Gal. 5 : 22, that "The fruit of the Spirit is love"; but what of the Spirit's own love for us? Do we ever pray in the feeling of a prayer quoted by G. F. Holden from the Short Office of the Holy Ghost, "Blessed Spirit, shed Thy purest light within us, delighting us with Thy love"? More than a century ago an English devotional writer, Ambrose Serle, expressed himself thus:

"If God be love, then the Spirit is love, because the Spirit is God. He, as one of the parties in the everlasting covenant, loveth His people with an everlasting love. By Him also they are made sensible of the love of the Father and of the Son, when He sheddeth forth His own love upon their hearts. Without the love of the Spirit, they could not know, so they could not come up to, the love of the whole Trinity; for by Him alone it is shed abundantly upon all that are His, both in earth and heaven."

It is not often that Christians so speak in these days of the love of the Spirit for their souls. No, the question to which consideration is asked is, whether by regarding the entire second half of Christ's Year as intended,—and that by the Holy Spirit Himself,—to keep His, the divine Spirit's immanence and omnipotence and love in their various aspects before the mind of Christendom throughout that long period,— by preaching and teaching and singing of the love of the Spirit and His manifold life-giving and life-saving operations,—we shall not immensely forward His work, and so hasten the coming of the day of God.

This volume contains many citations;—some will

say, a little multitude of them; and may ask the reason why. These three reasons I think will justify them. A large number of them give needed support to arguments and conclusions which being new may therefore appear doubtful. Again, the old fundamental truths, transcendent and glorious, have found in these passages from well-known writers clear, accurate, and sometimes beautiful, expression. Finally, to say nothing of Sunday School teachers and other lay-people, many clergymen, beside being long and hard workers, with little time for books, own small libraries, and have not easy access to the large ones; and it is hoped that such will welcome the quotations. I am convinced that this book is much stronger and richer for having them; and am personally grateful to the many authors at whose door I have knocked.

In strong sympathy for Thackeray's wittily expressed predilection for the letter *I* as being the straight line which was the shortest distance between his own mind and heart and those of his readers, sharing his dislike for the conventional third-person-manner of expression among authors, I have reserved the privilege of using the first-person form, by occasion and as seldom as conveniently possible.

What now shall by way of grateful acknowledgment be said of the kind people who have shown interest in this work; by a quick look of interest when its subject was named, or by words of encouragement; through actual assistance, by books lent or named, manuscript listened to or read; by helpful criticism and counsel, and last but not least by intercessory prayer? It would be a pleasure to name them all: many in fact are included in the Dedication. Some should be named: Professor

Robinson of the Philadelphia Divinity School, and Dean
Groton; my long-time friend, once a parishioner,
the Bishop of Bethlehem; the Bishop-Coadjutor
elect of Pennsylvania; the Rector of St. Timothy's
Church, Roxborough; Bishop Lloyd, and the Rector
of Trinity Church, New York; my son, the Rector
of Exeter, and the Bishop and Bishop-Coadjutor of
New Hampshire; my always courteous successor in
Bryn Mawr and my good Rector in Paoli, giving
or lending books, and often asking, How goes the
work? the author of the Consecration of the Eucharist,
Dr. Gummey; Walther Koenig, Ph.D., of the Library
of Congress; and finally Mr. Charles H. Clarke, of
The John C. Winston Company, to whom I am in
many ways greatly indebted. With him, as with all
the others, the loadstar and inspiration has, I am sure,
been the Subject itself. If this book be judged "any
good," and "worth while," to these good people
under God be awarded a large part of the credit.

J. H.

BROOKSIDE FARM
CHESTER VALLEY, PAOLI, PA.
ST. LUKE, EVANGELIST
1911

CONTENTS

CHAPTER I

THE HOLY SPIRIT

CHAPTER II

THE PRAYER BOOK AND CHRISTIAN YEAR

CHAPTER III

THE HOLY SPIRIT AND THE PRAYER BOOK

CHAPTER IV

THE TRINITY SEASON

THE TRINITY SEASON—CONTINUED

THE HOLY SPIRIT

Come, Holy Ghost, our souls inspire,
And lighten with celestial fire.
Thou the anointing Spirit art,
Who dost thy sevenfold gifts impart.
Thy blessed unction from above
Is comfort, life, and fire of love.
Enable with perpetual light
The dulness of our blinded sight.
Anoint and cheer our soilèd face
With the abundance of thy grace.
Keep far our foes, give peace at home;
Where thou art guide, no ill can come.
Teach us to know the Father, Son,
And thee, of both, to be but One;
That through the ages all along
This may be our endless song:
Praise to thine eternal merit,
Father, Son, and Holy Spirit.

And I believe in the Holy Ghost, the Lord and Giver of Life, Who proceedeth from the Father and the Son; Who with the Father and the Son together is worshipped and glorified.— Nicene Creed.

The Holy Ghost is the very essential unity, love, and love-knot of the two persons, the Father and the Son; even of God with God. And He is sent to be the union, love, and love-knot of the two natures united in Christ, even of God with man.— Bishop Andrewes.

Piece out our imperfections with your thoughts.—Shakespeare.

(2)

CHAPTER I

THE HOLY SPIRIT

A preliminary chapter upon the doctrine of the Holy Spirit would seem to be called for, were it only by reason of the acknowledged fact that this cardinal article of the Christian faith has been much neglected in the theology of our time. To me it appears that the absence of any treatise upon the subject I have chosen is but one illustration of the same general neglect of a truth expressly declared in the Creeds of the Church Universal.

Bishop Welldon, whose volume on the Revelation of the Holy Spirit, published in 1902, is one of three recent treatises on the Spirit to which the Church is greatly indebted, wrote (page 3):

"May it be permitted to me to affirm my own belief, that no doctrine,—apart from the Incarnation itself,—is such a solace and strength to Christian hearts in the present difficult days as the Personality of the Holy Spirit. * * * In spite of its historical interest this truth has not been realized in its full practical importance. It has not been uniformly felt as a living influence upon all that Christians believe, and all that they do. How few churches, for example, have been dedicated to the Holy Spirit! How scanty is the contribution which sacred art or music or literature has made in the Christian centuries to the thought of that Spirit as informing and inspiring the Church of Christ! Yet an oblivion of the Holy Spirit characterizes the dark hours in the religious life of a Church or of an individual soul.

"If the New Testament is the standard of value or importance as between the various doctrines of the Christian Creed, then the doctrine of the Holy Spirit necessarily claims little less than a primacy of importance in the devout and reverent thought of the Christian world.   It is there more prominent than the doctrine of the Church.   In the Epistles as in the Gospels long passages turn upon the gift of the Spirit.   The promise of the Spirit, His nature, His functions, His descent at Pentecost, His subsequent operation, His relation to the human spirit, His testimony, His influence, and the graces and virtues of which He is the author are subjects constantly present to the Christians of the New Testament, and strangely forgotten by Christians in the later history of the Church.

"It is more prominent in the New Testament than the Holy Communion.   Even when such passages as occur in the sixth and fifteenth chapters of St. John's Gospel are taken in due reference to the mystical doctrine of the Eucharist, it remains true that the doctrine of the Holy Communion does not occupy so large a space as that of the Spirit in the pages of the New Testament.   To emphasize the former and neglect the latter is to violate the 'proportion of faith' in the New Testament."

I

What may be termed the economy of divine revelation has consisted in a gradual making known to man of divine secrets which concerned him.   Truths were unveiled historically, by events, rather than in systematic and ordered instruction, and when believers in God were "able to bear them."   No deep spiritual truth,—no "mystery,"—was "shown" until the occasion for it had come, and until there were disciples —learners—to whom it was possible and right to say: "Unto you it is given to *know* the mysteries of the Kingdom of God."

The greatest and most winning practical truth of Scripture, the Fatherhood of God, was rather latent than patent in the Old Testament. In Christ as God's only-begotten Son, and in His filial character and life and teaching as being that Son, the divine Fatherhood was "brought to light." The same is true of the Son as a universal Saviour and King. The Old Testament Messianic passages glowed with a light of their own, but now they shine yet more brightly, lighted up as they are by Christ's Advent and the wonderful history that followed,—by the revelations concerning Him in the Gospels, and most of all by the writings of Apostles and Prophets inspired by the Holy Ghost.

Reflection on these things prepares us to expect the same gradual unfolding of the truth about the Third Person in the Godhead, of which Bishop Welldon said, "there is a sense in which it overshadows the whole Bible; nowhere is it absent from the sacred writers' minds." We do not expect to find the secret told out plainly, in the ancient Scriptures. It was a revelation Israel could not "bear." Surrounded by nations who worshipped "gods many and lords many," the great matter was to teach them the Unity: "The Lord our God is one Lord" (Deut. 6 : 4).

Yet, when one studies the Old Testament in all its parts it is remarkable how much is said suggestive of a personal Divine Spirit. The Spirit of God "moves,"— or broods,—upon the face of the waters, at the Creation. Pharaoh says of Joseph: "Can we find such a one as this is, a man in whom the Spirit of the Lord is?" Jehovah says to Moses, in respect to Bezalel, chief of the workmen selected for the construction and adornment of the tabernacle: "I have filled him with the Spirit of God." In Job 26 : 13 it reads: "By His Spirit the Heavens are garnished," and in chapter 33 : 4

Job says of himself, "The Spirit of God hath made me." In Proverbs 1 : 23 we find: "Behold, I will pour out my Spirit unto you." Psalm 104, describing God's works in nature, in reference to animal life, says: "Thou sendest forth Thy Spirit, they are created."

It is in the Psalms, the later ones especially, that we begin to find allusions to the Spirit as working His beneficent work in the human soul, searching the conscience, and instructing man in the ways of right-eousness; as in Psalm 139: "Whither shall I go from Thy Spirit?" It has been thought to be a sign of the lateness of Psalm 51, that in it occurs the prayer: "Take not Thy holy Spirit from me; restore unto me the joy of thy salvation, and uphold me with thy free (that is, thy willing) Spirit."

For it is in the later Psalms and in the Prophets that we find these more spiritual petitions, and expectations of spiritual help and deliverance, as also stronger suggestions of a personal Spirit; in Isaiah 11: "The Spirit of the Lord shall rest upon him"; in chapter 32: "Until the Spirit shall be poured upon us from on high"; and in chapter 59: "The Spirit of the Lord shall lift up a standard against him." It is in Joel 2 that we find the distinct and most comforting promise, cited by St. Peter on the day of Pentecost as having begun then to be fulfilled: "It shall come to pass that I will pour out my Spirit upon all flesh."

II

The New Testament doctrine of the Spirit begins where the Old Testament doctrine breaks off:

"The Holy Spirit of the Gospels and the Acts, of the Epistles and the Apocalypse, is still God exerting power, especially life-giving power; the Spirit of God which moved on the face of the waters, which inspired the Prophets and the Psalmists, which guided Israel and dwelt in the hearts of those members of the nation who were Israelites indeed. But his presence under the New Covenant is manifested in the Conception and Baptism, the life and ministry of Jesus Christ; in the regeneration and renewal of the members of Christ; in the common life and work of His mystical Body, the Universal Church."

Here, as in the older Scriptures, the revelation is progressive, but at once there are clearer intimations of the Spirit's distinct personality. At the Baptism of our Lord the Spirit of God "descends," while a voice is heard coming from Another. It is the Father, who says of Jesus: "This is my beloved Son."

To the disciples going forth to teach of Him, Christ says: "It is not ye that speak, but the Spirit of my Father that speaketh in you."

The most significant of the many references are, first, those which bear on the Spirit's relation to Christ in His ministry and sacrificial work; in His official anointing at the Jordan; in His fasting and temptation, to which He is led, yes, driven by the Spirit; in His teaching, in which He "speaketh the words of God, for God giveth not the Spirit by measure unto him"; in His mighty works, performed by His own testimony with "the Finger of God," or "the Spirit of God" (Matt. 12 : 28; Luke 11 : 20); in the atoning sacrifice, for it was "through the eternal Spirit" that Christ's sacred human will "conquered its aversion to death and for love to His Father and His people made Him a sacrifice for sin without blemish, as a perfect offering." It is evident from St. Paul's words in Romans 8 : 11, that he saw in the Holy Ghost the efficient cause of our

Lord's resurrection: "If the Spirit of him that raised up Jesus from the dead dwell in you, he that raised up Christ from the dead shall also quicken your mortal bodies by his Spirit that dwelleth in you."

The interest the inspired Apostle has in thus revealing the divine Spirit's personal agency in Christ's glorious resurrection is a distinctly practical one. As it was with our Saviour, so will it be with us. The Spirit it is, who will "re-unite our human spirit to the proper dwelling, not as a mere tenement, but as a home insusceptible of further death." But does not a like practical interest, as respects the members of Christ, attach itself to the gracious and all-powerful Spirit's relation to our Lord's life in the flesh from beginning to end?

It is a matter for regret, that Kenotists, even moderate ones, have in some points gone too far in their commendable endeavor clearly to bring out the extent and manner of the Son of God's dependence on the Spirit as very Man. The present writer has experienced something of this regret in regard to an occasional discourse of his own, delivered, and printed, many years ago. Words were employed respecting the degree and manner of our Lord's dependence on the Holy Ghost during His life in the flesh, which to-day he would guard himself from using. While saying this he desires also to discharge his individual debt of gratitude to Bishop Frank Weston, of Zanzibar, for a work entitled "The One Christ." In this notable volume on a subject of lasting theological and practical interest the author has endeavored to follow, and as it seems to many has succeeded beyond any former writer in following, faithfully, "the evidence of the

Scriptures, interpreted within the limits set by the decrees of the Catholic Church, in no case transgressing a dogmatic ruling of the Church, or refusing to allow for a fact recorded in the Gospels."

In the Synoptic Gospels there are three passages only to which reference need be made here. They all bear with great force on our subject. There is, first, our Lord's saying: "If ye, evil as ye are, know how to give good things to your children, how much more shall your heavenly Father give the Holy Spirit to them that ask him?" The second passage is the one concerning the sin of denying the Spirit: "Whosoever speaketh a word against the Son of man, it shall be forgiven him; but whosoever speaketh a word against the Holy Ghost, it shall not be forgiven him, neither in this world, neither in the world to come." Nothing could have been uttered more distinctly implying the Spirit's personality, and the supreme importance of His work for and in man.

The third word is the formula for the administration of baptism. Believers are to be baptized in (or into) the Name of the Three Divine Persons. "Had the words run simply, 'into the Father and the Son and the Holy Spirit,' they might have been interpreted as merely implying the incorporation of believers by Christ's baptism into the fellowship of the Holy Trinity. But *into the name* seems to suggest the further thought of proprietorship. The baptized person is not only brought into union with the Three, but he is devoted to Their service, living thenceforth a consecrated life."

It is in St. John's Gospel and the Epistles of St. Paul that we find the most advanced teaching concerning the Spirit. This is one of the features in which the Fourth

Gospel has something of the character of an Epistle, as conveying to the Church, after the Lord's Ascension, truths which the disciples had not been "able to bear," in other words, spiritually to apprehend, before receiving the supreme gift of the Spirit. In this Gospel there is found the fulfilment of the Lord's promise that the Spirit would bring to the Church's remembrance "things" He had said. There is also a showing of the truth about Christ and His "things," for which believers were not prepared while He was present with them in the flesh. We must look then upon the rich revelations in the Fourth Gospel and St. Paul's Epistles respecting Christ's Spirit, the Comforter, the Teacher, and the One who should henceforth dwell in the Church, as truths communicated by the Spirit Himself. It was for Christ, and in fulfilment of His gracious promise, that the Holy Ghost imparted these truths.

It will be helpful, then, to the purpose of this book to give special attention to St. John's words. Let Dr. Swete be our guide here. (H. B. Swete, "The Holy Spirit in the New Testament," pages 72–168.) He tells us that in the earlier chapters the Holy Spirit is revealed as the author of the spiritual life to men individually; in the later ones we have the relation in which He will stand to the future Church as a brotherhood, represented by the company assembled in the upper room. He is the *other Advocate*, or Defender of the Church, and "the *Acta Martyrum*, the whole history of the Church, and the lives of countless believers who have no place in history, bear witness to the fulfilment of this office of the Paraclete-Spirit in the Body of Christ."

The world will be unconscious of His presence, for

the Spirit is sent to the Church, to "those disciples who have learned to apprehend spiritual things through fellowship with the Lord." The Son had come to reveal and to glorify the Father; the Spirit comes to reveal the Son, and will teach all that belongs to the sphere of spiritual truth in Christ. The "reminding" of Christ will go much farther than a mere recovery of the Lord's sayings. It will enable those who have been present to live through His ministry again with a new appreciation of its meaning, form the basis of the Apostles' teaching, and be "ultimately the nucleus of that great stream of tradition which has moulded Christian belief and practice from their time to our own." "The Truth given in Christ will," as Dr. Hort has said, "need from age to age His (the Spirit's) expounding to unlock its stores."

The Eleven had had their training and experience with the Lord, but without the gift of Pentecost these would have been barren of results; but on the other hand the gift of Pentecost would have yielded widely different results if it had not fallen on men who "were with Jesus" and could testify to what they had seen and heard. "This collaboration of the human witness with the Divine extends to the whole life of the Church, which is a continuous joint testimony of the Spirit and the Bride."

The Spirit would convict the conscience of sin. The very men who had cried "Crucify him" and reviled Him would in the light of the Spirit "turned on them" perceive that they had rejected God's only-begotten Son, and cry, "What shall we do?" The Spirit brings home to men, that by the life and death of Jesus Christ judgment has been passed on the ruler of this world.

This judgment is still in force and fruitful of results. The Spirit is causing men to realize it, and they live henceforth as knowing that since the Lord's Resurrection "the issues of the great struggle are determined, and every day is bringing nearer the final victory of righteousness and the final doom of sin."

The Spirit would thus shift the whole standpoint of human opinion with reference to Sin and Righteousness and the conflict between them. That He has done this is "to be seen to-day in the changed attitude of modern thought and practice when it is compared with that of Græco-Roman society in the time of our Lord. The modern world is far from being under the control of the Spirit of Christ, but pagan as it may remain in heart it has been convinced of certain great ethical truths, and can never return to the worst vices or the heartless selfishness of the older heathendom."

The Spirit was not to "speak of," or rather from, Himself. Christ had not spoken from Himself, in other words, was not the Source of His own teaching, but spoke what He had received from the Father; and the Spirit will but carry forward the same teaching, "essentially one with that of our Lord, since its Source was the same." He will interpret and expand and apply the Christ truths.

"He will declare the coming things; the things of that great and untried life which was about to open before the Church at the Pentecost, and to reach its perfection at the Second Coming; the things of the new age, the dispensation of the Spirit; and, less distinctly seen, the things of the more distant future when God shall be all in all. Thus, while this promise includes the revelations of the Christian Prophets, it covers also the whole unfolding before the Christian Society in the Apostolic writings, in the work of her Bishops and Doctors, and in the experience

of life, the ideals, the polity, and the prospects of the Body of Christ."

The Spirit would "glorify" Christ. How? asks Dr. Swete. "Not by shedding upon the Person and work of the Lord any new glory from without. All that a Paul or a John has said under the teaching of the Spirit about the glory of Christ is but a disclosure of that which is His essential character, His inalienable possession. They have brought much to light, but they have added nothing to the glory which He had with the Father before the world was."

And so "the intercommunion and interchange are absolute," writes Dr. Swete. "The Only-begotten interprets the Father; the Spirit interprets the Son, and the Father in the Son. Thus the revelation of God is completed by the coming of the Spirit."

III

Passing to the Acts, we reach at once the tremendous event of the First Whitsunday. The promised Spirit descends upon the Church of Christ. Instituted by Christ in the days between His Resurrection and Ascension, and more particularly in the moment when He breathed upon the disciples and said, "Receive ye the Holy Ghost," we may say that the Spirit Himself took part in that institution. Our Lord spoke and acted in the Spirit during those forty days. We are told that Christ then gave commandments to the Apostles whom He had chosen, "through the Holy Ghost."

It was, then, through the Spirit that Christ imparted the "firstfruits," the "earnest of the Spirit," a prophetic and typical action of the Son, throwing light forward on the Whitsunday event as a *sending* of the Holy Spirit by the Father and the Son. This event itself, following upon the glorious Ascension of our Lord to the Father, when all power is given to Him in heaven and earth as the triumphant God-man, is a veritable Epiphany of the Third Person in the Godhead. He now in His turn has come into the world to be known as God, but as the Spirit of the Incarnate Son, risen and glorified and dwelling as Man in heaven. The "signs" with which His coming is announced are the insignia of a Divine presence and power. Scarcely would a Christian Jew who knew his Genesis, and his Job, and Psalms of Nature like the 97th, fail to recognize in the mighty wind and the fire evidences of the presence of the Creator-Spirit.

Named Acts of the Apostles, the Book we have now to examine is much more what the late Dr. A. T. Pierson was moved to call it, "The Acts of the Holy Spirit"; for, while engaged in carrying forward the work of Christ in the world, the Spirit is necessarily revealing Himself all through this first chapter in the history of the Church and of Missions.

Should we not anticipate this? Are we not taught to worship Him as no less than that

> "Creator-Spirit, by whose aid
> The world's foundations first were laid"?

The Agent in the incarnation of God's Son, and with Him throughout His entire earthly experience, He is present and active now as Life-giver and Guide to His Church.

If it be objected that in the New Testament Christ is set forth as the Builder and Maker of His Church, as also of the World at the beginning, in Colossians 1st, where it reads, "by Him were all things created," "by Him all things consist," in Hebrews 1st, "His Son, whom He appointed heir of all things, through

whom also He made the worlds"; I reply, that the
more correct rendering is, "in Him were all things
created, and in Him all things consist." What is
most striking in the Trinity as revealed in Holy Scripture, is the different yet perfectly ordered and harmonious working of the Three. The Father created all
things in heaven and earth in (or through) the Son, and
for Him; but by the Holy Ghost.

He is the Vicar of the ascended and unseen Lord.
The scene opens with Him at the head and in charge,
"the Lord, the Spirit." At the outset He is designated
the Holy Ghost through whom Jesus had "given
commandment unto the apostles whom He had
chosen." Matthias is chosen in the place of Judas,
a traitor in fulfilment of words spoken anciently by the
Holy Ghost. St. Peter's Pentecostal sermon opens
with the promise of the Spirit, in Joel. They upon
whom the gift comes, speak as the Spirit gives them
utterance. Always He is referred to as a Person, and
that a divine Person. When Ananias and Sapphira lie
regarding the price of the possession they have sold,
they "lie to the Holy Ghost." St. Stephen says to
the unbelieving Jews, ready to stone him to death,
"Ye do always resist the Holy Ghost; as your fathers
did so do ye." What more personal and divinely
authoritative utterance than the word to Philip, going
down from Jerusalem to Gaza and beholding the
Eunuch? "Then the Spirit said unto Philip, Go near
and join thyself to this chariot." When St. Peter,
obedient to a vision, has gone to the Roman Cornelius,
who obedient to another vision has sent for him, and
the first apostolic word to the Gentiles has been spoken,
the Holy Ghost falls "on all them which heard the

word," and clear it is that the visions have been sent, and this same forward step of the Church has been taken, in obedience to the Spirit.

Later, in Antioch, where prophets and teachers are assembled, fasting and praying and waiting for guidance, a yet more important step is taken, and the Holy Ghost it is who is described as ordering it. He appears here as Lord, as truly as Jesus is Lord; saith, "Separate me Barnabas and Saul for the work whereunto I have called them." They go on that unexpected and momentous missionary journey through Asia Minor, being "sent forth by the Holy Ghost."

The first Church Council is held in Jerusalem; and from it a message goes to the believers in Antioch in respect to the question in regard to circumcising the Gentile believers in Christ, Thus and so let it be done, for so it hath "seemed good to the Holy Ghost, and to us."

"The Holy Ghost," said St. Paul, "testifieth unto me in every city, saying that bonds and afflictions abide me." Perhaps the most remarkable indication,—in various senses remarkable, and suggestive as regards the divine method in missions,—is the instance of the Spirit's plain interference with St. Paul's plan to preach Christ in the little district called Asia, and, when hindered from so doing, again in the region named Bithynia. It was clearly the purpose of the Spirit not to sacrifice time then for the sake of work near home, but to push on with all speed to make Christ known in distant lands. It meant sowing the seed without delay in Europe. Nowhere can one perceive more distinctly the wisdom and the will of that Third Person in the Godhead to Whom the sowing

and gathering of the Lord's harvest had been committed. We Christians of the West were more concerned in that authoritative decision, and insistency,
of the Holy Spirit, than we have been capable of realizing the same. We may rightly feel that for us was
composed the verse of Hymn 262:

> "To Thee, O Holy Ghost, Whose gracious rain
> And living breath hath fed the ghostly grain,
>   We sing our Alleluia!"

IV

Having seen how clearly the Spirit's divine personality is manifested in action in the book named Acts, we
turn to the Epistles, and behold the same truth exhibited in a different way. It is in the way of thought and
interpretation. Rightly understood,—taken in connection with Christ's "promise of the Spirit,"—these
Epistles contain a fuller revelation of Gospel truth than
the Gospels themselves. I say this with emphasis.
Many have thought to find the purest, truest message
about Christ, if not the whole message, in Christ's
own words spoken on earth. How can this be the
case in view of His words regarding the Spirit as
Another Teacher, who should guide His people into
all the truth concerning Himself? that truth would
include His Sacrifice on the Cross, His Resurrection,
His Ascension to the throne of God in His glorified
Manhood. How could the deep and infinitely far-
reaching significance of those events be unfolded to
humanity before they had taken place? We may be
sure that fewer thoughtful and earnest Christians
would have made this mistake, had the doctrine of the
Spirit not been indeed "sadly neglected."

Taking up the Epistle of St. James, as probably the first inspired letter written to Christians, what do we find? At the outset it would appear that we find nothing. If, however, certain trustworthy commentators are right in interpreting the words in the fifth verse of the fourth chapter, translated: "The spirit that dwelleth in us lusteth to envy" (in the Revised Version: "Doth the spirit which he made to dwell in us long unto envying?"—in Mayor's free translation, "jealously yearn for the entire devotion of the heart?"), as referring to the Holy Spirit, we have one of the most touching utterances concerning Him in the entire New Testament. Moving and pathetic indeed were those passages in the ancient writings which represented Jehovah as yearning for Israel's love and devotion. One glance back to the verse before, "Ye adulteresses, know ye not that the friendship of the world is enmity with God?" convinces us that we are on the track of the divine thought. Father, Son, and Holy Ghost, the Three in One, love man with a love that has the first claim; and through the Pentecostal Spirit it is that this claim is now revealed, and every day pressed upon us, with a jealous affection.

Passing to 1st Thessalonians, also a very early letter, we find a like earnest word of St. Paul, which, as Dr. Downer has pointed out, leads the mind at once to the thought of Pentecost. "'Quench not the Spirit,'" he says, "looks back to the fiery tongues, which, though invisible, still burn in the Christian's heart."

The phrase, "God, who hath also given unto us his Spirit—the Holy" (chapter 4: 8), gives a strong impression alike of Personality and Divinity.

In 1st Corinthians 2 : 10, "The Spirit searcheth the

deep things of God," conveys the same twofold impression. (Dr. A. C. Downer, "Mission and Ministration of the Holy Spirit," pp. 147, 149.)

It remains to give a brief glance at other words in the Epistles bearing on this truth. In 1st Corinthians 12 : 11, we find the Spirit spoken of as dispensing different spiritual gifts to men as He wills; find in Romans 8 : 6, "The mind of the Spirit is life and peace." In Romans 15 : 30 the Apostle asks for the prayers of the saints, blessing them "for the Lord Jesus Christ's sake, and for the love of the Spirit." In Ephesians 4 : 30 he writes, "Grieve not the Holy Spirit of God in whom ye were sealed unto the day of redemption." It is as though he had in mind a careful housekeeper who has sealed and put away something she would keep pure and sweet, worthy of being brought forth and used on a day of joy and feasting. Think of her disappointment, in an hour when it is brought forth neither sweet nor worthy. So the Holy Spirit is grieved when men baptized, sealed, set apart for Christ, are found full of bitterness and wrath and anger, and the like. Dr. Torrey has asked us to think of a mother's grief, when a son, who has been brought up in ways of filial obedience and purity, forsakes them.

There is the remarkable passage concerning the Spirit's intercession, going on within us while God's Son intercedes for us before the Throne of heaven. It is the Other Advocate, befriending us in His own way, identifying Himself with our very personality. It is "with groanings that cannot be uttered." Silently, secretly, as when, by the Spirit's instrumentality, the wondrous gift was given to our race of which the children sing in the dear Christmas-tide, and as when the Christ-life is imparted to us individually at the sacred font, the same Spirit communicates to the soul the longing for divine forgiveness or help, which, "uttered or unexpressed," is prayer. Must it not be a Divine Spirit,—a Personal Spirit,—equal in essence with the Father and the Son, that can do this, and will in His love do it, in Christians "throughout the world?"

V

Coming, finally, to the Apocalypse, the same truth is conveyed to our minds. We are not confused by the mention of seven spirits before the throne. Seven is a mystical number in the Scriptures. It suggests completeness, and evidently these spirits before the throne are the various operations of the One Spirit who is on the throne. So do the seven Churches represent all the Churches that are, or ever will be, living branches of Christ's One Church Catholic. If, now, a message of grace and peace comes, through St. John, to these Churches, from the Eternal Father, and "from Jesus Christ," and also "from the seven spirits," must not the Holy Ghost be also an Eternal and Divine Person?

St. John has a vision of the Ascended Jesus in his glorified Manhood, and He, who, having been dead, is now alive for evermore, bids him, "Write." He writes a message to every Church; but at the end of each are the words: "Hear what the *Spirit saith* to the Churches." When we come to the end of the book, we have the Church earnestly praying for the second advent of her Lord; St. Peter expresses it, "hastening the day of the Lord" by her prayers; but the Spirit is, in like manner, inviting Him. In the words of Dr. Downer: "The great Book closes with the Spirit and the Bride, the Church of Christ, testifying in combination to the second coming of the Lord Jesus, and responding to His announcement, 'Behold, I come quickly,' with the intense and impassioned appeal, 'Come.'"

We shall have occasion later to make practical use of some of the truths which we have been engaged in noting; but before passing to the next section, shall we not pause to underline, as with a pencil, this one thought? Our Lord's promise to His Church, recorded in the fourteenth and fifteenth chapters of St. John, of another, evidently divine, Person, who should abide with it forever,—taken in connection with the first, great, inspired chapter of Christian missions, Acts of the Apostles, Acts of the Holy Ghost, and interpreted by abundant references to Him in the Epistles and the Apocalypse,—prove the Anglicized Greek word Paraclete to be a word of the richest and most comprehensive significance. The Spirit was to be,—and, when the Church will let Him and invoke Him to be, He is,— all that Christ could be to her. He is, as it were, Christ Himself to the Church, until Christ shall come again; not Teacher and Comforter, Advocate and Intercessor only; not merely "Fount of life, and Fire of love"; but also Guide and Leader. We must think of Him as called to the side of the divine-human Lord, as truly as to our side, His Paraclete as well as ours. Mystically He takes the place of Christ, being His Vice-gerent, or Vicar, in the Church Universal, for the time being deputed, or authorized, to perform His manifold divine functions, "the Lord, the Spirit."

The idea of the Latin Church, that our Lord would not have gone to the Father without leaving to His Church throughout the world just such a consoler, friend, and guide, in whom His own leadership and authority should be vested, was wholly true to our Lord's thought and purpose. Its tremendous, fateful, mistake has consisted in believing that such a glorious heavenly office could be occupied either by a woman, though it were His own blessed mother,—as Chaucer has it (cited in the Century Dictionary),

"He hath thee [the Virgin] maked vicaire and mistresse
 Of al the world,"

—or by a succession of men, fallible, or miraculously infallible.

God in His loving providence has prevented the error of Rome from being fatal to His Church and to humanity. He has overruled it, made it at times work for good, as we shall have opportunity to see. But it has also wrought an incalculable amount of harm. One evil feature has been that the false idea, the caricature, has for centuries veiled, if not hidden, the true one. The reprobate silver, being stamped with the image and superscription of the King, has served in great degree to depreciate the royal money. In other words, the dream of an infallible, supremely authoritative human Vicar of Jesus Christ on earth, has helped to obscure the prophetic vision, yes, the clearly announced, and at Pentecost clearly confirmed, truth, of an all-powerful, all-wise Leader, Guide, and Protector of the Church, the unseen, ever-present Paraclete.

Is it too much to affirm, that if the Church Catholic had conserved her unity, and integrity of credal faith, in the Spirit, been always conscious of His presence, invoked Him in Councils that were universal, and obeyed Him as the true Vice-gerent of Christ, she would have been practically infallible in every age?

VI

The task which now lies before is the comparatively easy one of ascertaining what has been from the beginning the Church's voice in regard to the Spirit, and the answer may in large part be given in the words of Dr. James Orr ("Progress of Dogma," 2d ed., page 125):

"The earliest age of the Church shows little trace of reflection on the doctrine of the Holy Spirit. From the first the Church acknowledged the Threefold name of Father, Son, and Spirit, and so, implicitly, may be said to have confessed the deity and personality of the Spirit. But there was no dogmatic treatment of the subject. The Church possessed the Spirit, and did not feel the need of discussing it. For long the wealth of material in the Apostolic Epistles lay unexplored. The Apostolic Fathers are for the most part content to use the Scriptural phrases.

"The deity and personality of the Spirit are fully recognized by Irenæus, Tertullian, Clement and Origen. Tertullian expressly calls Him 'God,' and lays stress on His unity of essence with Father and with Son. When the Nicene formula was written, in 325 A.D., it only said briefly as a kind of appendage to the Creed, 'And in the Holy Ghost.' It was apparently taken for granted that the personality and deity of the Son being confessed, that of the Spirit would be acknowledged also, as, in fact, it had not hitherto been challenged by any section of the Catholic Church.

"The subject came up in a council held in Alexandria, in 362 A.D., and the denial of the Spirit was there formally branded as heresy.

"It was when the Macedonian heresy came up, so named as espoused by Macedonius, the deposed bishop of Constantinople, 'a violent and unscrupulous man,' that the question was fully and finally settled, and in 381 A.D. the enlarged clause in the Nicene Creed was inserted, which makes explicit the divinity of the Spirit: 'And (I believe) in the Holy Ghost, the Lord, and Giver of Life; who proceedeth from the Father; who with the Father and the Son together is worshipped and glorified; who spake by the prophets.'"

It was a great step forward, and one that needed to be taken. To this voice of the Church Universal all Christendom has listened ever since, recognizing that it could only be the truth concerning Him into whose sacred Name, together with the Name of the Son and the Name of the Father, every Christian is baptized. Because he is so baptized, and not merely "Christened," made a member of that Body which, being the Body of Christ, is dwelt in and endued with all spiritual life and power by the Holy Ghost, there follows at once in that ancient Creed: "And I believe in one Catholic and Apostolic Church; I acknowledge one Baptism for the remission of sins."

It is a truth generally conceded, that the language of Christian worship is at all times likely to bear truer witness to what Christian people believe than does any theological statement. Hymn 446 of our Hymnal, beginning:

"Shepherd of tender youth"

was composed by Clement, of Alexandria. It ante-dates the Nicene Creed by about a century and a half, and it bears fullest possible witness to the Church's belief in Christ's Divinity. He is "our triumphant King," our "holy Lord," and the "all-subduing Word," the "great High Priest," the "Christ of God."

"Let all the holy throng
Who to Thy Church belong,
Unite and swell the Song
To Christ our King!"

Again, the New Testament Scriptures were for a much longer period than most Christians are apt to imagine known only in parts, and not equally everywhere. "For generations," writes Dr. John Fulton, "different Churches had different parts of Holy Scripture, and few had them all. But all of them," he adds, "possessed and held the Christian Faith." He might have said also the Christian Institutions. They kept Sunday and not the Sabbath. They celebrated the Eucharist as a remembrance of the Lord's Resurrection. This "breaking of bread" on every First Day, and the prayers and hymns which accompanied it, constitute a more venerable testimony to New Testament truth than the sacred writings themselves. As Dr. Fulton says, the latter, when better known and more used, "were regarded rather as means to faith than as objects of faith."

Having, then, heard the witness of the Scriptures, and of the Church voicing its conviction in General Councils, and in theological writings, regarding the Spirit's divine Personality, why should we not hear the testimony of the Prayer Book itself,—that is to say, in its oldest portions? What have these to tell us concerning the early Church's thought about the divine Personality of the Holy Spirit?

Let us look then at *Gloria in Excelsis*, which is, as Dr. Hart tells us, "an Eastern hymn, found in its full form, as is well known, about the year 450 A.D.; in the East it is a daily morning hymn, not used as with us in the Holy Communion." Of this early hymn to Christ, which begins with the angels' song over Bethlehem's hills, the final words are: "Thou only, O Christ, with the Holy Ghost, art most high in the glory of God the Father."

Te Deum laudamus is probably a little older than *Gloria in Excelsis*, being now thought to have originated about the year 400, and it sings how the Church throughout the world acknowledges not only the Father of an infinite majesty, and His adorable, true and only Son, but "also the Holy Ghost, the Comforter."

In harmony with these expressions are the words which conclude the ancient Prayer of Consecration in the Eucharist: "Through Jesus Christ our Lord, by whom and with whom, in the unity of the Holy Ghost, all honor and glory be unto thee, O Father Almighty, world without end."

The Service of Holy Communion has come down to us, with the *Te Deum* and *Gloria in Excelsis*, from what may be termed the Nicene age. Together with the two Creeds they bear the same witness to the truth of the Holy Spirit's personality which the Bible bears, from Genesis to Revelation. What is particularly to be remarked about the testimony afforded in this and other points by the Liturgy, is, first, that it represents the consciousness of the Church, rather than the dogmatic statements of a Creed like that of Nicæa and Chalcedon, and secondly, that it is a universal consciousness:

"The diverse liturgies, Syrian, Egyptian, Latin, and others, representing widely separated lands, are found all to agree so extraordinarily in a number of points as to prove conclusively that at some point in the Church's history there arose a tradition as to what a Eucharistic service should be, which tradition absolutely dominated the Church throughout its length and breadth."

The more one studies liturgical history the easier it becomes to receive this assertion, in its substance, and also in the manner of it, except, perhaps, in one point. If the Holy Spirit was to be the very Mind and Soul of the Church, interpreting the Will of her ascended Lord, might not the above mentioned and other dominating *traditions* better be frankly attributed to the Spirit, as patterns of sound words, and a deposit, distinctly committed to her by her unseen, ever-present Friend and Guide?

If the amendment I have ventured to offer be accepted, then is the witness of these most venerable portions of our Book regarding the Spirit,—like that in the Scripture and the historic Creeds,—a testimony of the Spirit about Himself. In all these ways the Holy Spirit, while showing us the things of Christ, incidentally, as it were, and yet to good purpose, shows us His own heavenly credentials.

Bearing this in mind, and resuming the argument, I bring forward certain Collects, demonstrably thirteen to fifteen centuries old, and in all probability many years older; and first, the Collect for Whitsunday, the Spirit's Day. Coming to us from the Sacramentary of Gregory, A.D. 590, we pray in it for the gifts of the Spirit, "through the merits of Jesus Christ our Saviour, Who liveth and reigneth with Thee, in the unity of the same Spirit, one God, world without end." The Trinity Sunday Collect, in which we implore "grace by the confession of a true faith to acknowledge the glory of the eternal Trinity," is derived from the same venerable source. A century earlier yet were composed the Collects for Ascension Day and the Sunday after, and both speak of Christ as "living and reigning with the Father and the Holy Ghost, one God, world without end." That for the Nineteenth Sunday after Trinity reads: "O God, forasmuch as without Thee we are not able to please Thee, mercifully grant that Thy Holy Spirit may in all things direct and rule our hearts."

Thus does the Prayer Book breathe the atmosphere and voice the belief of primitive Christianity as regards the truth with which this chapter is concerned. It shows what the Church had been holding as true in respect to the Spirit, during the three centuries since St. John died, while the doctrine of the Spirit was yet unformed, its "rational expression," as Neander termed it, not yet clearly manifesting itself. Strange that when His power made itself so mightily felt in the life as a new creative and forming principle, the consciousness of His identity with the essence of God was yet "far from being thoroughly apprehended and presented in conceptions of the understanding." Dr. Allen's thought is opportune here; that

"it was necessary that the Incarnation should become the full possession of the Christian consciousness before the life of the Spirit could be understood or appreciated. He was leading humanity into all truth, but His 'ways' had yet to be disclosed more fully to the reason in the long and painful process of experience,—the world that then was had to pass away, and a new world to arise, and grow, and reach maturity, before the life of God as the Spirit could be revealed in humanity as its actual possession, by which it shares on earth in the glory of the eternal Trinity, and moves forward to its destiny in attaining the fulness of Christ." (" Continuity of Christian Thought," p. 93.)

The results of deficient attention to the study and preaching of the Third Person in the early Christian centuries, and in the Reformation period, have appeared, according to Dr. Dowden (page 6):

"in dryness of spiritual experience, a low level of Christian life, formalism in worship, want of discipline in the Church, want of zeal in missionary enterprise, indifference to social improvement, and continual schisms embittered by partisan rivalry.

"Notwithstanding this failure, however, a list has been compiled of upwards of twelve hundred books, or parts of books, belonging to all ages of the Church, and written by authors of widely divergent views, together constituting a library of the literature of the doctrine of the Holy Ghost.

"During the last hundred years increasing attention has been directed to the subject, and many works by English writers have been issued, treating of one or more of its many aspects. * * * Missions to the unevangelized world are being treated by many contemporary writers as the characteristic outcome of Pentecost. The movement for the Deepening of Spiritual Life devotes its literature to the operation of the Holy Ghost upon the individual soul.   The literature of the Sacraments, which once took too little account of the necessary presence and action of the Holy Spirit, now seeks to remedy the omission.   The nascent movement towards Home Reunion gives opportunity for applying the teaching of the unity of the Spirit, a doctrine powerfully inclining Christian men towards a restoration of the broken unity of the Church."

A more hopeful sign of the times, spiritually speaking, a brighter harbinger for the twentieth century of the Church's life in the Spirit, could hardly be named than the appearance of many treatises, great and small, devoted in whole, or in part, to the Person and Work of the Holy Spirit, to the fruits of the Spirit in the individual soul, and, perhaps at this time most especially, to His relations to the Church as the Body of Christ, and to its World-Mission.

Let us recall again our Lord's word: "Unto you it is given to know the mystery (the secret) of the Kingdom of God." Shall we not take Him *at* His word, never turn from any secret revealed to us, either by Himself, or later by His Spirit? We are made in the likeness of God, to apprehend now, and eventually to comprehend, not God's things only, but God. Of the earth and earthy now, we shall bear the image of the heavenly, and understand all mysteries. The process has begun. The pure in heart already see and know God in the degree that they are spiritual, and desirous to be initiated.

It is sin which has separated man from God, and the knowledge of God. The Son of God has brought the possibility of fellowship and communion, and a corresponding increase of knowledge. Look at the story of Eden whichever way you will, as history or a parable, it is full of truth, and we must think of the cherubim at the gate as keeping the way, not only of the tree of life, but of the tree of wisdom and understanding; and before the believing and pure their flaming swords go down.

This is true of the Kingdom of Nature, which, equally with the heavenly one, is a Kingdom of the Creator-Spirit. In this natural and earthly kingdom we are surrounded by secrets. There lies a hidden and at present incomprehensible power which we call mystery under every truth of science or philosophy. The wiser the scientist or philosopher is, the better he knows it; and being a Christian confesses and rejoices in it. Gravitation, cohesion, magnetism, chemical affinity, electricity, are all at bottom divine secrets, and yet secrets in a measure told, and of vast practical importance.

The doctrine of the Spirit is no remote or esoteric thing, but that wherein God touches man most nearly, most familiarly, in common life. We can see why St. Basil, fifteen centuries ago, explained St. Paul's mention of the Spirit first, and then the Son and then the Father (1st Cor. 12 : 6) as being according to the nature of things. We come in contact first with the Distributor, then consider the Sender, then carry back our thought to the Fount and Cause of all good things.

All good things, natural or spiritual, temporal or eternal, are created and brought to us, and we are created to enjoy and use them, by the Spirit. "By the word of the Lord were the heavens made, and all the host of them by the breath of His mouth." It is the sending forth of the breath of God which is the giving to things of the gift of life; it is the withdrawal of that breath which is their annihilation. This is the teaching of the Scriptures about nature, and the early Christians were keenly conscious of it. They faulted Origen, because he seemed to exclude the Holy Spirit from nature, and limit His activity to the Church.

"Wherever the Holy Spirit is," wrote Ambrose, "there is life; and wherever life is, there is also the Holy Spirit." Hardly any truth is of greater practical importance, or has a more beneficial influence upon character, than this, that the spiritual world is the real and lasting world, and that only in so far as we are spiritual are we truly ourselves, and fit for an unending existence and undying joy. And because God is love and is holy, and His Spirit is a Holy Spirit, our spirits must be holy.

Our conflict is largely, chiefly, a struggle with spiritual foes, with the prince of the unseen "powers of the air," and we are to conquer these with spiritual weapons, as Christ the Second Adam did, by the Holy Spirit's help, with His sword which is the word of God, and by prayer in the Spirit.

The spiritual life, then, is the true and blessed life for every man, and nature being the creation and the daily, hourly care of the Spirit, is by all its marvellous operations, its wonderful unseen forces, its harmony and beauty, to remind us that we are spirits, and help us to be spiritual. One of the most interesting and suggestive features of Bishop Whipple's story of his life in the Episcopate consists in his testimony concerning the Indians (page 34):

"I have never known of an atheist among the North American Indians. They believe unquestioningly in a future life. They believe that everything in nature—the laughing waterfall, the rock, the sky, the forest—contains a divinity, and all mysteries are accounted for by these spirits which they call manidos. The Ojibways are not idolaters; they never bow down and worship any created thing. They have preserved a tradition of one Supreme God whom they call 'Kitche-manido,'—the uncreated, or the kind, cherishing Spirit."

Whence do these people, and these traditions of the Great Spirit come? Is it a cause for wonder that large numbers of them have responded as quickly as they have to the Church's message of an unseen Christ,—present by His Spirit,—and that a very large proportion of them have become Christians, not a few singularly genuine and noble Christians? For

us all as for them the first word of the Gospel is that
of our Lord to the Samaritan woman, "God is a Spirit."
For us all the powers and the gifts of nature are meant
to be symbols of the spiritual life, just as the Lord
made the water of Jacob's well to be one forever
afterwards for her: "Every one that drinketh of this
water shall thirst again; but whosoever drinketh of
the water that I shall give him shall never thirst; but
the water that I shall give him shall become in him a
well of water springing up unto eternal life."

THE PRAYER BOOK AND CHRISTIAN YEAR

He saith, the old is better.—Luke 5 : 39.

The Prayer Book is not the production of a single author or a single age. Its stately fabric, with a general unity of design apparent throughout, bears the impress of the thoughts of various epochs. The East and the West have conjoined to make it what it is. The well-instructed sons of the Church come to love it as the sons of some old historic house come to love the ancient mansion in which they were born and where they have grown up.—Dowden.

Next to a sound rule of faith there is nothing of so much consequence as a sober standard of feeling in matters of practical religion.—Keble.

Perhaps there is no one book, except the Holy Bible, which has been so much written about as the Prayer Book since the Reformation, and perhaps so much was never written about any one book which left so much still unsaid.—J. H. Blunt.

CHAPTER II

THE PRAYER BOOK

What is our American Book of Common Prayer, and whence does it come?

I

For a brief and clear answer to these questions we cannot do better than turn first to Dr. J. F. Garrison's Bohlen Lectures of 1887:

"The Book of Common Prayer, and administration of the Sacraments; and other Rites and Ceremonies of *The Church* is not a collection of ordinances and rules for the use of some local institution or temporary society. It is no mere arrangement of devout and proper forms for public worship and service. Its sacraments, ministry, and services did not originate with the founders of the American Church in 1789. They are not the product of the Reformation era, nor do we receive them solely as belonging to our honored mother, the great Church of England. On the contrary, they come to us on the authority of the one Holy Catholic and Apostolic Church, and we have and use them because our Church is a living member of this same universal body of the Lord. Hence it is from the Church that they derive their origin; it is to the Church we owe their preservation. They were ordained under the commission Christ gave His Church at its foundation, and through and by the Church they have been ministered through all the ages. As such they are received by us and truly named in our Prayer Book, 'The Sacraments, and other Rites and Ceremonies of *The Church.*'" (Page 22.)

"When the Church was first planted in England," Dr. Garrison continues (page 25), "its inhabitants were the Britons, a Celtic people akin in race to the Irish, the Scotch, and some of the tribes in Gaul. The precise date of its founding is not certain, but it was very early. And it was known all over Europe for many generations before a Saxon or an Engle had set foot in Britain, as a Church distinguished by its missions, and its long roll of saints.

"The chief features of our sacramental and other offices, derived from the English Church, and together with our Orders, and the Holy Scriptures, traced back through her in a valid and unbroken line to the age and authority of the Apostles, have been adapted to our own needs by the required modifications, and in the primitive Constitution of the Church such had been the manner in each national Church. Such had been the way in the West until Rome's power had overthrown the Church's apostolic organization. It is so now in all the Eastern Churches, and England has always retained 'full and complete power' over the services employed.

"Through all the varied phases of her history Briton, Saxon, Norman, English, down to the Reformation, she never allowed any other authority to interfere with her offices of public service than that which had been charged with this high duty. It had belonged of inherent right to her own bishops and her own convocations from the apostolic days, and it was so preserved by her through all the ages after."

Dr. Garrison says that Rome's efforts to induce or compel the English people to conform their liturgies to her order, as the Western Continental Churches had done, were unsuccessful until the time of Queen Mary, and even then they were yielded to only partially and under protest.

He quotes Archdeacon Freeman, saying, "It may be affirmed that no Roman or Continental priest can possibly, for many ages before the Reformation, have officiated at an English altar." All these are facts which every English and American Churchman ought to know. More than interesting, they call for devout thankfulness. They give a richer meaning and spiritual value to every Communion and service of Morning or Evening Prayer, to every Consecration, and Ordination, and Confirmation Service. If we prize our national privileges, and acknowledge the responsibilities of free citizenship, what of our anciently derived citizenship in Christ? If family descent has genuine value in our eyes, and "Noblesse oblige" speaks to the heart and conscience of many a sacred obligation, a social "calling wherewith we are called," God helping us, to keep bright and pure the name we bear, what of our historic lineage in the Church Universal?

To look a little farther here into our Church's history, and learn our exact relation to the great Latin Church, to which we owe many things,—though nothing in the way of allegiance,—we examine another passage of Dr. Garrison's work. He tells us that:

"The Church of the Britons belonged to a group of Celtic Churches, which, alike among themselves, differed in several matters from the usage of Rome. This Celtic Church, Catholic in doctrine and practice, had a liturgy of its own, its own translation of the Bible, its own monastic rule, its own cyle for the calculating of Easter, and presented both internal and external evidence of a complete autonomy. When it did come in contact, which, however, rarely happened in those early ages, with the Bishop of Rome, it allowed him a high post of honor, though second to that of Jerusalem, 'the place of our Lord's Resurrection,' but claimed to deal with him from the independent standpoint of an equal." (Page 25.)

It is not difficult to comprehend, that, when in 596, the Bishop of Rome sent Augustine with his forty companions to found a Christian mission among the fierce Engles and Saxons, who had virtually extirpated the old inhabitants from the East part of the island and made a heathen country of it, he was disposed to assume a superiority over the Britons and their Church. He knew little about them, it appears; and was he not the representative of the first Bishop in the Western Church? They indignantly refused to grant such superiority. They insisted that their customs were primitive and apostolic, and it appears that the offices of the Saxon Church as finally prepared by Augustine were shaped in many things after those of the kindred Celtic Church in Gaul, and "from these early offices," says Dr. Garrison, "have doubtless come most of the distinctive features which marked the services of the English Church through all the after-periods of her history, and gave them an impress they have kept even until now."

In 673 the Celtic and Saxon branches within the limits of the English territory agreed upon a settlement of their contentions, and "the common life of the two, thus united, became henceforth the one Church of England."

Dr. John Dowden, Bishop of Edinburgh, in "The Workmanship of the Prayer Book," says (page 69):

"Putting out of view the very large body of material derived from Holy Scripture, which we find in the Lessons, the liturgical Epistles and Gospels, the Psalms, the Biblical Canticles, and the Versicles and Responses, etc., we possess certain devotional elements whose histories extend back till they are lost in the mists and shadowy uncertainties that hang round much of Christian life and worship in the infancy and childhood of the Church. A striking example of these primitive elements is found in what is sometimes styled 'the lesser litany,' that pathetic cry of penitence and awe which finds utterance in the words:

> "'Lord, have mercy upon us,
>   Christ, have mercy upon us,
>   Lord, have mercy upon us.'

"It is interesting to observe that the services of the Latin Church, from which we have immediately derived this child-like utterance of the heart, have retained it in its Greek form—'Kyrie eleison, Christe eleison, Kyrie eleison.' And it seems reasonable to suppose that the use of the form in the West dates from the period when the early Christian Church at Rome was still, in the main, a Greek-speaking community.

"From Rome and the Italian provinces the use of the Kyrie spread (but not very rapidly) to the Church in Gaul. The use of it is enacted in the Council of Vaison, in 529, and was probably introduced about seventy years later into Britain by St. Augustine, of Canterbury. But it scarcely needs external evidence to its antiquity. It carries with it the almost unmistakable characteristics of primitive spontaneity. * * * It is as natural as a groan from a wounded creature. Its accents are the accents of pain, or of pity; but they are intermingled with a tone of hope! They are the tearful pleadings of a child with a merciful Father."

Of the Gloria in Excelsis, Dr. Gibson, of Leeds, is quoted as saying, "It cannot be later than the fourth century, while it may well be two or three centuries earlier"; and Bishop Dowden adds, "This magnificent hymn, a product of the Eastern Church, is characteristic of its source in 'the rushing storm of praise and jubilation with which it opens. Even the Te Deum pales before this superb outburst of adoring praise.'"

The earliest known manuscript form of this hymn is found in the great Codex Alexandrinus—"now what is perhaps the chief treasure of the British Museum"—which, it is claimed, may belong to the fourth, and cannot be later than the fifth, century.

These detached fragments of ancient services, coming to the Western Church from the East, and fitted into Western devotions, the Bishop says, "One may think of as of those fragments of rock left by some ice-floe on a shore far from their place of origin, and afterwards inserted in the structure of a human dwelling." It is different with the Te Deum, of which it may be said, "with all but absolute certainty, that its original language was Latin, and, with a high degree of probability, that the place of its origin was Southern Gaul. As regards its date, we cannot be far wrong if we assign it to some time between the closing years of the fourth century and the middle of the fifth. As we now possess it, or perhaps in a form with some curtailment of the concluding verses, it has been widely used in the Church for probably little short of fifteen hundred years."

The Litany has a long, complex, interesting history, into which we cannot enter. Its earliest known form, as a penitential service, belongs to the fourth century. It appears at Rome and at Vienne in Gaul in the fifth century, when, as Dr. Hart says (Book of Common Prayer, page 98):

"Men's hearts were failing them for fear and for looking after those things which were coming upon the earth. The barbarians were invading the empire, there were earthquakes and volcanic eruptions, famine and pestilence, present danger and fear for the future."

Among the very oldest portions of the Prayer Book is the *Sursum Corda*, etc. St. Cyprian suffered martyrdom in A.D. 258. In a little treatise of his on the Lord's Prayer is found a reference to the customary use in the Service of the exhortation, "Lift up your hearts"; and of the people's reply, "We lift them up unto the Lord."

A few words respecting the antiquity of the Communion Service. We cannot do better than quote from Dr. Hart's account (on page 139):

"We pass on now to the history of that worship as it has led to the forms of the Communion Office in the English Book and in our own. The earliest account of the eucharistic service which has reached us is contained in the so-called Apology (or Defense) for the Christians, written by Justin Martyr (of Samaria) to the Emperor Antoninus Pius in or about the year 152. As he describes it, the parts of the service on the day called Sunday, when all who live in cities or in the country come together to one place, were as follows:

"1. The memoirs of the Apostles (probably the Gospels) or the writings of the Prophets (meaning the Epistles of the New Testament prophets) are read as long as time permits.

"2. The President instructs and exhorts to the imitation of these good things.

"3. All rise together and offer prayers.

"4. We salute one another with a kiss [and alms are received for the poor].

"5. Bread, and wine mingled with water are brought to the President.

"6. He, taking them, gives praise and glory to the Father of the universe, through the name of the Son and of the Holy Spirit, and offers prayers and thanksgivings at considerable length, according to his ability.

"7. The people assent saying, 'Amen.'

"8. They who are called deacons distribute to the congregation the elements which have been blessed and carry a portion to those who are absent."

Dr. Hart, after giving us this most interesting record, "dating from within a half century after the death of St. John," comments thus upon it:

"We see here a definite order of the service while yet there is preserved to the officiating Bishop or Priest presumably speaking under divine or prophetic guidance, freedom of utterance in prayers and thanksgiving. That order has never been changed in any essential part of its outline. * * * The history of the service is the history of its modification along these lines, which had evidently been fixed so early that in a half century after the death of St. John they were the established rule of the Church."

We pass to the Collects. It can be safely assumed that not one in a thousand of our worshippers, even when a regular communicant, has a right idea of the antiquity of these petitions, connected, most of them, with the Eucharist itself. When the eye of a worshipper falls for the first time upon the Prayer of St. Chrysostom, he is likely to say to himself, "here we have an interesting relic of the early Christian times, imbedded in a service comparatively new." The fact is, however, that the venerable and beautiful petition dates probably from the ninth century, about five hundred years later than Chrysostom. On the other hand, the larger portion of the eighty-six Communion Collects in our book are from three to five centuries older than the prayer referred to.

"The Collects in our Prayer Book," writes Dr. Hart (page 116), "are for the greater part taken from three ancient Sacramentaries, or liturgical service books, of the Western Church. The oldest Sacramentary bears the name of Leo the Great, Bishop of Rome (440–461); the others are called by the names of Gelasius and of Gregory the Great. * * * The Collects first found in the Sacramentary of Leo, as it has come to us, are seven: those for the third Sunday after Easter, and for the 5th, 9th, 10th, 12th, 13th, and 14th after Trinity."

In the Sacramentary of Gelasius, bishop of Rome (492-496), we find, according to Dr. Hart's estimate, twenty-one of our Collects, among them that for the Fourth Sunday in Advent, "O Lord, raise up Thy power and come among us," and the Christmas Day Prayer of the glorious Incarnation, that in Him, born as at this time of a pure Virgin, we, being regenerate and made children of God by adoption and grace, may by the Holy Spirit be daily renewed. There is the most exquisite and touching Prayer for humility, for that Sunday before Easter when we come in full view of the Cross and Him who in tender love was sent to suffer death upon it, that we may follow the example of His patience and also be partakers of His resurrection. There we find the second Good Friday Collect, for all estates of men in God's holy Church, that every one may truly and godly serve Him; and then the Easter "cry" of the Spirit in our hearts, that by God's help we may bring to good effect those good desires which the Holy Week services and the Easter triumph have through His grace awakened in us.

The Collects first found in the Book of Gregory are twenty-nine. Those for St. Stephen's and St. John the Evangelist's Days and the Epiphany are among them, and the Collects for the five Sundays after Epiphany, for Ascension Day, and Whitsunday, and Trinity Sunday. Whether the noble prelate, the man of ardent and self-sacrificing missionary spirit,— who actually started himself to seek Britain and claim our fierce heathen forefathers for Christ, but was arrested and carried back to Rome to be made its bishop,—composed these prayers, we do not know; but earnest prayers they are, of such spiritual quality that we could easily believe that many of them were derived from the time of the Apostles, or early Saints like Ignatius and Justin Martyr and Polycarp.

Bishop Gregory I. died in 604 A.D., and the last Ecumenical Council did not take place until 680. The long list of corruptions and abuses, those errors and sins against the Faith and simple Polity of the Church, which have gradually created the wide gulf now existing between our own Church and the Church of Rome had not begun to be. Pictures and images, though used in the church toward the end of the fourth century, were not recognized as objects of adoration before the end of the sixth, and the final triumph of image-worship came only midway in the eighth century. The papal exactions in England were not made till five centuries later, nor Rome's claim to be the Church, outside of which there was salvation for no man, until nearly six centuries later. The Inquisition was not established before the twelfth century; the order of the Jesuits, which now controls the Vatican, was founded in the sixteenth century, a thousand years after those beautiful and scriptural Latin Prayers were composed, some of them more beautiful and more succinct and forceful in the Latin than they are now in the English.

That the dogma of the Immaculate Conception of the Virgin, and that of the Infallibility of the Pope, as being the Vicar of Christ in His Church universal, were not yet dreamed of, goes without saying; nor had that great loss and injury inflicted upon the laity in the withdrawal of the cup from them in the Eucharist entered yet into the heart or the imagination of the Latin curia.

II

REFORMATION PERIOD

It is not my purpose in this volume to do more than touch upon certain essential features of the Prayer Book and its long history, and thought shall now be briefly given to what was done in England in the sixteenth and seventeenth centuries to restore the ancient services. These, as rendered catholic and pure again, were taken over and adapted to the needs of the American Church in 1789.

"The leaders of the English Reformation," says Dr. Garrison (page 86), "next to their opposition to the Papacy, directed their efforts chiefly against the mediæval conceptions of the Eucharist, and the practical errors and evils which they regarded as essential parts of the doctrine as it was then accepted. The overweening assumption of the priesthood as the disposers, through masses and absolutions, of man's future destiny and present hope, the mechanical conceptions and uses of the Sacrament thus induced and fostered upon every hand, the palsying idea of religion as chiefly a matter of ceremonial and usages and official rites, and the innumerable superstitions and corruptions of the truth, which, in the course of centuries, had gathered necessarily around theories so little spiritual in their character, and seemingly so material in both their means and ends, these all were portions of the same one system, and neither in its principles nor its practices had they any Scriptural warrant or primitive authority.

"As the theology which had thus become supreme in Western Europe, and the evil results we have been tracing, were everywhere connected with a loss of that spiritual conception of the Eucharist which had been presented by our Lord, and embodied in the early liturgies, it is evident that the remedy was to be found in a return to the essentials of these ancient offices and the Scriptural truths which were inculcated by them.

"Indeed, these primitive services were from their authors and the conditions of their origin the highest and best expression outside the Bible, of the sacred verities with which they were concerned, and were in fact the forms appointed by the Apostolic founders of the Church to be for its continual guidance, pattern, and instruction, till the end of time.

"This was the fundamental principle on which the English reformers acted, and which the Church of England has embodied in her 'Order for the Administration of the Lord's Supper or the Holy Communion.' It is this same Liturgy in its general features that we have. We possess accordingly the restoration

of all that is essential both in form and doctrine, of the original
and catholic conception of the Eucharist."

Bishop Dowden, writing of the same period, says
(page 48): "It was a matter of common knowledge
among theologians, that the Greek Church made the
express Invocation of the Holy Spirit an essential in
the consecration of the Eucharist." He refers to
Cranmer's effort to incorporate a similar Invocation
in the English service, and to the fact that Bishop
Seabury, receiving the form from the Scottish Church,
put it forth for the Diocese of Connecticut in 1786, and
later the whole Church of the United States adopted
it in substance. He quotes the part of our service
containing, "To bless and sanctify, with thy Word and
Holy Spirit, these thy gifts and creatures of bread and
wine," familiar to every communicant of the American
Church, and adds: "This beautiful form is used
throughout the length and breadth of the United
States. Thus the quiet and scholarly studies of Archbishop Cranmer have at length borne most rich and
plentiful fruit."

He says further:

"In these days, when approaches have been made towards
the Holy Orthodox Church of the East, it is a matter of no small
importance that the Anglican Communions possess Liturgies like
the Scottish and American, in which the express Invocation of
the Holy Spirit has a place."

Dr. Garrison (page 58) lays great weight on this
element in our American service as having been prominent in the primitive liturgies.

"In all the primitive liturgies which we have in their original
Greek, the pervading thought and life of the whole service was

its dependence on the presence and operation of the Holy Ghost."

His final words are of great force,—and to us who have been dwelling, in the preceding essay on the Spirit, upon His place and part alike in the world of nature and of grace as the Lord, and Giver of life, they have the greater importance:

"Our Liturgy has thus in all its important elements preserved the forms of the early Church and of Apostolic origin. * * * With them it places the essence of the Christian life, and the personal value of every Sacrament and ordinance of the Church, in the operation and influence of the Holy Spirit. All the benefits which are promised are spiritual; the means are effectual only when blessed by the Spirit, and in our Holy Communion, as in them, the blessing sought, and if earnestly sought obtained, is the two-fold communion, on the one hand of our soul with Christ, in which we are 'made one with Him and He one with us,' and on the other of our hearts and lives in spiritual unity with 'the blessed company of all faithful people,' with whom we are thus knit together as one living body with Him" (page 92).

As regards Morning and Evening Prayer, all that needs to be done here is to refer to the restoration of the Psalter in its entirety, and of the Lessons, to this extent that substantially the whole of the Scriptures are read in the course of the year. The lessons of the old service-books had been taken, some from the Bible, some from legends of the Saints, some from the writings of the Fathers. They were now confined once more to the Holy Scriptures, including certain carefully selected parts of the deutero-canonical books of the Old Testament.

In respect to Collects and other prayers, admirable work was done.

"The artistic merits and literary beauty, no less than the devotional excellence of the Collects of the English Prayer Book," Bishop Dowden writes (page 119), "have been acknowledged with a remarkable fulness of testimony from various quarters. The great majority of these forms are either close translations, or, more commonly, somewhat amplified paraphrases of Latin Collects which can be traced to authorized devotions of the ancient Church of Rome. Many of them belong to the sixth, and some to the fifth century, or may even mount higher still."

As to Cranmer's part, Dr. Garrison speaks (page 156) of the services being "rendered into that devotional English of which Cranmer, beyond all men of his own, or we may say, of any age, was the most consummate master." We are told that the purpose was to "discharge the innovations of later ages, and bring things up to the primitive standard," and so the Church and people accepted them.

In regard to the Litany, there were much to tell; we must be content with quoting Bishop Dowden's remark (page 156) that it is worth observing that Cranmer's national sentiments did not prevent him from resorting to what seemed of value in the Roman, Lutheran, and Greek sources, as well as in the Sarum, York, and Hereford uses. The work is, on the whole, executed with masterly skill, and in a spirit that is eclectic and marked by a wise liberty of choice.

Bishop Dowden has words of warm commendation for the Revisers of 1661. He says that they, and Bishop Cosin in particular, ought not to be forgotten. They have left examples of entirely original work which may well stand comparison with the very best of the earlier Collects (page 132):

"Let the reader take his Prayer Book and read carefully the Collect for Easter Eve, and I think he will acknowledge that, judging by the standard of literary feeling and liturgical fitness, we have here a very delicate and exquisite piece of skilful workmanship."

This Collect as well as the "beautiful Collects" for the Third Sunday in Advent, the Sixth after Epiphany, and the First after Easter, we probably owe to Bishop Cosin.

These various points will be referred to again in a different connection in the next chapter, but regarding them simply as brought before us by Dr. Garrison and Bishop Dowden, they give cause for deep thankfulness. It means much to us to possess the sense of the original petition in dignified and harmonious English. "The diction of our Book of Common Prayer," wrote Macaulay, "has directly or indirectly contributed to form the diction of almost every great English writer. It has extorted the admiration of the most accomplished infidels, and the most accomplished nonconformists.

"It enhances our gratitude to reflect on the difficulties encountered. Of the thousands who thankfully use the services few realize that some of the more familiar formulas, which now run glibly over the tongue, were reached only after many tentative efforts. A sacred diction had to a large extent to be created. In the main it is to Coverdale's Bible and the Prayer Books of Cranmer and his colleagues that we are indebted for the language, so apt, so stately, so tender and winning in which religious thought and feeling has been wont to find utterance for the last three hundred and fifty years." (See Dowden, pages 175–189.)

Remarkable, too, is the fact that the great essential motives of the Services have been little affected by the transitory animosities of party.

THE CHRISTIAN YEAR

"Were the Christian year only now to be invented, the author of it would be compared with Luther or Wesley as one of the Church's greatest benefactors; and not without reason. Look at this majestic system of claiming all time for Jesus Christ, and filling every day in every year with His Name and His Worship! * * * Yet, because all this is but part of our inestimable inheritance as Churchmen, we hardly think of it as, even on popular grounds, a conclusive reason for being what we are, and as furnishing an irresistible argument against those who oppose themselves. * * * God has made it the distinction of the Anglican Church in divers parts of the world, to be almost the only witness for that system in His worship, in the great Congregation, which the Holy Scriptures show to have originated with the Divine Wisdom." (Bishop Coxe, "Thoughts on the Services," page 16.)

It is because of the profound connection between nature and man, and the Spirit's relation to both, and because the life of nature and the "operations" in the realm of grace are operations of the self-same Spirit, that those analogies between the two, of which our Lord made abundant use in His teaching, and St. James, and then St. Paul, made use after Him, are true and precious analogies. Now it is upon these same living connections and resemblances that the system of the ancient religious festivals seems to have been based, and the year of Christ, so dear and helpful now to the Church Universal, is in like manner founded. Sun, moon, and stars, trees and flowers, seed-time and harvest, and man, as created and as redeemed from sin and death in the Son of Man, are all bound up together.

We read in Genesis, "And God said, Let there be

lights in the firmament of heaven to divide the day from
the night; and let them be for signs and for seasons
and for days and for years." It was all in relation to
man's life; and centuries later, when mankind had
multiplied and replenished the earth, and when, by
the Spirit's influence, religious worship and customs
had developed in many lands, these words were
written, in Ecclesiasticus (33: 7, 8, 9):

"Why doth one day excel another, when as all the light of
every day in the year is of the sun? By the knowledge of the
Lord they were distinguished; and he altered (arranged) seasons
and feasts. Some of them hath he made high days, and hal-
lowed them, and some of them hath he made ordinary days."

This was true of the Sabbath, and it is true now of
Sunday as the Day of our Lord's resurrection. Upon
it the Spirit writes, as it were, His signature of divine
ownership, extending to all the days; as George
Herbert says:

> "The week were dark, but for thy light;
>   Thy torch doth show the way";

and the principle has a far wider and more profoundly
instructive exemplification in the system of religious
celebrations which we find pervading the entire Bible.
With these the who e Truth of the Incarnation is
bound up.

We have to begin by noting the agricultural, or
harvest-home, element which underlies all three great
festivals, and, indeed,—because the fact of Creation and
Re-creation or refreshment, go together,—underlies
the Sabbath, and the Lord's Day also. From the time
when Cain and Abel are described as bringing their

offerings of "the fruits of the ground" and "firstlings of the flock" to God, down through the ages, this element of thankfulness to Almighty God for life is ever present. Time would fail us to relate its history, running its roots as it does far back of Jewish annals into the early history of mankind. The harvest-home factor is present in the Passover, in Pentecost, in the Feast of Tabernacles. It is present in the shew bread, constantly renewed in the Temple. Always it meant, God is our Life.

It meant, also,—and that even in ancient heathen feasts,—not merely dependence upon God, or the "gods many," and grateful acknowledgment of it,— but fellowship with the divine. Sometimes there was only the thought of God feeding upon the offerings brought to Him, but this was a perversion of the original conception of a feasting with God at a table. Fellowship with the gods,—in Israel fellowship and communion with the One God, who had actually called Himself a Father to the people He had chosen,—this was the thought.

This Father-Creator was not only their Life, but their Providence, and again their Deliverer from Egyptian and from Babylonian bondage. He was a God of mercy and forgiveness. Together with the offerings of Bread and Wine went those of slain Lambs. These signified contrition for sin on man's part, and an ever-renewed welcome with a God of Holiness in the solemn sacrifice. For sin causes, sin is, separation. And separating men from God it separates them from each other, inevitably. Accordingly, with the thought of life from God and dependence on God in every way, redemption and forgiveness and communion restored in those holy feasts, there went the other thought of union and harmony among themselves. The three festivals were plainly intended to be a mighty social power, and a source of social happiness. The family and tribal life was to be strengthened and patriotism deepened. Was not this one reason of the divine promise that Jehovah would protect their homes while the men of Israel were absent, having gone up to the appointed feasts in the holy city?

The Lyric of Israel was immensely enriched by the religious, social, and national feelings awakened in these holy feasts. The songs composed for the purpose and sung by Passover pilgrims, and those who went up to Pentecost, and to the autumn feast of Tabernacles, or Booths erected in the vineyards,—sung as the people passed in bands along the roads, came in sight of the hills round about Jerusalem and in view of the beautiful Temple itself, or entered its gates,—we know them well. "Behold, now, praise the Lord; all ye servants of the Lord"; "Behold, how good and joyful a thing it is to dwell together in unity; I will lift up mine eyes unto the hills from whence cometh my help; I was glad when they said unto me, 'We will go into the house of the Lord'; Lift up your heads, O ye gates." We chant or read them in the wider, more privileged and more spiritual Church of the Ascended and Enthroned Son of Man, but scarcely realize the glory of their past associations, or the warm, rich light they can throw now upon the spiritual meaning and purpose of the Church Universal, the eternal Temple and Home of a humanity redeemed and re-united in Christ!

We appreciate too little their relation to our Lord Himself, as having partaken of our flesh and blood, and more than that taken "hold of the seed of Abraham" (Heb. 2 : 16). Being "by the operation of the Holy Ghost," as the Christmas-day Preface says, "made very man, of the substance of the Virgin Mary, his mother," we believe, and see how it could be true, that He was "tempted in all points like as we are" (Heb. 4 : 15), and is now a "merciful and faithful high priest" to us, in the things pertaining to an infinitely holy God (Heb. 2 : 17). Yet do we but feebly apprehend that such a complete self-identification with us involved an entering of Christ as a child and a man into the entire religious and social life of the chosen people from which He sprang. The Son of God became a true child of nature, and dependent as all men are on the Spirit who gives Life and nourishes it, in the realm of nature. As Man He drew in that life like ourselves.

He had entered into relations of time and place. Sunrise and sunset, the phases of the moon, seed-time and harvest meant the same to Him that they did to every pious Israelite, in truth much more, because He was "without sin," He was ever thinking gratefully of the Father from whom all good things came. As He grew alike in wisdom and in stature, and was permitted to go up to the solemn feasts in Jerusalem, He entered more deeply than could His pious kinsfolk and acquaintance into the manifold providential meanings of them, and loved the Songs of Zion with a love which they must have observed, and wonderingly commented upon.

However, whenever, the fact of His own personal relation to those joyous prophetic solemnities was borne in upon His human spirit, as being Himself the long-expected Messiah, they became yet more significant, and more dear. Already at the age of twelve we seem to see signs of this in His intense longing to linger in the precincts of the Temple, to listen to the doctors, to ask them questions about His "Father's Things." When His hour had come to teach the sacred truths of the Kingdom, the great Festivals not only afforded special opportunity for instructing vast numbers at once; they afforded types and suggestions of the fundamental truths themselves. It was at the Feast of Tabernacles that the libation of water took place,— brought from the fountain of Siloam in a golden pitcher,—one of the most notable Messianic types in the national history; and on the last, the great day of the feast, Christ applied it to Himself. "If any man thirst," He cried aloud, "let him come unto me and drink" (John 7 : 37). The rivers of living water which, beside slaking the thirst of believers in Him, would flow from them and refresh the souls of others also, He expressly pointed out, would be received from the Holy Spirit.

The harvest-home thought, underlying all three holy feasts, was perhaps especially prominent in the Passover, as being the Spring festival, when the first fruits of wheat and barley, of spelt and oats and rye, were offered. And was it not a great company of Passover pilgrims on their way to Jerusalem whom one day the Lord fed with the few loaves, and the next day taught the Truth that He was the true Life of the World? (John 6.) In a most important sense it was no new truth to them. If they but remembered it, the Passover itself taught that God was their Bread, their Life. He might have put a question to them similar to the one He asked Nicodemus. "Are ye

Israelites, going up to the Passover, and understand not to what these my words point?" What was new was that He was the very Son of God, and about to become by His Sacrifice the Life, not of Israel only, but of a redeemed world.

The second great thought in the Passover was that of deliverance out of bondage; and Christ, by His death to sin, and His resurrection, would be the Author of a far greater deliverance for Israel and for our entire race. This too some who heard Him were sufficiently "masters in Israel" and had learned already enough from Christ, or about Him, to lay hold of, in part at least; and we can apprehend it richly now, by His Spirit. We need not to dwell on it. There are, however, other elements of truth in the Passover, and in the Communion Service as instituted in connection with the Paschal Supper particularly, which even Prayer Book Christians are likely to overlook. These are the elements of fellowship and union, of social sympathy, of social harmony and joy. Atonement for sin and fellowship restored, and ever again renewed, with God, was the condition and basis of fellowship among men. Such was the ideal of that ancient system as planned by the Spirit of God to prepare the way in one small nation for Him who should be the Saviour and King of an entire race restored and re-united. Of course the ideal, like all divine ideals, was by many not realized and lived up to. Blind to the spiritual beauty of it, and cold at heart, these forsook the assembling of themselves together, as is the manner of many Christians now. But happy the bands of pilgrims who, with faithful regularity, trod the paths that led Zionward.

The Christian Year needs to be preached more than it is, and on broad lines. Historic sense, religiously speaking, is closely akin to Church sense, philosophic sense, yes, common sense, if by this last we mean a sense of what humanity most craves and needs. What it needs is just that which the Bible, and in those three great festivals most remarkably, exhibits, God and Man reconciled, and thereby the wide world of mankind drawn together in love and peace, in friendship and sympathy.

It were next to a waste of time to speak at any length of what Christmas alone is now accomplishing in the way of restoring the lost unity among Christians of every name. It seems impossible to believe that within two hundred years a man was put in the stocks in the State of Maine for celebrating the Nativity of our Lord on the 25th of December. From the beginning of Advent,—which, as Bishop Coxe writes, "answers to that Day in the Mosaic year," when "the Trumpet was blown in Zion," preparatory to the Feast of Tabernacles,—not the Church merely, but all Christians, if not all men and children, are thinking of Christmas. "All men are children" when that Day comes, and nearly all are friends. The heart of old Scrooge himself melts.

Still more profoundly, more spiritually, is it true that Lent and Holy Week, followed as they immediately are by the joyful Feast of Christ's Resurrection, are fostering—if one may dare coin the word—a spirit of *mankindness*. It becomes each year more strikingly apparent. "I, if I be lifted up from (or out of) the earth,"—and there appears to be a reference alike to His Death and His Resurrection,—"will draw all men unto me" (John 12 : 32). Good Friday and Easter, bound together as one, have this result, and by drawing us all to our Lord, they tend more and more to unite Christians in a world-wide brotherhood. Thank God for this benefit, through the increasing observance of the Christian Year.

We cannot but think that the Church Year is divinely intended to bring home to us more effectually the truth of our Lord's sacred humanity and the reality of His work and suffering on our behalf. George Herbert's lines regarding Lent,

> "Who goeth in the way which Christ hath gone
> Is much more sure to meet with Him, than one
> That travelleth by-ways,"

are true as applied to the entire first half of the Year. We are kept near to the Incarnate from Advent to Ascension. The Epiphany season, and Lent with it, are as truly a long epiphany of Christ's Manhood as they are of His Divinity. Taught to pray that we may after this life "have the fruition of His glorious Godhead," we learn each week better, that He has become one with us humanly. He will call us brethren forever. He conquers temptation and death itself in our nature, and the heavenly "fruition" is coming through our union with His humanity glorified in that human victory, and on account of it. It even appears that our future vision of God, and communion with Him, will be a vision and communion mediated, so to say, by the present transfigured humanity of the eternal Son.

How precious, in view of all this, the weeks which bring before us the infancy, the childhood, and, by suggestion and inference, the entire long, quiet, preparation of the Lord for His sacred Ministry! We behold Him increasing in wisdom as truly as in stature, and in favor alike with God and man. The human will joined with the eternal divine Will in a wonderful union becomes ever stronger to meet temptation, through the Spirit, given to Him without measure. His obedience is an ever riper obedience, made perfect, as the Scripture says, "through suffering." Always the beloved Son, always pleasing to the Father, His filial life is ever fuller, richer and more acceptable as a human offering. Every hour of the Redeemer's life in the flesh is part of His atoning work, rendering our humanity each moment more thoroughly *at-one* with God. For a work it is. When He says, "the Father worketh hitherto, and I work" (John 5 : 17), there is reason to think first and most of all of the inward labor and conflict, the tremendous work going on in the will and heart of our Lord, and becoming at moments,—especially at the last,—intense beyond the capacity of the most earnest Christian to conceive it.

So it is that He becomes more to us than the "Strong Son of God," even the Strong Son of Man, an unfailing source of moral and spiritual strength for our race. The power is, in the thought of Bishop Weston ("The One Christ," page 241),

"that of the Incarnate Son Himself, working with and through the Spirit, in two-fold relationship with Him, but always in the measure in which manhood was able to co-operate with divine power. He becomes strong, as the first Adam was intended to become and failed to do, in and through His temptations, becomes at last incapable of being tempted, as the first Adam might have done, and thus wins the glorious privilege of being our Second Adam. It is not primarily for our example. It is the great battle of God for our souls, in which the weapons are our human faculties, which are Satan's handles, but the power with which the Victor wields the weapons is divine. Therefore it is, that He is able to succor all who come to Him for help" (page 219).

It is not consonant with the purpose of this chapter to enter more fully into the details of this, the most decisive of all the "decisive battles in history." The motive here is merely to remind the Prayer Book worshipper how faithfully the first half of the Church's Year spreads before him the divine side, and the equally essential human side, of Christ's mighty work and contest with evil, in a manner to attract his attention, to deepen his love, and to quicken him anew with a lively hope in the Saviour of the world. It is the Truth of the Bible, and of the Nicene Creed in its fuller Chalcedonian statement concerning the One and the same Christ, recognized in the two natures, that has come down to us also in Services practically dating from the Nicene age.

THE SPIRIT AND THE PRAYER BOOK

Being by the right hand of God exalted, and having received of the Father the promise of the Holy Ghost, he hath shed forth this which ye now see and hear.—Acts 2 : 33.

The great Captain of our Salvation, our all-conquering Redeemer, was not so elevated with the pomp of His triumphs as to forget the captives that He released among the children of Adam. He received many donations from His Father on high to shower down among them upon His coronation day.—Ambrose Serle.

Through the Holy Spirit we are restored to paradise, ascend to the kingdom of heaven, recover the adoption of sons, may boldly call God our own Father, are made partakers of the grace of Christ, are called children of light, partake of eternal glory, and, in a word, enjoy the fulness of blessing both in this world and in that which is to come.—St. Basil the Great, born about 329 A. D.

I have long felt,—and conversation with others confirms my belief,—that the book sought for would be one on the subject the Christian Church needs so much to think about, pray over, the Holy Spirit. The dynamic we lack is His influence, and surely in view of the widespread desire for unity, we need, possibly as never before, His guidance. I cannot tell you how precious the truth of His power is to me: as I move among men of sterling manhood, Christian in the sense of admitting the truths of the Master's revelation, but generally indifferent to the claims of "formal" Christianity, I am compelled to feel that His power alone can do the things I desire, and this will come, I believe, as a blessing on my little efforts.—McFetridge.

CHAPTER III

THE SPIRIT AND THE PRAYER BOOK

I

By the testimony of the Scriptures in the Old and New Testaments, and by that of the early Church, in the Creeds, and in primitive portions of the Prayer Book, the truth of the Spirit as personal and divine,—although undeveloped in its doctrinal expression,—we have seen to be second only to the truth of the Divinity of our Lord and Sav·our Jesus Christ.

Creator of the world, and of man at the beginning, He is also the Maker and Builder, first, of the new humanity in the Person of Christ, and then,—after Christ's ascent to the Father in glory,—of the Body of Christ, the Church Universal, now gradually filling the world. The Vicar of our unseen Lord, the Spirit is conspicuously the Guide and Leader of His Church in its first great missionary campaign, recorded in what might be designated the Acts of the Holy Ghost. He is the risen Lord's Vice-gerent in every baptism, and the Consecrator of every eucharist. He is the Spirit of adoption, by whose indwelling life Christ's sonship is realized in us; the Spirit of prayer, who cries, Father, in every true Christian's heart, whether Jew or Gentile.

Prayer Book history, we have likewise found, points

5   (65)

back to the very infancy and childhood of the Church, considerable portions of it being derived from a period when, as it has been said, forces and influences at work in the apostolic age projected themselves with irresistible force into the age which followed it. A large proportion of its devotional elements are derived practically from what we may call the Nicene period of Church History. In the Liturgy we possess "the restoration of all that is essential, both in form and doctrine, of the original and catholic conception of the Eucharist." A wonderful "conformity to type, with certain differences in the different national Churches, is observable in this, the chief Christian Service, instituted by our Lord Himself. In the Scottish and American Church is found again the Invocation of the Holy Spirit which was prominent in the primitive liturgies.

We possess once more what the early Church enjoyed, and the mediæval Church lost, Common Prayer, that is, devotional forms in which the people have their part. The services are in the vernacular, which all understand and in which they can respond. In like manner the Eucharist has become what it was originally, the service of the Church as the Lord's Body. The laity have a complete Communion, with God and with each other, receiving as of old both consecrated elements. The words of an unknown hymn writer, translated by Dr. Neale,

> "Draw nigh and take the Body of the Lord,
>   And drink the Holy Blood for you outpoured,"

which lose half their meaning in the Roman Mass, for us recover their full significance.

We have considered the Christian Year, "that

majestic system of claiming all time for Christ, and filling every day in every year with His Name and Worship,"—based on the Jewish year, which, full of Messianic types, was also itself a means of spiritual uplifting and of social and national union and harmony, —and are ready to accept the assertion that this Year "is shown by the Scriptures to have originated with the divine wisdom."

II

The question now to be pondered, is whether a living relationship may be predicated between the Spirit whom we worship and glorify as God and these sacred and venerable Services. Is He, the Creator-Spirit, in a real and vital sense the Maker of these? It is possibly in some sort a new question; yet many a sincere lover of the Prayer Book must often in his heart have praised God for it as a good gift, a well-nigh "perfect gift from above." God has spoken to him out of it as truly as out of the Psalms and other Scriptures incorporated with it. If his conception of it as a divine work has not been clear and decided, may it not have been by reason of the fact that "the doctrine of the Holy Spirit has been neglected"? Conscious of the effect of His inspiration, we have failed to attribute it to Him personally.

Let us ask ourselves what we should have expected of One concerning whom our Lord said, "He shall be to you what I have been to you; He shall teach you all things." Should we not have anticipated that the promised Vice-gerent of Christ would teach His people to pray? He was to be the Church's Advocate, present at all times to befriend and counsel her; her Comforter;

and to comfort is more than to console. A friend who in hours of sorrow or difficulty leads me to the one true source of strength, is the best kind of comforter. St. Paul wrote of the Spirit as One who in our times of infirmity and need would Himself intercede within us; and was He ready and desirous to do this for the individual believer, but not for that mystical Body of Christ upon which He had descended at Pentecost to endue it with spiritual wisdom?

Precedent and analogy will help us here. A large part of the Old Testament Scriptures consists of praises and prayers. Intertwined with the record of divine revelations, made progressively to and through chosen individuals and a chosen people in the olden time, appears the response which they made to those revelations in confession, thanksgiving, and petition. Holy men not only "spake" otherwise, but sang praises and prayed, "as they were moved by the Holy Ghost." The Truths and the Prayers together make up the divine-human deposit which has come down to us. Many a psalm of that Psalter whose composition covers more than a thousand years, and which has been incorporated into our Book of Common Prayer, and which we regard as inspired, either begins, or ends, as a prayer. The last words in one of them are, "The prayers of David the son of Jesse are ended."

The Prayers of the Church Universal have taken more than a millennium to compose, as have the Hymns and Spiritual Songs which began almost at once to form a part of the New Testament Response, and it would evidently have been impracticable to embody them in the Scriptures of the New Covenant. So it was with the Liturgy. Though wonderfully "conformed to type," with its differences, characteristic of different nationalities, the Communion Service could not be in and of the Bible, as could the book of Leviticus,—full of divine directions concerning services typical of the One True Sacrifice on Calvary,—be in and of it. But Bible and Prayer Book, and Hymnal also, lie together by themselves on the Churchman's table, and are, so to say, bound up as one volume in his heart, a precious fruit and gift of the Spirit.

He is the Spirit of Order. "After this manner pray ye," said Christ, when, asked to teach His disciples how to pray, He gave them the "Our Father"; and the sequence of the Prayer Book praises and petitions, corresponding to the liturgical structure of the Lord's Prayer, has often been commented on.

The Holy Ghost is the Spirit of Universality, together with Unity. We perceive and admire this in relation to the world we live in, and more and more, as we come to know it, in that kosmos of which our earth is a part. The same mighty forces, the same principles and methods of working, manifest themselves in both; and withal an infinite variety. So works "the mind" of the Creator-Spirit in the age-long development of that two-fold library of sacred literature which we call the Bible. St. Cyril, of Jerusalem, teaching his catechumens, made a beautiful comparison between the rain, "one and the same," coming down upon all the world, yet becoming white in the lily, red in the rose, purple in the violets and pansies, with the Holy Ghost, "one and uniform and undivided in Himself," distributing His grace to every man as He will; and Cyril might with equal truth and suggestiveness have applied his figure to the Spirit in regard to the Scriptures. It was at sundry times and divers manners that in the ancient days the Spirit of God spake unto His people by the prophets, and almost the chief evidence of His part in it all is the unity in the different revelations concerning the One God, and in the promises of a universal Saviour. In the New Testament Scriptures there is in the different writings,—often as unlike in their special characteristics of expression as the rose and the lily, the vine and the palm-tree are unlike in their way,—the same unity of thought and motive, one and the same revelation of God as Father, Son and Holy Spirit, engaged in the glorious work of redeeming and restoring our race.

Now, what man can make faithful study of the historic Services, as they have reached us, and not find the "sundry times" and the "divers manners,"—so to speak, the rose and the lily, the palm-tree and the vine, the diversity and the unity,—in them also? I am tempted for a moment out of my path, to note Dean Goulburn's parallel between the wild hyacinths and primroses one may discover at the root of a decaying tree and the "bunches of fragrant, beautiful prayers," appearing when the old Roman Empire was in its last stage of decay, "giving token of a spiritual vitality below the surface of society." In these ancient Collects,—Collects we know by heart and teach our children,—joined to the Epistles and Gospels, mostly in the very place and order they have occupied for more than a thousand years, unfolding to man progressively the Truth of the Incarnate Lord, as also in the arrangement of the Lessons for Morning and Evening Prayer, he who runs his eye over the pages should be able to read signs of the directing "Mind of the Spirit."

He is the Spirit of Truth,—the truth of Christ, in its own distinctly marked unity and universality; the Spirit who, presiding unseen in the great Councils of the Church, when it was yet undivided, often very stormy and to the eye of man hopelessly discordant Councils, brought out at last a clear distinct witness to the Faith, as "once for all delivered to the saints." On every page the Prayer Book reflects to-day this historic Creed. We recognize everywhere in these ancient Services that truth which St. Paul held up before the Ephesian Church, and evidently all the Churches he founded: One Lord, one faith, one baptism, One God and Father of all, who is above all, and (in His Son) through all, and (by His Spirit) in us all. For there was, as he said also, "one body and one Spirit, even as ye are called in one hope of your calling" (Eph. 4 : 5, 6).

The Holy Ghost is the Giver of Life. "Wherever there is life, there is the Spirit of God." Ecclesiastes, speaking of the rain-clouds and the wind, and of seed-sowing on man's part to be attended to without too careful observation of these operations of God, speaking in like manner of the birth of the little ones in our homes, says, "As thou knowest not what is the way of the Spirit" in this matter, "even so thou knowest not the works of God who maketh all." Is not this truth, that we know not the way of the Spirit, as real in the realm of Christian life as it is in nature? Does it not hold in respect to all means of grace, and all divine institutions, whether before Christ's coming or since? Conformity to type, conformity to the hidden, wonderful, and yet perfectly evident principle of life, is to be looked for in all the operations of the self-same Universal Spirit. What we know not as regards the coming of the little children to gladden our homes,—know not concerning the marvel of Christ's humanity as born of a pure Virgin, to grow and become, when glorified, the new and living way through the veil of our sins and iniquities into the eternal Home on high,—we may not expect to know about the Lord's Church. Particularly will this be true of the child-life of the Church, as conceived in our universal humanity by the Spirit. Who can tell, or expect to tell, exactly *how it grew?*

For this is just the truth about the Church, that in every sense it grew. As it seems to me after years of reflection on the matter, not enough has been made of this principle as regards the Spirit and the Church. Often it appears to receive no recognition, and again but a partial one. Bishop Westcott recognizes it, when he says that after the close of the Apostolic age "the Christian societies silently, unconsciously, through the promised help of the Spirit, fixed the broad outlines of the Creed and the Canon of Scripture, and shaped a Catholic Church." He says, "The Christian Society has a life of its own, and we may dare to say that its thoughts are widened by the indwelling Spirit"; and again, "Of the formation of the primitive, the Apostles', Creed we can only say that it grew." The contents of both the Creed and the Bible "were fixed by common usage; that is, by the Christian consciousness."

Bishop Robertson wrote in Regnum Dei: "It does not surprise us that in the collective action of the

ANALOGY WITH OLD TESTAMENT 73

Society the guidance of the Spirit was most especially
counted upon." Why not apply this principle of
inner life and growth also to the Response of the
Church to the New Testament revelations, in united
praise and prayer; "dare to say" that also in this most
important particular the Church's thoughts were
widened and deepened by the indwelling Spirit?
Confessedly it had been thus under the elder covenant.
Dr. Downer says: "The Psalms, and the whole of the
Divine Lyric, represent the moral and spiritual breath-
ings of the individual under the teaching and discipline
of the Holy Spirit." If this is true, and if not the
Psalms merely, but, as we must surely believe, the
prayers of Abraham and of Jacob, of Moses and Job
and Elijah, of Jeremiah and Ezekiel and Daniel,—
Solomon's prayer at the dedication of the Temple,—
form a constituent portion of the divine Word, shall
we not with equal confidence ascribe to God's Spirit
those forms of worship, beautiful with the beauty of
holiness, which week by week and day by day now
draw the Christian's heart heavenward in our Prayer
Book Services?

"The Spirit is life," wrote the Apostle; and was it
not for this reason chiefly, and because "the letter"
would have proved to His future Church, to say the
least deadening, that our Lord, beyond the simple
formula of Baptism in the Triune Name, and "This
do in remembrance of me," and that simple form of
Prayer, the Our Father, appears to have left no positive
directions about worship? It would seem to be in
accord with this truer, safer principle of inward life
and growth under the Spirit, that beyond the appoint-
ment of the Eleven there was no regulation of a

Ministry, and again, no direction about Infant Baptism. Christ wrote no word, dictated none, to be read to His Church as a personal message. The entire New Testament deposit of Truth concerning Him is a "fruit of the Spirit." Again, as of old, holy men, evangelists, apostles, prophets, speak and write as they are moved by the Holy Spirit.

To refer again to the Canon of Holy Scripture, does not the remarkable history of its formation altogether favor our conception of the Church's entire life as being one of development from within, a divine-human process in the Spirit? Dr. Fulton, in his book "The Chalcedonian Decree" (page 50), writes:

"The old theologians held that 'the authority of Holy Scripture is from God alone,' not, as is sometimes foolishly said, from the Church; and therefore the acceptance of particular Scriptures has always been left to the free action of particular Churches, according to the light which they severally had." And the end, he says, "is a substantial agreement of all Churches."

How slowly that agreement came! It is difficult to conceive that the Epistle to the Hebrews, precious to every sincere and earnest believer in Christ's death upon the Cross as "a full, perfect and sufficient sacrifice, oblation and satisfaction for the sins of the whole world," was not everywhere accepted as canonical until the end of the fourth century. To enter further into this interesting and suggestive matter does not belong strictly to our subject, nor again to discuss that of the sacred ministry, which also would seem to me to have been a thing of growth, under the silent operation of the enabling Spirit. Sunday, the Lord's Day, on which day St. John makes it a point to declare that he was "in the Spirit," gradually superseded the Sabbath of the elder covenant by the influence of the same Spirit of life; and is it not by so much the more sacred and full of spiritual joy to Christians who thus regard it?

As to their origin, their present character, and their authority for our spiritual conscience, all these are things of the Spirit, and as such "things of Christ." Like the young Christ Himself, the young Church of Christ after its Pentecostal birth increased in wisdom and stature in the power of the Holy Ghost. Accordingly, it is more than a missing of our aim, with the result of disappointment and perplexity,—it is to obscure for ourselves, and to encourage the Church in continuing to neglect, the truth of the Third Person's characteristic mission,—when we anxiously endeavor to trace a clearly defined historical connection between the methods and institutions of the Church and particular injunctions of the Apostles or of our Lord. We must think of the historical link as being the blessed Spirit Himself. The whole early Church, as long as it lived on undivided, had, as St. Paul expressed it, "the mind of Christ." It was the mind of Christ as being the mind of the Spirit who was His Vice-gerent on earth.

Returning now to the Prayer Book in particular, as being, like the Scriptures, an integral part of the Church's inestimable inheritance, while it is perfectly appropriate to speak of the workmanship of it, especially after the manner of Bishop Dowden,—for a divine-human product it is—we must cherish the thought of the divine element in it as being no less than the unseen, present, Spirit of our Lord. It is right to say, with

Bishop Coxe, that our Blessed Lord is Himself the great Author of the Liturgy, and include in our thought what he says of those portions borrowed from or conformed to Apostolic and Primitive ordinances, if only we add, at least mentally, that nothing was ever "made that was made,"—and these sacred services were not,—without the co-operation of the divine Spirit. And the Spirit is life. When Dr. Waterman speaks of "some power" as having "impressed upon the Church's mind that certain things must be done" in the Communion Service; suggests the influence of "an authority so commanding that they could not but follow it," and when Dr. Garrison writes of the sacraments, ministry, and services, as being derived from the universal Body of the Lord, and "ordained under the commission Christ gave His Church at its foundation," we add,—maybe they in their thoughts added,—that the "commission" was given above all to the Holy Ghost, and the power and authority above all vested in Him as the Lord, the Spirit.

Moreover, the Spirit had come to stay. The Father, in answer to the Son's prayer, would give us another Comforter, that He might abide with us for ever. This promise we have a right to apply to the Church's prayers as enriched from time to time,—not a little enriched in quantity and in spiritual depth by the English Revisers in the sixteenth and seventeenth centuries. "Lord, teach us to pray," was a petition which Christ has been answering throughout the centuries. Alike the individual believer and the Church as a body, as time goes on and new occasions for divine succour and guidance arise, feel the need; and ever again the need is met. One instance is the comparatively new Collect for the Second Sunday after Easter: "Almighty God, who hast given Thine only Son to be unto us both a sacrifice for sin, and also an ensample of godly life." Of this Collect Goulburn says, "It summarizes the whole benefit of Redemption * * * perhaps we should not err in saying that it embraces more matter than any other Collect." In such an increase in richness and fulness of thought, expressed in what Goulburn calls "two masterly touches," may we not be confident of seeing a distinct proof of the Spirit's ever-continued ministration?

I fasten upon and appropriate, as true in this sphere of worship, Bishop Weston's remark respecting the Universal Councils, as speaking

"with the authority of the Holy Spirit both to Churchmen and on their behalf. For, first, the Spirit guides and assists the counsels of Christ's mystical body, enlightening the minds of the faithful generally, and directing their teachers to a clearer view of the things of God. Each age has its proper inspiration. And secondly, ascending Godward from the heart of the redeemed race, He makes articulate before God the joyful realization by men of the once hidden mysteries of redemption through the blood of Christ and communion with God in Him."

True it is that the Church of our fathers, in Cranmer's time and since, has been acting as a mere Branch of the Church Universal; but this could not be helped, and we may think that as such she has enjoyed her proper share of the heavenly gift, and been signally aided in making her belief in Christ "articulate" before His Father, and our Father, in Common Praise and Prayer.

That the leaders in Church and State in England

in the sixteenth century, held this view of the Spirit's
ever-continued guidance and help in all corporate
action concerning sacred worship, is plain from a certain sentence in the Act of Uniformity prepared, in
accordance with the instructions of King Edward VI
by the Archbishop of Canterbury, with other bishops
and learned divines, and carried through both houses
of Parliament, January 21, 1549.   It was not by these
godly and learned men thought enough to arrange
such an order,

"having as well eye and respect to the most sincere and pure
Christian religion taught by the Scripture, as to the usage in
the Primitive Church": they said also, This "rite and fashion
of Common and open Prayer and administration of the Sacraments has been by the Aid of the Holy Ghost, with One Uniform
Agreement, concluded by them, and is set forth by them in the
Book of Common Prayer." (Gibson's Codex, 2d edition
page 260, vol. I.)

We may claim to have found evidence of the Spirit's
divine watchfulness and care also in the preservation
of our ancient Services, as wonderful as the preservation of the Bible itself.   Like the gold and silver vessels
of the Temple, brought back by Zerubbabel, are these
vials (or vases) full of precious odors, which are the
prayers of the saints in the purest ages of the Church's
life, and which have been handed safely down to us.

The Holy Spirit was to be the Church's Teacher in
all things, and in no respect is the Prayer Book a mightier
instrument in His hands, than in that of its capacity
to communicate definite instruction to all sorts and
conditions of men in all ages.

"It was by means of the Liturgy, mainly," says Dr. Garrison
that "the faith of the Church was preserved uniform and un-

changed throughout the widely scattered Christian Church in
its early ages;" and again, "The liturgies of no portion of the
Church in any country or in any age have ever failed to keep
firm hold of the great central truths of the Gospel, and to present
to the people all the essential elements of the Christian life."
And in and by the very act of prayer "are these essential truths
infused into the life of our spirits" (page 201).

The Spirit of God is a Spirit, not of Wisdom and
Power only, but of Beauty. The exquisite beauty of
the floating summer clouds and of the evening sky,
of sea and lake and mountain, is of the Creator-Spirit.
To Him the world has owed the genius of Bezalel, and
Phidias, of Michelangelo and Raphael, of David
and Shakspere and Tennyson, of Mozart and Haydn.
The Bible has a spiritual dignity and beauty of form
all its own, and these we attribute in large measure
to the Mind of the Spirit; and few of the great masters
of literature in our day, if any, have failed to recognize
in the Prayer Book as a whole a nobility of expression
comparable to that of the Scriptures.

III

And now more than one reader, while fully inclined
to admit, first, that it would assuredly be the Spirit's
affair to create such a human response to the divine
revelations as the services of the Church Catholic are,
and secondly, that we do seem to see His signature
upon many a portion written, as it were, "in large
letters," like that of St. Paul at the end of Galatians,
may have a question to ask. If inspiration be predicated of the Prayer Book, in what sense, and in what
degree shall we affirm it? Is it like that of the Scriptures themselves?

To questions like these, however, who even among the wisest and most learned of Christians may undertake to give a categorical reply? Each one of us will have an opinion and feeling of his own as to what inspiration is, and as to what is inspired. Regarding the Scriptures themselves the Church Universal has never had any theory.

"It was content," wrote Dr. Fulton (Chalcedonian Decree, p. 98), "to profess its faith in the Holy Ghost, the Giver of all life, physical and spiritual, who of old times spake to the fathers through the prophets * * * no theory of inspiration is, or ought to be, any part of Christianity * * * the Christian religion is not bound up with any theory on that subject," and Bishop Gore has said, "We cannot make any exact claim upon any one's belief in regard to Inspiration, simply because we have no authoritative definition to bring to bear upon him. Those of us who believe most in the inspiration of the Church will see a divine purpose in this absence of dogma, because we shall perceive that only now is the state of knowledge such as admits of the question being legitimately raised."

That there are, alike in the Old and New Testament Scriptures, degrees of inspiration manifested in the human response to divine disclosures of truth progressively made, few if any biblical scholars will deny. The Magnificat moves obviously on a higher plane of inspiration than the song of Hannah, which it resembles, and the Benedictus and Nunc Dimittis in certain respects occupy a yet higher one. If we can conceive of our Lord's blessed mother giving utterance to her joy and gratitude thirty years later, having learned with St. James and St. John what spirit we "are of" in the new dispensation, can we not think of her magnifying the Lord because He had "filled the hun-

gry with good things," while saying naught of the rich
being "sent empty away?"

Will not the Spirit in our hearts Himself best enable
us to answer questions relating to the Prayer Book as
an object of His creative energy and loving solicitude?
If the method in this chapter has appeared strikingly
tentative and interrogative, a way of meeting one
query by putting forward others, it will not, I trust,
be set down to anything else than a due and natural
discretion; the dislike to seem, still more to be, wise
in my own conceits, and above that which is written.

> "So runs my dream, but what am I?"

Not quite, it is hoped, like Tennyson's infant,
"crying in the night," or "crying for the light," yet
possessed with a certain sense of loneliness until voices
shall be heard, saying, some, "we are with you," others,
possibly, "we have always thought so." If my feeling
and opinion, read in the lines and between them, appears
too pronounced, let it be qualified by the judgment of the
learned and wise. All that can be asked is that what has
been written shall receive consideration, and with it Dr.
Fulton's question (page 100): "Who would presume to
set up a theory of inspiration which would virtually
deny that the various and partial inspirations of the
Holy Ghost who spake by the prophets were generically
different from the diversities of gifts by which that
one and self-same Spirit now guides and inspires
Christ's Church and its members? In the hard and
fast theories of inspiration which have prevailed in
modern times, nothing is so pitiful as the unconscious
but real assumption that the Holy Ghost, which
spake of old to the fathers in the prophets, speaks no

6

more in the new and fuller dispensation of the Spirit which our Saviour promised." These vigorous sentences of Dr. Fulton will have force with us who have inherited "Services substantially the most ancient now in use in Christendom." "Ours is the Church of the Nicene Age restored." Grateful for this high privilege, grateful that "such as the Church was then in the days of martyrs, such is our own Church now," we shall be grateful too for every sign of the Spirit's presence with and in her, and desirous that due recognition, and a more definite expression of it shall be included in the new and ampler development of the Doctrine of the Spirit in our day.

IV

The reader will believe that Dr. Downer strikes a chord in my heart when, having spoken of his own need of Divine grace

"to think rightly, to write truly, to act faithfully, in all that pertains to this sacred and wonderful Person, who is the Lord and Life-giver," he adds: "If in any degree the realization shall answer to the aim, I would hope that these chapters, together with the writings of better teachers, may contribute to render the doctrine of the Holy Spirit the characteristic study of the twentieth century. When it shall become so, we may look for a fuller, richer life and experience in the Church; a deeper longing after personal and corporate holiness, with a clearer view of the method of its attainment" (page xiii).

To me there is pleasure merely in the hope of imparting by the present study a slight impetus to so noble a movement of thought,—of stirring some one or more of the "better teachers" to deal with my theme in particular as it might be dealt with.

The entire second half of the Christian Year, named after the Trinity in our Book, remains to be treated. It is hoped that in the course of this treatment more light may be thrown upon the proposition I have sought to establish. Certain it is that the clearer signs we can discover, that the Book of Common Prayer is,—what we ourselves are as Christians,— the Spirit's "workmanship," the dearer and more sacred it will become to us. And on the other hand, so much the more precious will be the truth of the Holy Ghost, Sanctifier of the Faithful, that "blessed Spirit, whom, with the Father and the Son together, we worship and glorify as one God, world without end. Amen."

THE TRINITY SEASON

How profoundly we are indebted to the Bible for knowledge of spiritual things, and how as the ages move on does new light under the illumination of the Spirit break forth from it! Constantly too, it seems to me, the orthodox and conservative faith becomes at once no less firm as to fundamental truths long held, and comprehensive of all shades of truth, new and old, that have been held apart from their full relations; so that the faith as intelligently held ever broadens.—Letter of Dr. James E. Rhoads.

I think one reason that the great crowning festival of the Christian Year, Whitsunday, meets with such slight regard is the very spirituality of it. Our lives are so *coarsened,* if I may coin the word, with the continual friction of the world around us, that we lose sense of those finer things which lie beyond the claims of ordinary life. Now the principle on which we neglect the future life in our absorption in the present is just the same as that on which we neglect the Festival of the Descent of the Spirit on the Church, in comparison with those of the birth and of the resurrection of our Lord. * * * Without the Spirit, the events of our Lord's career must ever be purely external to us. And being purely external they will be incredible. It is He that makes the life and death and resurrection of the Christ anything more to us than a picture is to a blind man or a symphony of music is to a deaf man.—Bishop Reichel.

CHAPTER IV

THE TRINITY SEASON

I

Dr. Blunt, in The Annotated Book of Common Prayer (page 114), writes as follows:

"The Octave of Pentecost has been observed in honor of the Blessed Trinity from a very early age of the Church. In the Lectionary of St. Jerome the same Epistle and Gospel are appointed which have always been used in the Church of England; and the Collect is from the Sacramentary of St. Gregory. But the name "Trinity Sunday" was general until a later period, though it has been used in the English Breviary and Missal since the time of St. Osmund, and may have been adopted by him from still earlier offices of the Church. In the Eastern Church this day is the Festival of all holy Martyrs; a festival which has been observed at this time in the East, even in the days of Chrysostom and the Emperor Leo, who have left respectively a Homily and an Oration upon it.

"It appears to have been regarded as a separate Festival in the western world only by the Church of England, and those Churches of Germany which owe their origin to the English St. Boniface, or Winfred. Both in the ancient English and in the ancient German Office books all the Sundays afterwards until Advent are named after Trinity; whereas, in all Offices of the Roman type they are named after Pentecost.

"It seems probable," continues Dr. Blunt, "that this distinctive ritual mark is a relic of the independent origin of the Church of England, similar to those peculiarities which were noticed by St. Augustine, and which were attributed by the ancient

British bishops to some connection with St. John. In this case it is, at least, significant that it was St. John through whom the doctrine of the Holy Trinity was most clearly revealed; and also that the early Church of England was never infested by the heresies on this subject which troubled other portions of the Christian world.

"The general observance of the day as a separate Festival in honour of the blessed Trinity was first enjoined by a synod of Arles, in A. D. 1260. * * * It seems to have become generally observed by the Roman as well as other Churches at the end of the fourteenth century; but the Sundays after it are still named from Pentecost in all the Catholic Churches of the West, except those of England and Germany."

It will not be necessary to quote the comments which follow upon the fitness of a Festival so named, coming after the Services which commemorate our Lord's life, His death and glorious resurrection and ascension, and the resulting revelation of the Holy Spirit.

"In the festival of Trinity all these solemn subjects of belief are gathered into one act of worship, as the Church Militant looks upward through the door that is opened in Heaven, and bows down in adoration with the Church Triumphant, saying, 'Holy, Holy, Holy, Lord God Almighty, which was and is and is to come. * * * Thou art worthy, O Lord, to receive glory, and honour, and power; for Thou hast created all things, and for Thy pleasure they are and were created.'"

Every sentence in these paragraphs will interest the Prayer Book worshipper, not the least those having reference to the independent origin of our branch of the Western Church, and the probable influence of the title, Sundays after Trinity. It is not difficult to conceive that the name Trinity, printed on page after page of our Service Book during so many centuries, has done much to strengthen the orthodoxy of Church people.

On the other hand, whoever realizes that the manifestation of the Third Person in the Trinity on the first Whitsunday was as real a turning-point in human history as the Birthday of Christ, will feel no surprise that Dr. Blunt's comment, read for the first time many years ago, became a subject of much thought with me. It raised this question: Do these twenty-five Sunday Services, which were not anciently named after Trinity, and are not now so named in the Latin Church, have in fact the event of the Spirit's descent, and the consequent outpouring of new life and power from heaven, for their dominant thought and motive?

The event, I say; for it is rather events than truths to which men build monuments, and appoint days of commemoration. The Nativity of Christ was an event. So was His Manifestation to the Wise Men, who, coming from the East, represented nations that eventually would sit down with Abraham's children in the kingdom of heaven. Easter marks an event. If Christ be not risen, our faith is vain; there is no Gospel. And it is the same with Whitsunday.

What have other writers on the Prayer Book said on this matter? Turning to Procter and Frere (page 548) we read:

"In early days the Sunday following Whitsunday was kept merely as its octave. The service of the Trinity came into existence first as a Votive Mass; it then became customary (apparently first in England, and in the tenth or eleventh century) to use this upon the Octave of Pentecost, as a day more especially appropriate; and from this arose the festival of Trinity Sunday, designed to sum up all the dogmatic teaching of the first half of the year in a solemn commemoration of God

the Blessed Trinity.   Following the English custom, the succeeding Sundays are in the Prayer Book reckoned after Trinity and
not after Pentecost."

In respect to the Epistle and Gospel for Trinity
Sunday it is noted (page 549) that "these are the same
that were read in the old Octave of Pentecost, the last
day of the more solemn time of baptism, to which the
Gospel refers," and it may be added, the *Whit*, or
White in the name Whitsunday refers, because candidates for baptism came to the font clothed in white
raiment.

Further, it is said (page 550), that the Epistles for
the Sundays after Trinity, taken in the order in which
they stood in the Sarum Book, "are a series of exhor-
tations to the practice of Christian virtues."

Carrying our question to Dr. Samuel Hart, we
receive practically the same information, with this
point added, that "the special observance in honor of
the Holy Trinity is attributed to St. Thomas à Becket,
about 1165; but it would appear to have been older
by at least a century" (page 128, Book of Common
Prayer).   We are told that, "whereas in the former
half of the Christian year, from Advent to Trinity,—
which brings before us the successive events or lessons
of the Lord's life,—the Sunday Gospels contain the
special teaching, and the Epistles are chosen to illustrate and emphasize that teaching;" in the latter half
it is the other way: "on the Sundays after Trinity,
it is the Apostles who are teaching, and the Lord who
'confirms their word' by His signs and His lessons of
truth."

Bishop Coxe, having said ("Thoughts on the Services," page 231) that the Epistle and Gospel for

Trinity Sunday are the more striking because the ancient ones for the Octave of Pentecost were not specially selected with reference to the Trinity, remarks (page 233):

"So far (in the Church Year) we have seen that the Son of God was 'manifested'; now we are to learn how He destroyed 'the works of the devil.'" Commenting on our mutual weakness and need of grace, and calling attention to the Collect, "O God, the strength of all those that put their trust in thee," he continues: "Like the rod of Aaron, the rod and staff of our Creed must now blossom and bear fruit in piety; so we pray for the life-giving Spirit, that we who are by nature dead in sin, may become plants of grace in the garden of God."

The Bishop is greatly impressed by the difference in the teaching and entire spiritual atmosphere of the two periods, that from Advent to Trinity, and that from Trinity to Advent.

"As the whole book of the Acts is a record of the Spirit and has been called the 'Gospel of the Holy Ghost,' we continue to read it at this season in the Daily Lessons and also on Sundays after Trinity Sunday. Indeed, the residue of the year must be conceived of as a continuous commemoration of the Spirit, just as the earlier half of the year is dedicated to the Eternal Word. The feast of the Holy Trinity serves as the clasp or bond by which the whole is made a unit. Thus the Lord, and Giver of Life, receives due honour, while His divine personality and blessed offices are prominently kept in view. May all who profess to worship the Spirit do so in Spirit and in truth" (page 223).

Clearer and more forcible expressions than these none could ask or expect. No such testimony, however, is borne later by Bishop Coxe to the Epistles and Collects of this period as regards the Truth of the Spirit; for example, on the Fourteenth Sunday, in whose Epistle the Holy Spirit is named five times;

and on the Nineteenth, when we pray that God's "Holy Spirit may in all things direct and rule our hearts," and are taught in the Epistle not to "grieve" Him.

Dr. Blunt, after furnishing the above-mentioned information in regard to the late origin of the name Trinity Sunday in the English Church, and the suggestive comments thereupon, makes slight reference to the Spirit in his often quite full comments upon the Epistles.

There seems, then, to be good reason for devoting thought to the subject of this chapter; and encouragement to do so has come from the conviction that others have had our question in mind, yet have not sought the answer. In a letter from a wise bishop, lately deceased, was the remark: "I have never considered fully the reason for designating the Sundays after Trinity as we do, in preference to the Roman use, though not confined to the Romans, of designating them Sundays after Pentecost."

II

Taking up our task of examination, and remembering the fact just noted, that the Epistles give the leading thoughts in the Service from Whitsunday to Advent, we turn to them first, and chiefly. Bishop Coxe, and other authorities, have supposed the reason for the choice of these Epistles to lie in their capacity to "build up the members of Christ's Church in personal holiness." This they assuredly do, and a blessed end it is. The Holy Ghost is here to make every Christian soul His temple, and the comforting and uplifting books which are continually being written upon this aspect of His ministration, are none too numerous. But there are wider aspects of it revealed in the Epistles, and, as we shall see, in those appointed for this season especially. It must be the case, if He is indeed the Creator-Spirit, who in Christ's name and as His Vice-gerent is laying the foundations of the Church, wherever they are laid in the whole world, or, as Dr. Downer expressed it, "conducting the missionary campaign of the Ascended Lord." If the season which stretches from Whitsunday to Advent, equalling in length all the other Church Seasons together, is, as I hope to show, the Spirit's Season, we may expect to find in it hints, at least, of many elements of His personal greatness, and of the breadth and power of His sacred mission.

The Apostles apprehended these elements, but, as Dr. Fairbairn has said, "the Fathers were slow in discovering them." We are all slow to realize them, even we who "worship and glorify Him" as "the Lord, and Giver of Life. His work," writes Dr. Fairbairn, "was as great and as necessary, and expressed attributes as divine, as those of the Father and the Son— ubiquity, holiness, truth, infinite energy, ever exercised and ever resultful." ("Place of Christ in Modern Theology," page 490.)

Our work must begin with a brief study of Whitsunday itself, of which Bishop Doane, in the Mosaics, has written as follows:

"The Church, taken out of the side of the Second Adam in the deep sleep of death, got on Whitsunday her share of the breath of life, the Spirit given without measure unto Him, and became Eve (life), the result of breathing, the spiritual 'mother of us all' who live unto God."

It was the Epiphany of the Third divine Person, completing the revelation of the Triune God. It was marked by many signs, insignia of a kingly Presence and Power.

"The Holy Ghost was never incarnate," wrote Dr. Ewer, "but there is a certain sense in which we may regard Pentecost as the birthday of the Spirit; for it was then that He descended from Christ's Body Natural upon the Catholic Church, and filled it with His presence, His light, and something of His power. From all eternity He had dwelt in God the Son. Now, when that Son became incarnate, it could not but be that the Spirit should pass into the Human Body and Soul which the Divine Son took into eternal and hypostatic union with Himself.

"Furthermore, when the God-man framed, so to speak, and united the Body Mystical to Himself, it could not but be that the Spirit should pass into and dwell in It also. * * * Thus at Pentecost the springs of life and light for the human race were extended from the Natural to the Mystical framework of the Body of Christ. * * * As the Son revealed the Father to the world, so it was one of the functions of the Spirit to reveal the Son to the Church.

"Here we have then the Catholic Church as a Body illumined with all truth and designed by God to be perpetually present among men as a Divine Teacher of the world."

Our Lord had used more than one name to convey to the disciples what the Spirit would be to the Church Universal and to the world. The word "teacher" did not cover it. "Comforter" did not, especially in the familiar, secondary sense of one who consoles. Its primary sense of strength-giver is more nearly adequate, and yet not entirely so. The Greek word "Paraclete" is not, because it meant one who has been called, or sent, to stand by another, to support and defend him; whereas Christ had said also, "He shall be *in* you."

A divine Person, and in fact the Creator and indwelling Life of the world and of humanity, could only be indicated by many signs. The Dove seen at Christ's baptism meant one attribute,—that of gentleness; perhaps also the brooding, fostering care of motherhood. The Water of the feast of Tabernacles signified inward life and refreshment.

Wind, breath, and air, are one, and are associated with the great gift, life. The Spirit had breathed life into man at the beginning. It is through the all-encompassing atmosphere that He sustains vegetable, animal and human life to-day. How profound the significance of the Fire to disciples who had been with the Lord! When they beheld tongues or forked flames of fire above each others' heads, would they not remember Christ saying, "I am the light of the world," and, on another day, "Ye are the light of the world"? It was in the Spirit that these different truths became one.

He had said, "The Spirit shall bear witness of me," and again, "Ye shall receive power after that the Holy Ghost is come upon you, and ye shall be witnesses unto me." The Spirit has come; the fire over their heads means that He has, and means that He, and they in Him, shall take up the work of testifying to Christ. With the light there comes a warmth of zeal for God and for man such as the world has never seen. In the new, heroic courage to proclaim Christ, bear all hardships, suffer death itself in order to proclaim Him, we discover similar evidences of another divine Epiphany.

It was Light of Light of Light, the thrice holy light of the Godhead, made known at last. Perhaps the greatest wonder consisted in the clear vision and intense feeling of the Church's universality, at once realized by all. Christ had said, "Greater works [than mine] shall he do who believeth on me; because I go to the Father;" and the early believers did perform miracles; yet the supreme Pentecostal miracle was the breaking up of Jewish exclusivism, the new longing to save "all that were afar off," and a sublime effort to accomplish it.

To take in the truth of Whitsunday, merely in outline, will be to agree with Bishop Reichel's words:

"Pentecost is the most important festival of the Christian Year, and our thought about it and manner of celebrating it inadequate and unworthy. Looked at on all sides and in its practical relations to men as individuals, to mankind as a whole, it is greater than Christmas and Epiphany, greater even than Easter."

The Passover was distinguished by the waving of a single sheaf of wheat, emblem of the harvest's beginning, and such was our Lord Christ, "the firstfruits of them that slept." Pentecost, calling for yet deeper and warmer gratitude for the harvest completed, was a symbol and prophecy of the glorious ingathering of an entire race, risen and transfigured in Christ. It is

"Christ for the world we sing,"

and on no other day of the year should those words of Hymn 262 have such a rich meaning for us:

"Yea, West and East the harvest men went forth;
'We come' has sounded to the South and North;
    At morn sing Alleluia."

III

Let no man say, then, that one day's services, or one day's preaching,—were Chrysostom himself the preacher,—or twenty-five such days, or weeks, can exhaust the riches of the Pentecostal Truth. Convinced that they cannot, and opening our Prayer Books at Trinity Sunday, we are not surprised to find that it is the Spirit's day almost as much as Whitsunday itself. The Epistle marks the Trinity Truth; but in it we read of the "seven lamps of fire burning before the throne, which are the seven Spirits of God," —suggesting the various operations of the one Spirit; while the Gospel contains Christ's word to Nicodemus concerning the new birth "of water and the Spirit." The first morning lesson is the story of the Creation, and the second contains the Baptist's announcement that our Lord would baptize with the Holy Ghost, and the account of the Spirit's descent upon Christ at the Jordan.

We might expect this, knowing Trinity Sunday to have been anciently regarded as the Octave of Whitsunday, but what of the next Lord's Day? Here the Holy Ghost's signature is not written, so to say, over the portal of the service; but we think we find it, reading, "Love is of God; and every one that loveth is born of God," and "Hereby know we that we dwell in him, and he in us, because he hath given us of his Spirit," and remembering that of the nine fruits of the Spirit love is by St. Paul first named.

Love being first, and being the "fulfilling of the law," and "the greatest thing in the world," we are not surprised to find it spoken of two Sundays in succession. At any rate, here it is again in the Epistle for

7

the Second Sunday, and here again is the Spirit named. Hereby we know that Christ abideth in us, "by the Spirit which he hath given us."

No mention is made of the Spirit on the Third Sunday, nor is humility anywhere named as one of His nine "fruits." This must be said, however, that humility is the very first *necessity* in a Christian. It lies at the base of all the Christian graces, and is well nigh hardest to attain. By pride the angels fell, if not man also. The Good Friday Collect implies that Christ saved us by His "great humility." It is because He humbled Himself even to the death of the Cross, that He sits as Man at the right hand of God, and has earned the right to send the Spirit of His own, divine-human, love and humility to us.

Moreover, in the Gospel for this Sunday we find the parable of the woman lighting the candle and sweeping the house to find the one lost piece of silver. In this woman's solicitude to recover her lost possession more than one commentator has thought to discover a touching image of that sympathy for lost mankind which is characteristic of the Comforter.

We have reached the Fourth Sunday, and the eye falls on the word "firstfruits," and "the Spirit," as also on "the whole creation." How closely bound up together are the whole creation and man, the child of nature, we have seen in Chapter I. There is a mysterious connection between man's sin and the present condition of the earth and of the entire animate world. In a very important sense the earth is redeemed with man, and there will be a new heaven and a new earth (Rev. 21: 1), to receive the new humanity, transfigured and glorified in Christ.

Now the Spirit is—to use the homely phrase,—*in all this*. He created the earth and man, prepared man and the whole creation for Christ; Himself co-operated in the Son's Incarnation, and sustained and empowered the Son as Man through childhood and manhood, and in His agony and patient, holy death. When "the adoption" comes for which earth and man are waiting, how large a share of the "glory and honour and thanksgiving" will belong to the gracious Spirit!

IV

No age of the Church's chequered life was more momentous than that of the persecutions; and it was in that period that the Collect for the Fifth Sunday seems to have originated. Found in all three ancient Sacramentaries, it is a cry for the Peace of the Church, that it may joyfully serve its Lord "in all godly quietness." In the words of St. Peter: "The eyes of the Lord are over the righteous, and his ears are open to their prayers," and "If ye suffer for righteousness' sake, happy are ye; be not afraid of their terror, neither be troubled;" in Christ's word, "Fear not," to Simon Peter in the sinking vessel on the lake, associated with the thought of the manifold troubles of those early Christian centuries, we have grave situations depicted, and for these situations divine comfort promised which can cheer the Church and individual Christians in every age.

The Church is the Spirit's creation and the Spirit's care, and our cares for her and ourselves we are to cast upon Him. Care turned over to the Comforter ceases to be "an enemy to life." And He, as the Spirit of Missions,—His first great aim being that of catching and drawing in all mankind into the kingdom,—would not have us fail to mark in this connection the lesson in this Sunday's Gospel. The multitude of fishes taken, the broken net, the call to the partners for help, the two ships more than filled, and Christ's final word to Simon, "Henceforth thou shalt catch men," bear on the chief purpose for which "the Spirit was given," and for which the Church lives and moves and has its being in Him.

The Sixth and Seventh Sundays suggest the Spirit indirectly, yet forcibly, because in the Epistle for the one Baptism is the subject, and in the other occurs the word "fruit," always suggestive of the Giver of Life. "Ye have your fruit unto holiness, and the end ever-lasting life," is to be realized by us only through our new life in the Holy Spirit, and into this new life we are initiated by our baptism. In the words of Dr. Du Bose, "the substance of Christianity is to realize our baptism."

Four times the Spirit is named in the Epistle for the Eighth Sunday, and in connection with the Gospel truth of our new filial life, through union with the eternal Son. To join us to the ascended Son of Man, forever at home with the Father in heaven, is above all other things the Holy Spirit's delight, and to preach this new life of adoption and freedom was the special affair of Christ's, and His, Apostle to the nations of the West. It is a favorite note with him, and clear and strong it sounds here in Romans, like the keynote of a sweet hymn-tune played on a cathedral chime, heard at hours of prayer across the house-tops and fields: "As many as are led by the Spirit of God, they are the sons of God,— ye have received the Spirit of adoption—The Spirit itself beareth witness with our spirit, that we are the children of God."

The Epistle for the Ninth Sunday contains no distinct reference to the Spirit, yet has a vital connection with the realm of grace over which He presides. The Corinthian Christians were warned not to tempt Christ as the Israelites had tempted Him of old. Although "baptized unto Moses" and eating "spiritual meat" and drinking of "the spiritual Rock that followed them," these had displeased God, and "were overthrown in the wilderness." We Christians are taught that the same thing can happen now in the New Testament Church, enjoying the rich means of grace which those ancient supernatural gifts prefigured. It is upon this passage that Godet has written the following striking comment:

"It has been justly observed that in this passage we find for the first time the combination of the two sacred acts of Baptism and the Lord's Supper as forming a complete whole; the one representing the grace of entrance into the new life, the other the grace by which we are maintained and strengthened in it. The combination of these two acts, under the particular name of *sacraments*, is not therefore an arbitrary invention of dogmatics."

In the Epistle for the Tenth Sunday the note of the Spirit is struck again, not merely nine times, but with singular power. Nowhere in the Scriptures do we receive a stronger impression of the divine Personality of the Spirit. Men say, "the will is the man," and we receive a distinct impression of the Spirit's Will, where the Apostle declares that "no man can say that Jesus is the Lord, but by the Holy Ghost," and that all the different "gifts," wisdom, knowledge, faith, healing, and other endowments, are conferred by the Spirit, "dividing to every man severally as He will."

V

Attention should be invited at this point to the existence of certain groups of Sundays,—that is to say, of Sunday Epistles. We have passed such a group from Romans, and shall find one from Galatians, and another from Ephesians. Now the Tenth, Eleventh and Twelfth Sundays take their Epistles from First and Second Corinthians. All three speak of gifts of grace. While the Tenth deals with gifts conferred by the Spirit upon different members of the "great congregation," as manifestations of the Spirit's presence, to be used for mutual edification, the Eleventh and Twelfth speak of gifts for the Ministry in particular. They cover what is now designated the grace of Holy Orders.

It will be impossible to discuss this subject,—grace in general, grace in the "diversities of gifts" enjoyed by the many, grace given to the sacred Ministry. Enough to say, that wherever the word occurs, as, for example, in the Collect for the Eleventh Sunday, "Such a measure of thy grace," we are to remember not Christ alone, but the Spirit also. The Benediction contains indeed the phrase, "The grace of our Lord Jesus Christ"; is it not, however, His Spirit's special function to minister this grace to redeemed men? In the language of Dr. Downer:

"As soon as the catastrophe took place which we know as the Fall of Man, a second or new creative work began. This is the Economy of Grace, or the manifestation of God's love and mercy to those who by sin had forfeited His favour. Here the Blessed

Spirit finds His truest and most characteristic sphere. His re-creative work within the soul of man began at once, and from the first it was coupled with the promise of a Mediator. The first phase of this new work of the Spirit is Regeneration:—The Holy Spirit gives effect to all the Church's means of grace."

As to the grace of the Apostolic Ministry, it is more than interesting to note how the theme is carried over from the Eleventh to the Twelfth Sunday. "By the grace of God I am what I am; His grace which was bestowed upon me was not in vain—I laboured more abundantly than they all: yet not I, but the grace of God which was with me," are utterances followed up and confirmed on the next Sunday by words even more forcible, and of extreme beauty, from the Apostle's second letter.

We need to weigh the words as truly as did the Corinthians. Many who are in Orders, and more who are not, appreciate the spiritual efficiency and "glory" of the New Testament ministry as little as did they who received two Apostolic letters on the subject; and of the twenty-six Sundays after Pentecost the two in which the Spirit in the Church brings them before us are none too many.

It is as true for us as it was for the Apostle, that our sufficiency,—efficiency,—is of God. We too are "able" ministers only as being ministers of a "new testament." All the "life" we have, all the power we have to inspire men, to communicate life in Word or Sacrament, is derived from the Holy Spirit, or, as He is termed in the last part of this wonderful chapter, "the Lord, the Spirit."

Except in that the power to do unto God "true and laudable service" is the gift of the Pentecostal Spirit, and that we pray for it on the Thirteenth Sunday, He is not named on that day. On the Fourteenth He is suggested as the Giver of all life in nature and in man by the word "increase" in the Collect, and named in the Epistle five times, three times in a way which emphasizes His personality. The thought of His *enmity* to human flesh, contending against His *spiritual motions*, is distinctly personal. The phrase, "If ye be led by the Spirit," gives a like impression. The word "fruit," and the nine fruits named, correspond to the words "*increase* of faith, hope and charity" in the Collect.

VI

The last nine Sundays may be considered as forming a group, or as a "movement" in the long Pentecostal symphony. The keynote of this movement is the thought of the Church as a Body. We hear it in the Collects. In that for the Fifteenth Sunday the prayer is, "Keep thy Church with thy perpetual mercy"; for the Sixteenth, "Let thy continual mercy cleanse and defend thy Church"; for the Twenty-second, "Lord, we beseech thee to keep thy household the Church in continual godliness."

Where the Church is not actually named, one can see that Christians are thought of chiefly in their relation to that divine Society formed at Pentecost, of which the Spirit is the bond of union. The virtues and graces enjoyed are such as tend to conserve the unity and foster the life of the Body. The sins reproved in the Epistles are sins which wound and rend Christ's Body and make it the opposite of winning in the eyes of the world. On the Fifteenth Sunday the Church is prayed for as endangered by the "frailty" of its members. It is a "new creation" in Christ, and "as many as walk according to this rule, peace be on them, and mercy, and upon the Israel of God." Not "circumcision," but baptism in the Spirit has created this new and wider Israel.

Five Sundays the Epistle is taken from Ephesians. The Epistle to the Ephesians was not written, as Dean Alford has said, on account of peculiar circumstances, but addressed to Christians in a cosmopolitan city "as a type and sample of the Church Universal." It was intended to "set forth the ground, the course, the aim and end of the Church of the Faithful in Christ." Entirely in accord with this purpose is the fact noted by Dr. Downer (page 165) that it has several important references to the Spirit, and that the first of them, which is Pentecostal, is the opening passage, "The God and Father of our Lord Jesus Christ, who blessed us in all blessing of the Spirit," the aorist participle used "pointing to the great act by which this blessing was originally conveyed to the Church."

In all these Sunday services, and in fact until Advent, there is a certain depth and largeness which belong to what has been called by Alford (Commentary, Vol. III, page 19) the Life in the Holy Spirit. If they may be rightly compared to a movement in a symphony, *largo* should be thought of as inscribed on nearly every page of the music. It certainly belongs over the passage in the Epistle for the Sixteenth Sunday, beginning, "For this cause I bow my knees unto the Father of our Lord Jesus Christ," and ending, "Unto Him be glory in the Church by Christ Jesus throughout all ages, world without end."

The Rev. Dr. Waterman, of the Diocese of New Hampshire, in a sermon preached at the Fortieth Anniversary of Bishop Niles' Consecration, said:

"Our Bishop has taught everywhere, as St. Paul taught, that the Church is a Body. It is not merely a Society, made so by the fact that good men felt the need of coming together and co-operating with one another. It is not merely an organization provided by men's wisdom with more or less useful machinery. It is an Organism. It is a Body. No less a word will do. It is a Body, made so by the fact that it is the vehicle of a supernatural life. It is a living body, it is the Body of our Lord Jesus Christ, in which He shows Himself alive on earth to-day."

This is the truth of Ephesians, and in Ephesians, as in the New Testament generally, the Holy Spirit is the Soul and Energy of this corporate Christ life. It is the truth of our Book of Common Prayer, and in the eucharistic services of the Sundays of which we are now speaking *all* of "the important references to the Spirit in Ephesians" are found. In that for the Seventeenth Sunday is the passage beginning, "Endeavouring to keep the unity of the Spirit in the bond of peace." In that for the Twentieth we have, "My brethren, be strong in the Lord, and in the power of his might. * * * Take the sword of the Spirit which is the word of God; praying always with all prayer and supplication in the Spirit, and watching thereunto with all perseverance and supplication for all saints, and for me."

The Collect for the Nineteenth Sunday is noticeable not merely as being the only one which invokes the aid of the Spirit by name: it refers to Him as being already present, not praying that He may be "sent," or crying, "Come, Holy Spirit." One of the oldest

Collects, found in the Sacramentary of Gelasius, it
reflects the original thought of the Church, that, sent
to dwell in the Church, the Spirit is *here*. If now He
is here, by Christ's and the Father's Will especially
near, and *in charge of us*, we appreciate the better the
force of the word, "Grieve not the Spirit," found in the
Epistle for this Nineteenth Sunday. Does it not belong
just here? Is it here possibly by the blessed Spirit's
own arrangement? Certainly it can help to bring home
to men Bishop Gore's words, that "in humanity made
after the divine image, it was the original intention
that the Spirit should find His chiefest joy," as also
Bishop Webb's touching thought of His self-humiliation
in connection with His long labor of love in human
hearts, comparable even to the self-humiliation of the
Lord Jesus Himself.

In the Collect for the Twenty-third Sunday we pray
that God may hear the devout prayers of His Church,
and the Epistle speaks of the heavenly "citizenship"
which will be fully realized in that great Day of the
Lord, when the body of our humiliation shall (by the
Spirit's power) be changed, and made like unto the
body of Christ's glory.

The Epistle to the Colossians contains but one
reference to the Holy Spirit, and we find it here, *i. e.*,
in the Twenty-fourth Sunday. All Saints' Day is
near, and we have a reference to "the Father, which
hath made us meet to be partakers of the inheritance
of the saints in light," but also, be it observed, to the
love of the Colossians for "all the saints," that is to say,
in the Church Militant, and to their "love in the Spirit,"
reported to their Apostle by Epaphras, his dear fellow

servant, and a faithful minister of Christ for them. The words *wisdom, spiritual understanding, fruitful, increasing* in the knowledge of God, suggest the Spirit; and more particularly in His personal relation to Confirmation.

Then comes the Sunday next before Advent with its prayer that God's people may plenteously bring forth "the fruit of good works" and by Him "be plenteously rewarded."

VII

Throughout the first ten Sundays of this Season the Second Morning Lessons are taken from the Acts. Called in the New Testament Acts of the Apostles, they are in truth Acts of the Holy Spirit. Dr. A. T. Pierson wrote in the Introduction to his book:

"This brief study is the announcement of a *discovery* made by the writer, that this narrative is a revelation of the Holy Spirit in His *relations to believers as Christ's witnesses,* and *to the Church as the witnessing body;* and that from the opening chapter on there is a *progressive unfolding of this great theme.*"

On the ten Sundays referred to there is a noticeable selection of events, which are distinct turning-points in what Dr. Pierson characterizes as the Active Mission and Ministry of the Spirit of God, the Divine Paraclete. First, it is Philip planting the Church in Samaria and baptizing an Ethiopian eunuch. We then have the conversion of the future Apostle to the nations of the West. We witness next the baptism of Cornelius the centurion and his household by St. Peter, the first reception of Gentiles into the Universal Church. The preaching of the Gospel in Antioch follows; and on the Fifth Sunday we are with Paul and Barnabas in Lystra and Derbe.

On the Sixth Sunday we are at Jerusalem, at the First Council of the Church, which settles the vital question concerning the attitude to be assumed toward the Gentile element in regard to circumcision, and sends out the letter with the decision, and the sentence, "It seemed good to the Holy Ghost, and to us." Already the next Sunday we are with St. Paul on Mars' Hill, and hear him tell the men of Athens, how God, the Lord of heaven and earth, dwelling in temples not made with hands, has made of one blood all the nations of the earth; tell them of a judgment day, and of a Man appointed to be the judge, whom God has raised from the dead.

Each Sunday brings us to a new turning-point in the first chapter of the long story of Missions in Foreign Lands, under the guidance and in the power of the mighty Spirit. The rapidity of our progress in the reading of it may serve to remind us of the marvellous speed with which the Church was borne along by the breath of the Holy Ghost in those days after Pentecost. On the Eighth Sunday we are in Ephesus; on the Ninth in Cæsarea, where St. Paul answers for his life and doctrine before the noble Felix; on the Tenth Sunday, last in this series, we come to one of the great scenes in the Apostle's missionary experience, his defense before King Agrippa.

VIII

Two points are likely to suggest themselves to a thoughtful worshipper in the long season which we have been studying. One is, that the order of the truths presented to us is much the same as the order in the last section of the Catholic Creeds. We have first the Holy Spirit Himself, "the Lord, and Giver of Life, who proceedeth from the Father and the Son." We behold Him, worshipped and glorified, speaking by the Old Testament Prophets, and more fully and clearly by the inspired writers of the Gospels and Epistles. Then follows the "one Catholic and Apostolic Church," which was by His divine instrumentality conceived and born in our humanity, and which He informs and guides; and here, as in the Creed, Baptism for the Remission of Sins has its due place, "the realization" of which, as bringing mankind into living union with the Son of Man in heaven, "is the substance of Christianity." The Resurrection of the dead, and the Life of the world to come, round up the teachings of the Christian Year just as they do the historic formula of our Belief.

The other thought will be somewhat like this,—the Spirit of God is the Creator both of nature and of man, the immanent presence and energy of God in both. Of the fruits of my orchard and the flowers in my garden and of the increase of faith, hope and love in the garden of my heart, He is alike the divine author. Such words as *increase* and *firstfruits*, frequent in these Summer and Autumn services, as also the Epistle, from St. James, in the beautiful Thanksgiving Day Service, are there in part to remind me that the various beneficent works of the mighty Third Person in the kingdom of nature are one long parable of His more blessed and glorious operations in the kingdom of grace.

IX

What now are the results of our investigation? We will look at them primarily from the point of view of figures; and first as regards the Lessons. The Holy Spirit is referred to by name in the Sunday Lessons from Advent to Trinity fifty-six times, whereas He is named in the Trinity Season, on seventeen Sundays, only thirty-one times. It will be remembered, however, that a large proportion of the fifty-six references either occur in connection with the Nativity of our Lord, and of John Baptist, or consist of promises of the Spirit made by Christ just before His Death and Ascension, promises *fulfilled after Pentecost*. Moreover, the Second Lessons of ten Sunday mornings after Trinity, as we have been noting, relate to Acts of the Church under the continual influence of the personal Spirit, often unnamed.

In the Collects and Epistles and Gospels of the different Seasons from Advent to Trinity the Spirit is mentioned thirteen times, whereas He is named forty-two times in those of the remaining Sundays of the year.

When we give this last-mentioned fact its due weight, looked at simply in the way of numbers, and add the more important fact of the inward significance of the references, as I have tried to exhibit them in the foregoing pages; and lastly when careful attention is given to the teachings concerning the Spirit in relation to the Church and to individual believers, in the Morning Lessons for the Sixteenth, Twentieth, Twenty-first, Twenty-third, and Twenty-sixth, and in the Evening Lessons for the Twenty-third, Twenty-fourth and Twenty-fifth Sundays, it becomes difficult to understand expressions used by certain writers on the Prayer Book, while commenting on this Season.

For example, can these Twenty-five Sundays be rightly designated "uneventful"? It is true that no new event is related, worthy in itself to be compared with the Nativity, the Crucifixion, or the Resurrection, of our Lord. No star rises on faith's horizon which matches the star of the Spirit's own Epiphany. But so glorious is His, the Whitsunday, manifestation, that the world and even the Church which He founded have not yet rightly estimated the power and the beauty of its light. May not the season we have been studying seem uneventful to many, because in general "study of the Person and Work of the Holy Spirit has been neglected by the Church throughout her history"?

The more men do study it, the more thoroughly they will be convinced that twenty-five Sundays in the year, nay, fifty-two, are none too many to exploit the treasures of meaning which the Pentecostal Event possesses for mankind. Indeed it is less the meaning than the dynamic of Whitsunday which Christians come short of appreciating. The instant that one of those mysterious forces of nature which man is learning to harness to the chariot of progress in modern times is discovered, he sets himself to work, to learn how best to set *it* to work for human advantage. Yet no force ever discovered meant so much to the world as the new spiritual power of Pentecost. The philosopher Comte wrote on "Social Dynamics"; but the true social dynamic has been the motive of Christian love and fellowship, and of undying hope for our race, born on the first Whitsunday.

The new force with which believers in Christ then came into contact, and which influenced them to a degree in which His own presence and teaching had not, evidencing the truth of His saying, that it was expedient for them that He should go away, was interpreted at once by a new heroic behaviour and action. Selfishness gave way to love, even a love like unto that of the Lord Himself. It was this new love and courage in the Spirit, which wrought the acts of the Apostles, and began at once to change the face of the earth, and create a new civilization. It resembled that other force of the Spirit, gravitation, in that it drew men together in the Lord, as they had not been drawn even by Christ Himself, in the flesh. It was like the mystery we call life, but a spiritual life. There was a new and deeper consciousness of sin, a new understanding of the soul's need of a Saviour, and of the ascended Lord as being that Saviour.

It is not easy to comprehend, that a writer on the Christian Year who certainly believed in the Holy Ghost as the Giver of life, and who had already spoken of the Trinity Season as a "continuous commemoration of the Spirit," should afterward speak of the second half of the year as "devoted to duty primarily, and to doctrine only as reduced to practical piety," say, that the Christian Year is "divided between the Creed and the Decalogue," say, that in the earlier half of the year "our affections are warmed and our feelings healthfully excited," but in the latter half "no such impulse is supplied,—our spiritual joys must be purely those of faith and duty,—physical as well as spiritual efforts must be made if we would keep our souls alive and growing."

Is not the "doctrine" of an ever-present, omnipotent Spirit a glorious doctrine in itself, an essential and most important part of the Creed? Is He not the immediate Source of Love, and Joy, of Life and spiritual spontaneity? The Decalogue was given on Mt.

Sinai, and our Whitsunday Lesson teaches,—all through the following weeks we are to remind ourselves of it,—that in the Church of Christ we are not come unto Mt. Sinai, but unto Mt. Sion, the city of the living God, the heavenly Jerusalem.

The law is good, but as a schoolmaster to bring us to Christ, and the Spirit of Christ is the Spirit of sonship, and of that love which is in itself the fulfilling of the law. Rightly understood, faith, love, filial obedience, all the Christian graces, live and grow in us, in the Spirit, as the grass and the grain and the roses grow in the Summer sunshine, also in the Spirit. Through the long Whitsuntide we go to school to the Spirit, and it is going to school to our mother, that we may come by the filial spirit, as it were, by breathing it in. Duty, when filial, knows no effort. Brotherly and sisterly duty knows no effort. That was a favorite story of the late beloved Bishop of Pennsylvania, of the little girl seen carrying a robust specimen of babyhood, who, asked whether her burden was not heavy, answered, "Na, it's me brother."

The truth that duty done in the filial spirit is transfigured, is admirably brought out by the development of thought in Wordsworth's Ode to Duty. The first line,

"Stern daughter of the Voice of God,"

has the effect to repel us. Why should this daughter of heaven be stern? Already in the second verse there is a warmer light:

"There are who ask not if thine eye
Be on them * * *
Glad hearts! without reproach or blot;
Who do thy work and know it not."

The third verse is more winning still:

> "Serene will be our days and bright,
>   And happy will our nature be,
> When love is an unerring light,
>   And joy its own security."

And what of the sixth?

> "Stern lawgiver! Yet thou dost wear
>   The Godhead's most benignant grace;
> Nor know we anything so fair
>   As is the smile upon thy face:
> Flowers laugh before thee in their beds,
> And fragrance in thy footing treads;
> Thou dost preserve the stars from wrong,
> And the most ancient heavens, through thee
>   are fresh and strong."

Wordsworth was a Christian; and perhaps unknown to himself the truth of the Spirit lay between all these lines. Whether it did or not, the fact is,—and the New Testament and the Prayer Book are full of it,—Duty would wear no smile, nor would fragrance tread in her footing, the example of the ever punctual sun and planets would have no influence,—nor would that set us by the blessed Christ Himself,—had not His Spirit descended. As Bishop Reichel says ("Cathedral and University Sermons," page 191):

"It is the inner spirit,—first our own, and then the Spirit of God acting on and through our own,—that makes the life and death and resurrection of the Christ anything more to us than a picture is to a blind man or a symphony of music is to a deaf man."

"The conclusion of the whole matter," as regards the latter half of the Christian year, can for us "members

of Christ and children of God" scarcely be this, that
we have now simply to "fear God and keep His commandments." In this era of the enabling, trans-
forming, Spirit such were "a lame and impotent
conclusion." To enter the period of which Whitsunday is the gateway, over which the legend is inscribed,
Love, Joy and Peace in Christ the Son, is like crossing
into the promised land; "of brooks of water, of fountains and depths that spring out of valleys and hills,
of wheat and barley, of oil olive and honey."

The fountains by which the soul of the believer is
refreshed are not like the quickly dried springs which
descend the rocky sides of Horeb. They are inex-
haustible, living, waters which gush, as it were, from
under the walls of New Jerusalem. It is Hephzibah's
land, it is Beulah, "for the Lord delighteth in her, and
her land shall be married." Her bridal presents are
the inward spiritual gifts earned by her Lord's Labor
and Passion of thirty-three years, and brought to her
from on high by the gracious and loving Spirit.

It goes without saying that we need to enter upon
such a season of privilege desiring these inner gifts.
About a hundred and fifty years ago John Berridge,
Vicar of Everton, wrote:

"Every one who is born of God is made to hunger for implanted
holiness, as well as to thirst for imputed righteousness. They
want a meetness for glory, as well as a title to it; and know
they could not bear to live with God, unless renewed in
His image."

It is the Trinity Season which more than all the
others appears and appeals to us, as a period of implanted holiness; when week by week the Prayer

Book Christian will hope to realize in every thought and motive the truth of the Apostle's words (1st Cor. 1 : 30): "Of him are ye in Christ Jesus, who of God is made unto us wisdom, and righteousness, and sanctification, and redemption;" a Season when, meadows and trees turning green, and then gold, "the King's daughter" will be moved thereby to make good progress in becoming "all glorious within." Green, the students of ecclesiastical colors tell us, symbolized in the Eastern Church the Life of Grace; and Nature for her part now decks her outdoor altar to the Spirit in green. Putting on, as it were, her broad green stole, she preaches, in union with the Church, of grace, and all the blessed fruits of it, in the Spirit's sons and daughters.

Probably few readers of this book,—whether clergymen or laymen,—will not plead guilty to a desultory, unsystematic, habit of effort and prayer in the Trinity Season. All of us are more or less accustomed to lay aside ordered and definite reflection upon religious truth and conduct until the trumpet of Advent sounds again. This results in a serious loss of growth and power. Our study must convince us that such is not the conception and purpose of the Spirit as revealed in the Prayer Book. We are meant to be,—He is ready to help us to be,—growing Christians, and to arrive at each new Advent wiser and stronger. How is it with us? Many, it may be, have come upon a tree cut down in forest or orchard, which sawed and not hewn shows all its rings. A little difficult to distinguish at the centre, they become better defined and easier to count as one proceeds outward; and each ring tells of another year of growth.

Is it this way with the years of our life in Christ?

Can the Spirit who dwells in us, and longs to be the strength of this life, discover any rings?   And do these show thicker, because each season we have been more rapidly growing in grace, and in the knowledge of our Lord and Saviour Jesus Christ?

THE TRINITY SEASON—(CONTINUED)

He (the Spirit) dwelleth with you, and shall be in you.—John 14 : 17.

I tell you the truth; It is expedient for you that I go away.—John 16 : 7.

When he the Spirit of truth is come, he shall guide you into all the truth.—John 16 : 13.

I shall show you plainly of the Father.—John 16 : 25.

As many as are led by the Spirit of God, they are the sons of God.—Rom. 8 : 14.

Unto you it is given to know the mystery of the kingdom of God.—Mark 4 : 11.

The Spirit searcheth the deep things of God.—1st Cor. 2 : 10.

> Teach us to know the Father, Son,
> And thee, of both, to be but One.
>
> —Veni, Creator Spiritus.

No man can say that Jesus is the Lord, but by the Holy Ghost.—1st Cor. 2 : 10.

Whitsunday, as connected with Trinity Sunday and leading to it, seems to me to contain the most marvellous and blessed witness of the whole year, and that without which all the rest would be in vain.—F. D. Maurice.

The great intellectual struggle of our day turns mainly on the question whether there is a Holy Ghost.—Thirlwall.

The doctrine of the Holy Spirit has been, hardly less than that of the Resurrection of our Lord, too much neglected in the theology of our time.—Milligan.

A science without mystery is unknown; a religion without mystery is absurd.—Darwin.

Life precedes organization.—Huxley.

> Flower in the crannied wall,
> I pluck you out of the crannies;
> Hold you here, root and all, in my hand,
> Little flower: but if I could understand
> What you are, root and all, and all in all,
> I should know what God is, and man is.

I feel that we shall never see a real revival in the Church, or in any individual soul, until the "Veni Creator" is said as a real prayer addressed to a real Person.—Bishop Ingram.

The Church Catholic is the Spirit-bearing body, the special home of the Holy Spirit's activities. * * * Amongst the gravest signs of the times is the attempt which is being made to eliminate the idea of the Church in education. * * * In this gift of all the gifts, the Holy Spirit, resides the secret of the harmonizing of Reason and Revelation. He will help us to *wait* in patience for the reconciliation of seemingly hopeless antagonisms, show us that religion has everything to hope for, and nothing to fear in, scientific conclusions. Above all, He will enable us to see that both Reason and Revelation come from the same Giver of all good gifts; that the one is the complement of the other; that they are the truest of friends; that the God of Nature is the God of Grace, and that what God hath joined together man must not put asunder.—Holden.

The Triune God of the Nicene Creed is the only God in which modern science has left it possible to believe.—Fulton.

The purpose in what has been written in the preceding chapters will not have been attained, unless my readers have received a somewhat clearer idea of the personality of the Holy Spirit, and of His agency in the creation and development of our venerable

Services, and finally of the fact that the so-named Trinity Season, in our Book, is substantially a continuous commemoration of the Epiphany of the divine Paraclete and of the various "gifts" He brought, and is now year by year and day by day dispensing to the Church and to mankind, for the sake and in the name of the ascended and glorified Son of Man.

It will perhaps be helpful to consider further what these three facts practically mean, or should mean, to the Christian mind and heart, and to the entire race; and how such a Season,—equal in length to the other Seasons of the Year of Christ united, may be most profitably commemorated. If the Holy Ghost is in truth the Lord, and Life-giver, the Vicar of the unseen Christ, and if it was really "expedient" for us that the Lord Jesus should "go away," in order that He might thus be manifested, and if Whitsunday does actually "contain the most marvellous and blessed witness of the whole year," and is the spiritual dynamic for all the needs in all the years, till the great Head of the Church shall come again, then certain points are evident. It is clear that not a single Truth, however glorious and convincing in itself, revealed to man in the teachings of those other Seasons, is so glorious, and so effective to win, and to sway humanity, as it *becomes* when brought into connection with the truth of this blessed Season.

The saying in 1st Corinthians 12 : 3, "No man can say that Jesus is the Lord, but by the Holy Ghost," contains a principle capable of wide application. No man can say, *i. e.*, believe in his heart and witness to his brother men, that the Christmas truth is true and Jesus Christ, God's only Son, "was made very man of the substance of the Virgin Mary his mother, without spot of sin, to make us clean from all sin," without the help of the Holy Ghost by whose personal "operation" the blessed Nativity took place.

The Epiphany truth, that Christ is very God and a Universal Saviour, was made known to St. Peter by the Spirit,—our Lord implied this, saying: "Flesh and blood hath not revealed it unto thee, but my Father which is in heaven,—" was by the Spirit made known to St. Thomas before the Ascension, in the same supernatural way; and again was made known gradually in its rich fulness, and in all its wide bearings upon philosophic thought, to St. John, that in his old age he might bear personal witness to it, to the Church then coming in contact with great systems of thought. And no man, woman or child in the world to-day believes it without the aid of the self-same Spirit.

So is it with the other side of Christ's Epiphany, namely, His sacred, spotless, Humanity,—without which there were no salvation for the great human family,—brought out by St. Luke, the converted "pagan," in what Renan has called "the most beautiful book in the world." This human side means more and more to us every year. It was a truth only partially developed in the early days, and it is not yet developed in its fulness and beauty, or seen in its many practical bearings. The Spirit it was who in co-operation with the Father and the Son wrought the wonder of that perfect humanity in the Person of Christ Jesus, and He alone can make it a reality to human faith.

The divine Fatherhood, a New Testament revelation, and a truth exhibited on nearly every page of the Prayer Book,—which Bishop Westcott somewhere says is

perhaps the chief message of our Church to the men of
this day,—is easier to read and hear of than to embrace
with the heart. But the Third Person is pre-eminently
"the Spirit of adoption." By Him, it reads, we cry,
Abba, Father (pater) in our hearts, to the One universal
Father. At first we almost necessarily miss the point of
the two names, the one Hebrew and the other Greek,
thus joined together. *Abba* spoken by Hebrews and the
many races akin to them, and *pater, padre, père, vater,
father,* spoken by Greek, Roman, Italian, Spanish,
French, German and English tongues, sum up practically all mankind. It is the Spirit's delight, and He
is that divine Person whose function it is, "to make
all men" see, in this Pentecostal era, that God is the
Father of all, and has redeemed us all in His Son.

And so is it with the complementary truth of Christ's
Sonship, to come into vital union with which is Life
and Freedom, is Rest and Peace, while to fall out of it
into the legal, unfilial, life, is to "fall from grace."
"Come unto me,—I will give you rest,—my yoke
is easy, my burden light" (Matt. 11 : 28-30) as the
context shows, refers to the filial relation which is
first His, and then ours in Him. But it is the Spirit
who can persuade us of it, and enable us to be sons
indeed.

Of that supreme Gospel Mystery, or secret, which
God permits, yes, invites us to look into and "know,"—
imparting "wisdom and understanding" that we may
in some sort apprehend it,—the truth of the Holy
Trinity, the same is to be said. It is an exalting and
a comforting truth even mentally. It is not contra-
dictory to our reason, approached as it should be
"through the doctrine of the subordination of the Son

and the Spirit to the Father" (Mason, "Faith of the Gospel," page 51). Canon Mason writes also:

"If we say that before creation was, the infinite love of God was infinitely expended upon Himself, we cannot but feel that such an expression would be shocking to all our best instincts, if (as Arius taught) God is a single person. A monstrous selfishness is the only picture which such language could suggest. It can only be morally true to say that God loves Himself, if there be eternally within the Divine nature a real Distinction of Persons, whereby one Divine Person may lavish the infinite wealth of His love upon another Divine Person who is infinitely worthy of receiving it. * * * Hard though it may be to understand the Church doctrine of the Trinity, it is much harder to conceive how God could be eternally love, if He were a solitary unit."

The Spirit can and will in answer to prayer help us to apprehend the glorious heavenly reality, and in the "Veni Creator" we do pray:

> "Teach us to know the Father, Son,
> And thee, of both, to be but One."

It is not the heart only, but the intellect also that He quickens, when the heavenly Dove comes to Christians "with all His quickening powers."

No season of the Christian Year brings home to us as does this one the truth that "the Catholic Religion is a reasonable religion." It is true that the natural (psychical) "man receiveth not the things of God," but *in Christ* we are something higher and better than natural, even spiritual. "The Spirit searcheth the deep things of God," that He may tell the glorious secrets to us. There is no department of human knowledge so uplifting and no exercise of man's god-like reason so strengthening to him, as are those of which we speak.

Whether we think of the eternal divine "purpose" to found a new universal family among the nations,—which is also called a mystery,—or again the wonderful secret of our resurrection, after the manner of our Lord's resurrection, "Behold I *show* you a mystery; we shall not all sleep, but we shall all be changed"; or that of the Church's union with her Lord, to be compared with the sacred union of man and wife; "This mystery is great; but I speak of Christ and the Church;" it is always the same. The Spirit is, or one day will be, the efficient cause of the marvels themselves, and the Spirit it is who lets us into the truths which mean so much to us, and which angels desire to look into (1st Pet. 1 : 12). God Himself will have His "manifold wisdom made known through the Church" to those "principalities and powers in the heavenly places" (Eph. 3 : 10), nor would He leave us out, who *are* the Church.

As no man can say out of his heart that Jesus is the Lord but by the Holy Ghost, so none can without the same inward help confess the truth of Atonement, by which nevertheless the Bible is pervaded from Genesis to Revelation. The Jewish Festivals owned it, incorporated with the harvest-home thought, "God is our Life." The first half of the Christian Year embodies it. The Incarnation was, at once and in itself, a reconciliation. Christ's perfect filial life, His holy childhood and youth, with which, already, the Father in heaven was "well-pleased," was an *At-one-ment* between God and Mankind. The Lord's victories great and small obtained over His and our Tempter, were in so far a closing of the gap sin had made, *justifying* our humanity. And the greatest victory,—that of the Passion and the willing Death,—which every Eucharist now thankfully celebrates, closed the gap entirely, and forever restored our fellowship with the Father.

And yet the Spirit alone makes this real, to the Church as a Body representing mankind, and to the individual soul. It is a revelation of the Spirit to me, that *I* am justified, received and through eternity united to God in this mighty Act of vicarious self-giving on the part of the Son of God made man. Theories of the Atonement are good, in so far as they are true theories, that do not infringe upon the truth of God's Fatherhood and Christ's and my sonship, but none of these can make the reconciliation real to me, and help me to appropriate it—like the rude Maori chief, who, seeing a crucifix by the roadside, cried, "Come down, Christ, that is my place,"—without the Spirit. No man or woman can rightly say, "my Lent was a good one,—I had a good Easter," but by the Pentecostal Spirit.

Connected with this, however, is the other fact of sin. Over and over again the Prayer Book tells us, that "if we say that we have no sin the truth is not in us," speaks in the Communion Office of our Lord's perfect self-oblation as "made for the sins of the whole world." But it is easier to listen to the words than to acknowledge the truth of them for ourselves, saying from the heart, "we acknowledge and bewail certain manifold sins which we from time to time have grievously committed." If any one, even a near and dear friend, calls our attention to such offenses, it may break the friendship forever. Four centuries before Christ a little man, with an interesting though almost

ugly face, and a powerful mind, went about the streets
of Athens, saying to its citizens, "Know thyself; live
an honest and pure life." He lived justly himself;
but they condemned him to die. Our Lord reproved
sin, and though men heard Him gladly, and He was
without sin, He was crucified.

Now it would appear that He must have been
rejected, and at last crucified, in great part, because the
Spirit was, as He said, "not yet given." Behold the
change, when in about two months the Spirit had been
given in power. The very men who have put Him to
death, or looked on approvingly, pricked in the heart
are crying "What shall we do?" They act on St.
Peter's word, "Repent and be baptized every one of you
in the name of Jesus Christ unto the remission of your
sins." Now to any man reading this record, and
reflecting on his own, at least possible, connection with
this matter, considering who Jesus Christ was, three
points will stand out clearly. He will see first, that
to have a share in the remission of sins he must perform a certain outward act easy enough to be performed; secondly, he must repent of all sins of which
his conscience accuses him; and thirdly,—which is of
prime importance,—it must be the Pentecostal Spirit
who can enable Him to repent. The Holy Ghost must,
can, and in answer to prayer will, quicken his conscience,
doing for him what Socrates could not do for the people
of Athens, and what even the Lord Jesus might not
do for the people of Jerusalem without the Spirit.

Just this the Lord promised that the Spirit would
do: "He shall convince the world of sin, of righteousness and of judgment." That is, He would assist
every man who should invoke the Spirit upon his

conscience, to see and in some degree feel and acknowledge, that the "sorrow which" was "done unto"
Christ, the pangs and afflictions, and the awful desola-
tion, which forced from His sacred lips the cry, "My
God, my God, why hast thou forsaken me?" were
sufferings endured on account of our race; and therefore
have a moral value for him.

The fact is,—and one needs to think of it often in
Lent, or Advent, or whenever one would practice
self-examination,—there is no such thing, there is no
self-knowledge possible, "but by the Holy Ghost."
We all have to go to God to get examined; say,
"Examine me, O Lord, and prove me: try out my
reins and my heart"; open sins and secret ones, sins
of thought, word and deed, sins of *omission* and commission; and He answers the petition through that
Third Person, whose Epiphany is commemorated
throughout the entire second moiety of the year. To
speak in frank confidence, bringing in the priestly and
pastoral *ego*, were I to begin again to teach and preach
of "sin, and of righteousness, and of judgment," I
would strive to do it more than ever before in the
power of the Spirit. In this and in all the sacred
seasons I would at times ask my hearers to lift up
their hearts and listen *in* the Spirit, because no man
can say in his heart that Jesus is a Redeemer from the
guilt of sin, and that he in particular needs and wants
this redemption, but by the gracious Spirit's assistance.

In the "intermediate state," regarding which the
Scriptures have not told us much, and yet have said
enough to lead a Christian to look forward and count
upon it not a little for himself and others,—in which
we shall be led by Christ's Spirit in paths of truth, which

are only *vistas* now,—the wisest and purest of believers
will be purged of many faults and enlightened as to
many misconceptions. He will have much to show
them of two at present half-told secrets; "the mystery
of iniquity," allowed here of God to "work" more or
less in all hearts, and the other mystery of atoning and
purifying Love revealed in the Son of Man. Only
when, in the Spirit, we shall have mastered and taken
home to our inmost consciousness these spiritual facts,
our personal need and God's most costly remedy, shall
we be able to behold our Lord face to face, and to "read
our title clear"; in other words, see our "names
written" large "in the book of life of the Lamb slain
from the foundation of the world." (Rev. 13 : 8.)

If the truth of the Trinity be made a subject for treatment in the Trinity Period, in the simple and real way
in which it certainly can be, and in which the Bishop
of London has treated it most helpfully, there should be
a great deal to say concerning the love of the Spirit,
especially as a love not to be *grieved* or *quenched*. The
reason why sin against the Holy Ghost was spoken of
by Christ as a sin not to be forgiven calls for and
admits of statement. There is a peculiar nearness of
the Spirit to our race, to which St. Basil referred.

The "signs"of the Spirit convey distinct and very different lessons, both to the Church and individuals, and
some of them, like Fire, Water, the Earthquake, invite
treatment in sermons the more urgently, because they
cannot with ease be represented suitably in Christian
art.

The Family has a large place in that Epistle which
occupies perhaps a more important position in the
Prayer Book, particularly in this Season, than does any

other Epistle; namely, the Ephesians.   In the Christianized family we possess, in my opinion, the truest, highest,
and most suggestive figure of the eternal Triune Life
on high.   Marriage is not a mystery.   It was the sacred
union of Christ and the Church which the Apostle
called a mystery, while comparing it with marriage.
But the triune life in the home is, and would seem
originally intended to be, a type of the Triune Life
in heaven; most remarkably as respects those principles
of Authority, Subordination, and Obedience, together
with Equality, Respect, and Love, which produce
harmony in heaven and earth alike.   It has been a
wonder to me to find so little made of this truth.   Canon
Mason said, "The only approach we can make to a
right understanding of what is revealed of the unity of
the blessed Three lies in the doctrine of the subordination of the Son and Spirit to the Father."   Now parallel
with this, surely, is the fact that the only approach to
actual peace and true progress, in the life of humanity,
is in the realization of this same principle first in the
home, and then in the state, and in every sphere of
human life.   This is one of the pressing truths for
our day and generation.

Is there any time when in our present circumstances
it is not in order,—will it not be especially in order
in the long Whitsuntide?—to preach and teach of
the Spirit as the fount of Unity in heaven and therefore on earth?   Called "Osculum Patris et Filii"
He is the bond of unity between the Father and the
Son, and His essential function is that of *uniting*.
In our present unhappily divided condition as Christians, the surest road out of our difficulties will be
through a clearer recognition of the Spirit's relation

9

to Christian life and conduct. We must believe that
we should not long differ if we betook ourselves more
to Him in earnest petitions for a right judgment,
and for a right temper and feeling in this whole matter
(*vide* G. F. Holden, The Holy Ghost the Comforter,
pages 4, 12, 13).

The Communion of Saints in this life,—in the Church
Militant,—is a theme for this period. Who but the
Spirit of Unity and Love shall impart to us "the love
which" we *ought* to "have to all the saints" here
and so make us "meet to be partakers of the inheritance of the saints in light" hereafter? It is to be
observed that alike in Romans and Ephesians, read
nine times in all in the Communion services of this
Season, the virtues inculcated are such as tend to
heal prejudice, create sympathy and every way foster
the Church's corporate life. And these two Epistles
are in their doctrinal portions almost entirely devoted
to this aspect of the Christ-life in us. Many books
have been written within a few years upon the Holy
Ghost, but attention has been confined in them mostly
to the individual life of Christians in Him. There
is a call for a wider outlook, and the Scriptures read
in the Trinity Season greatly favor this broader vision.
They should inspire Prayer Book worshippers to
think, to study, to labor, and to pray with one heart
for the prosperity of God's holy Apostolic Church;
to ask for a ready will to obey His word, and a hearty
desire to make His way known upon earth, His saving
health among all nations, and,—in order the better
to promote these glorious ends,—to work and pray
for unity and co-operation among Christians everywhere.

Now the quickening thought, yes, the motive and the motive-power, for this corporate spirit and prayer and effort are to be found in the personality and energy of the Holy Ghost, which as we have seen are either in the foreground or the background of all this Season's services.

I would not be understood to favor constantly repeated references to the blessed Spirit, such as the purposes of this volume have seemed to require. These would tend to weary one's hearers, if not to offend them. We may in this matter, as in many another, "take a leaf" so to say "out of St. Paul's book." For a while the Spirit is not named by him. It is only by study and comparison of passages that we learn that he is thinking of Him, as his readers are supposed to be doing in the Pentecostal age. And then how he takes us by surprise by naming the Spirit again and again! It is like the strokes of a hammer driving in the nail fastened by this "master of assemblies;" or, better, the strokes of the clapper of a sweet-toned bell. So he sends home the truth of the mighty Spirit's presence and indwelling life.

While writing this book I have looked into sermons of distinguished preachers, in our time and before it, to see whether many or any of them have imitated the great Apostle to the Western world in this respect. I have found no instances of it. It seems to me that it were good to imitate him. For example in the Epistle taken from Galatians (Fourteenth Sunday after Trinity) the Spirit is named five times in quick succession; and in the eighth chapter of Romans He is named nineteen times in thirty-nine verses. So doing we should soon bring back to the minds of our people the neglected if not forgotten truth of the Lord, the Spirit.

The process would be hastened by singing the beautiful Whitsuntide Hymns oftener than we have done during this Season, and at other times. These hymns are prayers, to the Spirit and for Him. The "normal" method of prayer is to the Father, through the Son, for the gift of the Spirit. Yet in the Litany we directly address Him. We do it in the "Veni Creator," and in the Hymns. Why should we not do it, if He is what Christ promised that He would be to us, if He loves us with a love of His own, and if He is a Spirit whom we can *grieve?*

"Years ago," wrote Holden (page 13), "I remember Dr. Liddon saying at Oxford, that if any one would but try the experiment of saying the 'Veni Creator' once every day for a year, he would be astonished at the end of that time to find how much spiritual insight had been granted. To those who are called to advise others there is no condition so certain to secure counsel and guidance, as that of abiding union with the same Blessed Spirit."

The remainder of this work will consist of sections in which themes are treated, now at some length, and again briefly,—always imperfectly,—which appear to me worthy of consideration in this Season. It has seemed to me that the thought of Missions should have the same first place in this book which it will have in every soul of which the Holy Ghost has taken complete possession. Dr. Downer has said,

"Acts 1 : 8 shows the Holy Ghost to have been given for the missionary purpose, and for other objects only as they subserved that purpose. Had the Apostles refused, or neglected, to undertake the duty, can we doubt that the gift of the Spirit would have been withdrawn from them? And does it not follow that failure to discharge the missionary obligation has been the direct cause of the dry, arid, unspiritual condition into which the Church has fallen at such times, owing to the retirement of the Blessed Spirit from His active and vitalizing operation within her, grieved at her disobedience to the standing orders of her Lord, or at least by her forgetfulness of them? * * * There are many treatises setting forth the nature of the Divine Spirit, His administration in the Body of Christ, His work in the individual soul; but few dwelling upon this, assuredly one of the foremost of His functions."

"O Holy Spirit, who proceedest from the Father and the Son, teach us to do the truth, that Thou mayest unite us in a mysterious bond of love to the Father and the Son, from Whom Thou proceedest so ineffably." (Mozarabic Liturgy.)

"Heavenly King, Paraclete, Spirit of Truth, who art everywhere present and fillest all things, the Treasury of good things and the Bestower of life, come and dwell in us, and purify us from every stain, and save our souls in Thy goodness." (Midnight Office of Eastern Church.)

MISSIONS

I will make you fishers of men.—Matt. 4 : 19.

Go ye therefore and teach all nations.—Matt. 28 : 19.

The Holy Ghost said, Separate me Barnabas and Saul for the work whereunto I have called them.—Acts. 13:2.

To me, who am less than the least of all saints, is this grace given, that I should preach among the Gentiles the unsearchable riches of Christ.—Eph. 3 :8.

The Book of the Acts of the Apostles does not in any complete sense justify its title. What it does give is the great leading Acts of the Holy Ghost, not in every place, or through all the chosen servants of the Ascended Lord, but on various critical and exemplary occasions, sufficient to show to all succeeding generations the principles and methods of the Divine Spirit as He dwells in and energizes the Body of Christ. It is this that renders the book of such transcendant importance as the hand-book of the Church in all ages.—Downer.

Missionaries, native Christian workers, and leaders of the missionary activities on the home field, while they differ on nearly all questions pertaining to plans, means, and methods, are absolutely united in the conviction that the world's evangelization is a divine enterprise, that the Spirit of God is the great Missioner, and that only as He dominates the work and workers can we hope for success in the undertaking to carry the knowledge of Christ to all people.—Mott.

Each new race which is introduced into the Church not only itself receives the blessings of our religion, but reacts upon it to bring out new and unsuspected aspects and beauties of its truth and influence. * * * How much of the treasures of wisdom and power which lie hid in Christ awaited the Greek intellect, and the Roman spirit of government, and the Teutonic individuality, and the temper and character of the Kelt and Slav, before they could leap into light! And can we doubt that now again not only would Indians, and Japanese, and Africans, and Chinamen be the better for Christianity, but that Christianity would be unspeakably also the richer for their adhesion,—for the gifts which the subtlety of India, and the grace of Japan, and the silent patience of China are capable of bringing into the city of God.—Bishop Gore, on Ephesians.

The few commands Christ gave to His followers while in the flesh became after the descent of His Spirit upon them rather inward motives than commands. So it was in regard to the Eucharist as a grateful memorial of Him, and so it was as to the commands, Let your light shine, and, Preach my Gospel to all the world.

The light shines because it is light. As soon as the promised Spirit dwelt in Christians, and the Love and the Light were in their hearts, the great work of missions was inaugurated. As Bishop Brent has said, "The Christian tree does not grow because it is bidden, but because it is a tree * * * unexpansive religion is dying religion." Is it too much to say that the Churchman cannot sing or say from the heart, "The Holy Church throughout all the world doth acknowledge Thee" without desiring to do his part toward making the words entirely true in fact?

The Psalmist wrote, "Make me a clean heart, O God, establish me with thy free Spirit; then shall I teach thy ways unto the wicked, and sinners shall be converted unto thee," and the Spirit it is who now on a broader scale communicates missionary love and energy to the Church. Dr. Downer remarks on the verse, "Ye shall receive power when the Holy Ghost is come upon you; and ye shall be my witnesses * * * unto the uttermost part of the earth," that a more important verse it is impossible to find. It is the key, not only to the whole of the book in which it occurs (The Acts), but to the entire record of Church history."

The "nations" are in their turn to become witnesses for Christ; "not the cultured Greeks alone, nor the military and conquering Latin race, but the barbarous people of Gaul and Germany, the mixed races of Asia Minor, the dark-skinned tribes of Africa, the Goths and Vandals, the Keltic Britons and the fair-haired Saxons." The rivers of living water which are to flow out of Christians as individual believers and as Christ's Body are rivers of missionary influence. They are "bright as crystal," they are life-giving and refreshing to all around, because they have their source in the Spirit who dwells in them.

It may be an overstatement in Dr. Trumbull's work, "Our Misunderstood Bible," that we make a mistake to think of the Holy Spirit as given to us for any other purpose than to make us faithful and valiant witnesses to Christ in this world; yet it is noticeable that in the Proper Preface for Whitsunday this is the dominant purpose. It represents the Holy Ghost as "lighting upon the Apostles to teach them and lead them to all truth; giving them the gift of divers languages and also boldness with fervent zeal constantly to preach the gospel to all nations."

We think of Advent and Epiphany as missionary seasons, but the above-mentioned Whitsunday Preface, and the fact before referred to, that the Acts of the Apostles—"Acts of the Holy Spirit"—are read on the first ten Sundays after Trinity, and read on week-days from June twenty-third until August fifth, together with other features of the Services yet to be named, show this second half of the Christian Year to be pre-eminently the missionary season.

One lesson in this "first chapter in the history of Christian Missions," read on a week-day in July, we could wish were always read on Sunday, throwing light as it does on the Spirit's office as the Vice-gerent of Christ, and the supreme organizer and controller of the missionary campaign for all time.

It is humiliating to think how "neglect of the doctrine of the Spirit" generally has caused the Church to neglect in particular this event in the career of St. Paul as bearing on the Spirit's method in what we term foreign missions. Eager to cover the ground

near home, in the limited region called Asia and then
in Bithynia, the Apostle is overruled, one might say,
rushed along to ancient Troy, and then beckoned to
from across the sea by the "man of Macedonia."
The whole account is a lesson to the Church in every
age. To one who knows anything of the narrow, wind-
ing channels and dangerous rocks, and the rarity of
winds favorable to "a straight course" to Samothrace,
then to Neapolis, and then to Philippi, it seems as
if the winds and waves must have been obedient to
the voice of Christ as they had been once on Gennesaret. The breath of His divine Spirit seems to be
filling the sails.

Surely it was so. It was the Mind of the Spirit,
His holy Will, to lose no time in flinging out the banner
of the Cross in the great cities of the West. Is it not
His mind now? The field is the world. The Gospel
seed is in all ages to be scattered widely. We are not
to favor the intensive at the cost of the extensive
method of cultivating the field.

What Mr. John Mott,—whose name has become
almost a household one in the Church and Household
of Christ, through his connection with the Edinburgh
conference,—says of the "unmistakable signs of the
awakening of great peoples from their long sleep" is
unquestionably true. He declares, that

"through the whole of Asia a ferment is in process which has
spread from the intellectual leaders, and is fast taking possession
of the masses. It affects over three-fourths of the human race,
including peoples of high intelligence and ancient civilization."

Now is not this in great measure an answer to
prayer for "opened doors," and have we not been

losing time through neglect of prayer, and slowness
to behold as in a vision the man of China, and the
man of Japan, and the man of India, beckoning to us?

Mr. Mott's book is called the "Decisive Hour
of Christian Missions." Doubtless there are these
decisive hours with God. It is true that with Him
"a thousand years are as one day," that we may not
hurry God, nor force His hand. But is it not also true
that He waits for us, and that we keep Him waiting
by our slowness of heart to obey the motions of the
Spirit and discern the signs of His presence. "Our
wills are ours," and for what? To make them His.

The whole Pentecostal era was intended to be a
long, glorious, decisive period of missions. We have
but to study the Acts, and mark the rapid, continuous
march of events and expansion of method to see this.
It is humiliating to reflect how little broadly and intelligently Christians have interpreted the Apostle's
word, "Now is the accepted time; now is the day of
salvation." A glance at Isaiah 49 proves that the
borrowed phrase was a prophecy of the conversion of
the nations to Christ. St. Paul uses it with the same
thought, and in an age when "all things" have "become
new," because God is in Christ, "reconciling the
world unto himself." Accordingly "Now" means not
this or that "decisive hour" when "Jesus Christ is
passing by" as in the days of His flesh. He is the
risen, ascended, glorified Christ, to whom all power
has been given, and whose Spirit is always with us,
never passing by in the sense that He was not here
and strong to save yesterday, or will not be to-
morrow. All that is needed is that we receive not
this grace in vain, but give up ourselves to walk, to live,

to preach, to teach, work and give in the Spirit
unceasingly.

The Augustinian, and Calvinistic, but non-Pauline,
doctrine of election,—together with words like those
in the Westminster Confession of Faith, that as "God
hath appointed the elect unto glory," * * * so
"the rest of mankind was He pleased according to the
unsearchable counsel of His own will * * * to
pass by, and to ordain them to dishonor and wrath for
their sin, to the praise of His glorious justice,"—will
surely have had some effect to deaden feelings of
concern and responsibility, in many Christians, for
individuals and nations upon whom no light had
apparently shined. It was largely the fault of Christians, if it had not shined. According to St. Paul
(1st Tim. 2 : 3), it is the will of God "that all men
should be saved and come to the knowledge of the
truth." His Son is a universal Saviour.

It was a pity and a shame that the Reformation,
operating within the Church and diffusing spiritual
light and holiness among her members, resulted in
small gains for missions, owing to unhappy difficulties
and divisions which occupied the attention of the
reformed communions.

> * * * "The scambling and unquiet time
> Did push it out of further question."

It can be said for the Church of the Prayer Book
that the Whitsunday Preface already twice referred
to dates from the Reformation period. But outside
of the petition, "That thou wouldest be pleased to
make known thy saving health to all nations" and the

comparatively new prayer, beginning, "O God, who hast made of one blood all nations of men," the missionary thought finds meagre expression in the form of distinct missionary prayers.

So far as the choice of Scripture passages is concerned, the Prayer Book is true to the Spirit's mind in the Advent Season. "The things written for our learning" in the Psalms and Prophets, and quoted by St. Paul in Romans,—words compared by Godet to a duet in which the nations, gathered together into one body in the most cosmopolitan of all the Churches, sing Glory to the Father and to the Son,—bear distinctly upon missions. In the Collect, however, "Blessed Lord, who hast caused all holy Scriptures to be written for our learning," one discovers no trace of the missionary thought.

No race in the world owes more to missionary love and sympathy manifested in the early Christian Church than does the race to which we belong. Shall we forget? Shall we fail to recall the conversion of ancient Britain, probably due in part to Christian soldiers of the Roman cohorts in their encampments of the far North-West? Shall we forget our debt to Gregory and Augustine of Canterbury? With entire justice has Dean Church, in one of his Village Sermons, made application to the English conscience of what Gregory under the Holy Spirit's guidance did for England, and, we must add, for us.

"The Christians of those days, who lived as we live in more settled countries, who could have their share of ease and quiet without troubling themselves about distant barbarians, felt that the Gospel was not to stop at themselves, felt themselves debtors even to those unknown barbarians, to try and bring them within their Master's fold,—trusted that God would do what seemed impossible to man.

"Here is in a word the *human* cause of the conversion of England. A minister of God, living far away from this island, was inflamed with love and pity for its people, our *then* heathen countrymen and forefathers. He desired for them the heritage of the angels in heaven. He could not go himself, but he got others to go. A few humble, helpless men, with the Cross of Christ and the Book of God, landed on our shores. There was opposition, there was difficulty; there was labor that seemed in vain. Over and over again all seemed lost; over and over again the work had to be begun anew. It was not done in a generation or in a century. But that good man who longed for the conversion of heathen England has had his wish. He did not see it. He only saw then what seemed its feeble and hopeless beginnings. But his work went on and prospered. What could not be done at once has been done in time.

"And here is this great realm and church of England, not the least of the kingdoms of the world which acknowledge the name of Christ, the mother of new nations, the planter of new churches,—where through its length and breadth, in cities and cottages, the Light of the World is shining,—owing all its blessings, owing its knowledge of the Gospel, owing all to the warm love and far-seeing faith and hope, which refused to be frightened, of one old man far away."

How has our English-speaking race developed in the thirteen centuries since Augustine landed in Kent! In the five centuries since aged Gaunt is made to call our mother country

> "This happy breed of men, this little world;
> This precious stone set in the silver sea,
> Which serves it in the office of a wall,
> Or as a moat defensive to a house,
> Against the envy of less happier lands,"

how have her character and her sphere of world-action, —not least, her knowledge and her language,—expanded and ripened! Her language, which is ours, is the most widely spoken language in the world. As the ruler and guardian of India and Australia and Canada, she, together with her daughter America, is vastly different from the old-time

"England, bound in with the triumphant sea."

Bishop Montgomery's analysis of the present character of our type of manhood, our position in respect to the other races, our opportunity and our fitness to spread Christ's kingdom everywhere,—found in the Introduction to the valuable work entitled "Mankind and the Church,"—possesses intense interest for a Prayer Book Christian. Still insular,

"this man has had a wonderful world-experience and training." Almost color-blind by nature to certain aspects of truth, "his defect has compensating advantages, inasmuch as when, by a kind of divine surgical operation, he gains his spiritual vision, no man is more fervent in his desire to bring his conduct into close line with his beliefs. * * * Used to holding in dim fashion that our blessed Lord must have been born in London for the express benefit of his own race alone, he has become one of the greatest of missionaries. The day was, when he declared that it was almost ludicrous to suppose you could convert a Chinese or an Indian, and when in consequence, with kindly eyes, we had to say to him, 'If God Almighty has converted you, do you really suppose there can be real difficulty with any other race?' To-day he is earnest in impressing upon all men the Faith of the Gospel."

The record of the Church of Britain, before Augustine came to Canterbury, and after that, was a noble one in respect to missions. It is enough to mention Columba and Aidan in the former period, and Wilfrid and Boniface in the latter. It is plain in this our own day, that a special calling wherewith English-speaking

Christians are called, is to be a missionary people.
One of Macaulay's most brilliant passages is that in
which he has described Rome's loyalty to her early
vision, and her purpose, unabated to this day, to
touch the uttermost part of the earth with truth as
she understands it. But her day is passing. No
longer can it be said that she is "full of life and youthful vigor," that "the number of her children is greater
than in any former age." Bishop Montgomery writes:
"It is not for me to prophesy about the future of that
marvellous engine of spiritual power, but I may suggest what, again, experience of many lands has taught
me. The time-spirit is against the Latin Church
among every race except the Latin."

It would appear according to this writer that the bells
in many a tower are chiming in the era of the English-
speaking Catholic Church. It is the call of the Spirit.
Four things are necessary to the people and the communion who shall respond to and fulfil this high calling,
and with these the Spirit has been fitting us by natural
endowment and a long education and discipline.

We may name first a racial genius and bent which
many strains and many strands have contributed to
make what they are, and a wonderful history has developed and improved. English or Americans, John
Bullish as we are by our reserve, independence, and
force of will, a "little world" still, or a large one, in
ourselves, we were fitted to learn, and have learned,
intellectually and every way,—after the manner of the
great Shakspeare himself,—to sympathize with the
greater world of mankind. German thought and
knowledge, or French or Oriental, we can appreciate
and assimilate them all. Nothing that is human is

quite foreign to us. In all this training and equipment of universality the Spirit of the divine-human Lord has had His part. To Him, not to us, it chiefly belongs. This, like our language, prepares us to be the greatest of all missionary races.

English and American experience with independency has been of inestimable value. Finding out its weakness and instability, its sad failure to command the respect of the people as a whole, and keep them loyal to the fundamental truths of Christ, we have also been learning the patience and forbearance of God, and His wisdom and power to overrule sectarian division and rivalry for good. The lesson our blessed Lord taught at the very beginning in the correcting word, "Forbid him [or it] not; for he that is not against us is for us," so often forgotten, we have been learning over again, by our personal observation of His Spirit blessing the work of many at home and abroad, and sometimes in a wonderfully abundant way, who are casting out the evil spirits in Christ's name while following not with us. We have learned to admire in them a missionary zeal and devotion surpassing our own; seen that they were in fact more catholic than ourselves, partly in their strict obedience to the Lord's great missionary mandate, and partly in their conscious and oft expressed dependence on the Holy Ghost as before all else a Spirit of Missions.

In the third place, there is the important principle of nationality. Free and bold to maintain,—from the early times, and even when the Papal power was at its height, and asserted its false claim most insistently,— her autonomy as a member of the Church universal, the English Church has recognized our right to the

same ancient privilege. She, like the American
Church, is ready and glad to cherish the desire for
autonomy and establish national Catholic Churches
in every land. Almost as little as what the sometime
Bishop of Tasmania terms "the Latin straight-jacket"
is suitable to be fixed upon every race in the world,
is an English or American one, catholic or non-catholic,
adapted to Christians in the Orient or Africa. Christianity is "universal in essence and purpose." As
Bishop Brent has reminded us, "Christ is the Orient.
The father of His immediate herald called Him 'the
dayspring from on high.' In taking Him to the East we
take Him to His own." How think then to force His
religion upon the East in its Westernized form and habit?

But perhaps more important to be named than
either of these three features, is the heritage of Faith
and Worship and Order which we have to pass on. It,
too, like the Founder of our universal religion, was of
Eastern origin, was born, as Bishop Brent says our
blessed Saviour was, "in a country that was the border-
land between East and West." Accordingly it, too,
was created to live and be a blessing to countless generations East and West. Bishop Montgomery's thought
on the Church as a continuing Church is one to be
remembered:

"There are vast organizations, denominations, Churches,
whatever may be the name they desire to be called by, outside
this ancient and to us stable Church. Their devotion and work
has been magnificent; for all their great achievements for
Christ's kingdom throughout the world we love them; we gaze
upon them as one would look upon a splendid athlete winning
race after race: but the old Church of this nation notes also,

10

and with foreboding, a look of delicacy in the athlete's fac
it is often so with athletes, and we ask, will he live the ordina
span of life? then we shake our heads. I can only give my co
viction, formed chiefly in regions outside the motherland, th
the stability of Christianity depends upon the Catholic Chur
and its order and temper. The only anchor that can hold t
the end in spite of any storm from whatever direction, is t
Catholic anchor with its long, unbroken chain.

"If this be so," the Bishop continues,—and it is a solemn wo
for American Christians who have their hands also upon t
historic unbroken chain and anchor,—"then, since we a
responsible to the fullest extent of our power for the stability
the Faith one thousand years hence, the order and temper a
attitude of the Catholic Church is part of the 'deposit' which
too sacred to be parted with for any consideration whatsoev
and becomes an essential part of our contribution to the rac
of the earth. It is possible, fortunately, to say this with unfeign
respect, with genuine affection, for those who do not agr
with us."

The lesson is doubly solemn and imperative fo
American Churchmen, by reason of the two-fold manner
in which our country is now coming in ever closer contact with the people of other lands.   They are pouring
in upon us to become an integral portion of our vast
commonwealth, while we are reaching out more and
more, to shape and influence their development at
home.   Alike here in the field of domestic missions and
in missions beyond the seas, we are bound to furnish
them,—ought to love and long to give them,—

"a Faith which will be stable and living a thousand years hence;
all that has been of late summed up and implied in the phrase,
the historic Episcopate; the ordinances, the definite attitude, the
simple Apostolic belief, the atmosphere, the taste, the 'sort of
perfume almost,' which inhere in the Church and Prayer Book,
the Spirit has made ours that we may give them to others, and
that you discover best when you step outside its limits."

To American Christians home missions are foreign missions. On the other hand, to plant missions abroad which shall result in stable and autonomous Churches means in the end to confirm and enrich our religious life here. Alike at home and beyond the oceans, far-seeing, broad-minded Christians perceive each year more clearly the necessity of establishing everywhere a united Christianity. Not the one Spirit only is to be sought and found, but the one Body. "Amiable but aimless," says Bishop Doane, commenting on the Epistle for the Seventeenth Sunday after Trinity, "is their endeavour who, seeking to keep the unity of the Spirit, sacrifice as of no importance the unity of the body. Keep oneness even at the cost of peace." It is a Scotch Presbyterian, Dr. Milligan, who tells us that the Church will never enjoy the fulfilment of our Lord's promise, "greater works than these shall he that believeth on me do, because I go unto my Father," unless believers are one in Christ as He is one with that Father. Out of this truth flows all that is most characteristic of the Church.

"She must not only be one, but visibly one, in such a sense that men shall themselves see and acknowledge that her unity is real. * * * The world will never be converted by a disunited Church. Bible circulation and missionary exertion upon the largest scale will be powerless to convert it, unless accompanied by the strength which unity alone can give." ("Resurrection of our Lord," page 201.)

The Spirit of Unity is the Spirit who has given us a Book of Common Prayer which embodies so wonderfully the Faith and the spiritual aspirations of the undivided Church. And the self-same Spirit is it, who in marvellous ways prepared the nations to receive a universal Saviour. Long before His Incarnation, Christ, coming into the world by the Spirit, was lighting every man, and every nation. The better acquaintance our missionaries make with the Eastern peoples and with their religious and philosophical ideas, even the crude ideas and beliefs of the Negro race, and the Papuans, the clearer become the evidences of the Spirit's witness in ancient times. They discover how far the foreign field is from being a field barren and poor. There is immense encouragement in this. The vision of St. Paul in Troy repeats itself in other fashion in our day. It is the vision of such a new humanity in Christ as Christendom itself has not dreamed of. "As surely as every river in the land ultimately reaches the sea," writes Bishop Brent, in "Adventure for God," "so surely the religion of Jesus Christ will receive into itself those lesser faiths wherein God did not leave Himself wholly without witness. There comes a tremendous enlargement of interest and a full flood of hope with the thought that the first duty of the missionary is to find Christ rather than to give Him among those to whom he is sent" (page 89).

It will be when all the great races have been gathered in, and a world-wide Christian Church and Civilization has taken form, and begun in truth to live, that the rich meaning of the New Testament phrases, the "perfect man," and "the measure of the stature of the fulness of Christ," and "the breadth and length and depth and height," will dawn upon the world. These expressions, found near together in that great Epistle upon the Church, Ephesians, come to mind when one reads the book just quoted from so freely, "Mankind and the Church." It is called an attempt to estimate the contribution of great races to the fulness of the Church of God, by Seven Bishops. Rather expecting to be styled "the Seven Dreamers," they are not ashamed of, —nor will their readers, especially preachers on Missions in the Trinity Season, fail to be profoundly interested in,—their visions of "the things which Christians now have a right to believe shall be hereafter," through the love of Christ and the wisdom and power of the Universal Spirit dwelling in a Universal Church.

Their Apostle asked for the saints in Ephesus that the spirit of wisdom and revelation might be given them in the knowledge of Christ; and one may perhaps presume to think of the dreams of the Seven Bishops as in the same long line of inspired thought with the visions of St. Paul while a prisoner of Christ in Rome; of St. John in Patmos, "in the Spirit on the Lord's day"; of St. Augustine in Civitas Dei; of the author of "Adventure for God"; of Bishop Westcott, in "Lessons from Work"; of Mr. Mott, in the "Decisive Hour of Christian Missions." Books like the last-named, and sermons suggested by them, together with items of news almost daily coming in from the missionary fields, are creating a wide-spread interest in Missions in the Churches, and making truer the saying, that "the signs of the times are full of hope, and missionary interest and endeavour a veritable power."

"It is unique and inspiriting," says Bishop Brent, "that in the heat of a political campaign a President of this Republic should call men to confer with him regarding a missionary opportunity in a non-Christian land, which it seemed to him should be seized. * * * When the highest post of honor in a leading school for girls is the presidency of the missionary society, and when the head master of a great school for boys publicly proclaims that he would rather see one of his pupils a foreign missionary than in the Presidential chair, surely the vision of adventure for God is a living force in our midst!"   ("Adventure for God," page 30.)

THE ANTE-NATAL LIFE

The various Symbols of the Pentecostal Spirit's presence, taken from the sphere of nature in which He has ever been active, suggest parallels too often passed by unnoticed. Our Lord could not make use of them in His parables, before the Spirit was manifested; but to us who live in the era of the Holy Ghost it ought to be evident that in grace, as in nature, without Him not anything was made or done that was made or done.

Freer application of this principle should long ago have been made to the study of human history, before the Incarnation and since; but to many it has become clear that, while sin was everywhere, none would seem to have been totally depraved, and that of this God's loving mercy was the cause.

"No sooner had man sinned," wrote the first American Bishop, Seabury, "than God was in Christ reconciling the world —human nature—unto Himself. 'The seed of the woman,' said God, 'shall bruise the serpent's head.' Something wanted to be done within man—in the very centre of his being—in order to save him. He had gotten a crooked, perverse and serpentine nature, which required to be bruised, crushed, brought to nothing in him, that the holy, heavenly nature which he had lost might be renewed in him. He now, as I take it, imparted to Adam, and consequently to his whole posterity, a new principle, or sensibility of goodness, called the seed of the woman—something of the holy nature of Christ."

On the Feast of our Lord's Nativity we read that He "was the true Light which lighteth every man which cometh into the world." Whichever way we understand this, whether as meaning that Christ, "on His way to the world, advancing by preparatory revelations, in type and prophecy and judgment," was lighting every man; or that he lighted each soul as it came into the world, it is the same. It meant prevenient grace, and that on a universal scale; beginning to "strive with man" everywhere, for the sake of a world-Saviour who should be manifested and accomplish His redeeming sacrifice in the fulness of time. It meant a gift of grace co-extensive with human sinfulness, and that no such thing as "total depravity" or total unfaith existed, except possibly in cases where the human will resisted the Spirit to the last degree.

Was it not owing to this same new principle of life, imparted to Adam and his whole posterity, that the men of Athens could understand the Apostle speaking of all men as living and moving and having their being in God, and that certain of their own poets had written "We are also his offspring"? Does it not account for the possibility of Nineveh's conversion, for the history of the noble Cyrus, for Socrates and Plato and Epictetus, and for Confucius; for the faith of the Roman centurion, and of the Syrophenician woman?

The words of Bishop Seabury, quoted above, are cited by Dr. James Craik in his book entitled, "The

Divine Life," written more than sixty years ago. If out of print, it ought to be published anew; and though a clergyman had but a dozen books at his disposal, this ought to be one of them. It brings to view the truth that God does not now call upon men everywhere to believe, without first having empowered them to believe and to turn from sin. Bishop Otey, of Tennessee, quoted by Dr. Craik, referring to the "world-wide restoration of man's spiritual capacity, the gift of God in Christ,—a free, unmerited gift to every human being endowed with a rational soul," had even said, "in this subordinate sense all men may be said to be regenerate. For thus argues the Apostle: 'By the righteousness of one [that is Christ] the free gift came upon all men unto justification of life.'"

Wherever signs of this, which may be termed the ante-natal life, are discovered, they bear witness to His presence and power who is the Lord, and Giver of Life, in the realm of nature and of grace alike. As in the month of March there is life before birth under the brown soil and in the leafless trees and vines, so was there moral and spiritual life in the wide Gentile world; and we discover it to-day in heathen lands, in many at home who do not call, or it may be even think, themselves Christians.

In the Scriptures, and therefore in the Prayer Book, baptism with water and the Spirit is called the New Birth, and this it is as introducing us into the Church, the Spirit's own creation and care. Conversion, which is the distinct turning of the individual will to God, — and Confirmation, which is a blessing on that personal free choice of Him and His holy will as our true end,— determine, seal, expand and enrich the soul's life.   But prior to these, and before the so-called New Birth itself, exists the universal, perfectly free gift, corresponding to the hidden life in the soil and the plant.

It is this which, as conveyed to multitudes in heathen lands, by means of ancient traditions, or institutions, and by the direct influence of the Spirit, is proving each year a more interesting study to our missionaries, and is persuading them that Christ has been there before them. Those are significant words quoted by Herbert W. Horwill in *The Atlantic Monthly* for April, 1911:

"'There is no reason whatever for Christian propaganda,' they conclude, 'unless the missionary has something new to proclaim; but it is equally certain that there is no basis whatever for the missionary appeal unless the missionary can say, "Whom therefore ye worship in ignorance him declare I unto you." Even where the native faith itself seems to offer few points of contact with Christianity, there is sure to be in the minds of the people some upward impulse, some desire for deliverance from evil powers, some vague aspirations for a higher life, which may in some measure be used as a *preparatio evangelica*.'"

In "Mankind and the Church," by Seven Bishops, the Archbishop of the West Indies writes (page 11):

"If even some missionaries, when first realizing the depth of native degradation, should have concluded that the African with whom they came in contact was without the knowledge of God, this would not be surprising. But whatever may have led, in any such case, to such a conclusion, it is a profound mistake. * * * They know of a Being superior to themselves of whom they themselves say that He is the Maker and Father. * * * It may be considered quite certain that the negro mind even in his original savagery, is strongly imbued with a belief in the existence of a great Creator and Ruler. * * * It is in keeping with the original bent of the negro mind, though modified and developed by Christianity, that the negro Christian is especially strong in the habit of realizing the presence and power of God in all nature, in all life, in all circumstances; recognizes in all the providences of human life the hand of a loving ever-present Divine Father."

Of the same kind,—and to be acknowledged thankfully as signs of the universal saving efficiency of our Lord's Sacrifice, and as fruits of the personal Spirit,— are the good impulses and desires of non-Christians discoverable by the stethescope of our sympathetic faith,—even conspicuous acts of kind and just dealing, deeds of self-denial, equal if not superior to the actions of many professing Christianity. No man thoughtfully observing these, and knowing the testimony of the Scriptures regarding the Spirit's relation to mankind as redeemed in Christ, will ever declare, as Romans do, that "in Baptism grace is first infused"; or on the other hand assert, with the popular, loose theology of dissent, that grace is given only after or at conversion. Nor will he be of those who, as Dr. Craik expresses it, are accustomed to refer the manifest good that is in all men to what they style "mere human virtues,"—carefully abstracting from the said human virtues all possible influence of the Spirit of God. As Dr. Craik shows at considerable length, all the expressions of the Prayer Book are consistent with the truth of the universality of divine grace. If only Churchmen themselves had always spoken and acted in accordance with it, *giving glory* to that Spirit, "whom with the Father and the Son together we worship and [say that we] glorify as one God!"

Had they but taught and lived by this heavenly truth there would have been less reason for that religious enthusiast, of pure life and unimpeachable sincerity, George Fox, to arise and bring forward his

doctrine of the *universal inward light*.   Robert Barclay
would not have needed to proclaim that

"God out of His infinite love, who delighteth not in the death
of a sinner, but that all should live and be saved, hath so loved
the world that He hath given His only Son a light, that whosoever believeth in Him should be saved; who enlighteneth every
man that cometh into the world. * * * Therefore Christ
hath tasted death for every man; not only for all kinds of men,
as some vainly talk, but for every one, of all kinds; the benefit
of whose offering is not only extended to such as have the distinct
outward knowledge of His death and sufferings, as the same is
declared in the Scriptures, but even unto those who are necessarily
excluded from the benefit of this knowledge by some inevitable
accident; which knowledge we willingly confess to be very
profitable and comfortable, but not absolutely needful unto such
from whom God Himself had withheld it."

Curteis, in the Bampton Lectures in 1871 on Dissent
in its Relations to the Church of England, writes (page
264):

"I fear not to say that within the Church of England, no less
than among the Dissenting Communions, this doctrine of the
Holy Ghost and of His indwelling light has been far too little
heard.   And therefore, when in the seventeenth century a
fragment (as it were) of her substance was thrown off on this
account, and began to revolve, not far away, but yet in a separate
orbit of its own,—it were well to acknowledge that even thus,
too, good may be brought out of evil * * * that no small
debt of gratitude is due to one who first (even amid some error
and extravagance) recovered for us the true prominence of the
third great section of the Nicene Creed."

If only this prominence of the Spirit-truth could
have been re-asserted by the Friends without causing
a new division in Christ's Body, and losing out of sight
other precious verities!   To go back a thousand years,

—if only this all-inviting truth, having been more fully exhibited in Christian theology from the beginning, might have been present to the mind of the great Augustine in his controversy with Pelagius! It would have been a controversy earlier and more happily settled, could Pelagius have been shown that, correct in asserting the existence of good in every man, he would have been wholly so, acknowledging that good to be due to the dim and partial light which went before, and which was to prepare the way for, the life in the free air and sunshine of the Spirit in the Church.

The error of Pelagius still lives. Men still "vainly talk," denying the fault and corruption of our nature, and that we are,—in the Church and out of it,—"far gone from original righteousness." On the other hand they vainly talk who continue to speak of total depravity, failing to recognize the partial recovery and restoration of all mankind in Christ through His Spirit's world-wide influence. This blessed doctrine tends to reconcile truths and men alike. The sympathetic and genial preaching of Phillips Brooks would have proved even more convincing and winning than it did, had the personal Spirit been distinctly brought forward as the immanent, efficient cause of the spiritual capacity in men, which the preacher constantly recognized, and of those good impulses to which he appealed. There can be no harm, but only benefit, when our better selves are appealed to, if we are not allowed to forget that the Author and Finisher of these new and better selves is the mighty Spirit of our Ascended Lord.

The truth that no man is without a measure of the quickening, enabling Spirit helps us all to realize better our dependence upon God for every good gift. It is, as Dr. Craik contended, the precise refutation of Pelagianism; because it takes the very facts relied upon for the support of that error, and accounts for those facts by proving them to depend upon the gift of the Holy Ghost. Throughout our whole life, as a race and as individuals, one kind or degree of spiritual assistance is ministered after another, or is ready to be ministered. One kind is the reward of another that has been well-used. It is intended to be a golden chain of inward gifts and powers. As Bishop Westcott explains "grace for grace," each blessing received has become the foundation of a greater blessing. "The Church of Christ," he says, "has been appointed the last, the fullest, and the most perfect of the means and instrumentalities for the nurture and development of the Divine Life, from its embryo existence as a power in the soul of man, through all the successive stages of growth, to the maturity of perfect manhood in Jesus Christ."

Hundreds of the people whom we are liable to meet any day, and whom we honour as fellow citizens, and maybe love as friends, need to be guided to this truth of the Spirit; and particularly to His gracious preliminary work long going on in their own hearts, made possible for them, as for all, by the patient and willing sufferings of the Redeemer. They need to be made aware that there is nothing to be waited for and *much yet to be done;* to pass on and upward to higher and more lasting things in Christ and the Spirit. The Sonship of the Race, which they have been faintly conscious of as being for themselves, is rudimentary, and as it were a matter of course. The capacity for receiving the Divine Life which these recognize as in a degree existing in them is, so to speak, native to all; and of this also our Lord Jesus Christ has paid the price. But the actual realization of their sonship is possible only through Christ, and it is through the Spirit that this final and more glorious possession will come, if they will co-operate with Him,—will receive Him, and live and walk in Him.

Is not the Season of the Spirit a season in which to press this truth home? to tell the thousands of whom it would be true, "Alive you are indeed, thank God, according to the Scripture; nevertheless, —according to Scripture, and by your own failure to understand and act,—not yet born."

THE CHURCH AND PREDESTINATION

I am the light of the world.—John 8 : 12.

Ye are the light of the world.—Matt. 5 : 14.

The Spirit of truth shall testify of me.—John 15 : 26.

Ye shall be witnesses unto me,—unto the uttermost part of the earth.—Acts 1 : 8.

To the intent that now unto the principalities and the powers in the heavenly places might be made known through the church the manifold wisdom of God according to the eternal purpose which he purposed in Christ Jesus our Lord.—Eph. 3 : 10, 11.

Whom he foreknew he also fore-ordained to be conformed to the image of his Son, that he might be the firstborn among many brethren.—Rom. 8 : 29.

The eternal purpose which he purposed in Christ Jesus our Lord, in whom we have boldness and access in confidence through our faith in him.   *   *   *   To apprehend with all the saints what is the breadth and length and height and depth, and to know the love of Christ, which passeth knowledge, that ye may be filled unto all the fulness of God.—Eph. 3 : 11, 18, 19.

God our Saviour; who willeth that all men should be saved, and come to the knowledge of the truth.— 1st Tim. 2 : 4.

The predestination of which Paul speaks is not a predestination *to* faith, but a predestination to glory, founded *on* the prevision of faith.   *   *   *   What the decree of predestination embraces is the *realization of the image of the Son* in all foreknown believers.   *   *   *   God wished to have for Himself a family of sons; and therefore He determined in the first place to make His own Son our brother.   *   *   *   Thus what comes out as the end of the divine decree is the creation of a great family of men made partakers of the divine existence and action, in the midst of which the glorified Jesus shines as the prototype.—Godet.

Much is said in Scripture of God's will that all should be saved, and of Christ's death as sufficient for all men; and we hear of none shut out from salvation, but for their own faults and demerits.   More than this cannot be inferred from Scripture; for it appears most probable that what we learn there concerns only predestination to grace, there being no revelation concerning predestination to glory.—Bishop Harold Browne.

The ecclesiastical instincts of average catholic churchmanship had grown up in an atmosphere of Free Will equipped with sacraments, to which the Augustinian doctrine of Grace was not, nor ever could become, wholly congenial.   Augustine himself never reached a real synthesis of the two.—Bishop Robertson.

The originator of the later doctrine of predestination was St. Augustine, one of the greatest, if not the very greatest, of the Fathers of the Church, who, nevertheless, by his teaching of that doctrine, poisoned and corrupted the religion he professed.—Fulton.

The theory of the Westminster divines is not the theory of the apostle Paul.   When he speaks of God as electing men, choosing them, foreordaining them, predestinating them, he means something very different from what Calvinism means by the same words.—R. W. Dale.

The chapters in Romans on the election of Israel have been by scholastic theology put to uses for which they were never intended. They are not a contribution to the doctrine of the eternal predestination of individuals to everlasting life or death. Their theme is not the election of individuals, but of a people. * * * Still more important is it to note that election is not conceived of as an arbitrary choice to the enjoyment of benefits from which all others are excluded. Election is to *function* as well as to favour, and the function has the good of others besides the elect in view. * * * In the teaching of Christ the elect appear as the light, the salt, and the leaven of the world. It is a vital truth strangely overlooked in elaborate creeds large enough to have room for many doctrines much less important, and far from recognized as yet even in the living faith of the Church, though the missionary spirit of modern Christianity may be regarded as an unconscious homage to its importance.—Prof. Bruce.

Text-criticism, careful study of the context, pitifully neglected in former times, and especially "higher criticism" as applied to the time of composition, circumstances, and leading purpose of the respective writings, together with the personality and soul-experience of their inspired authors, have all tended to shed a new and warmer light upon many books of the Bible. This is notably true of three books which fill a large and important place in the services of the Trinity Season; namely, The Acts, Romans, and Ephesians. The first, read ten Sunday mornings in succession, beginning at once after Trinity Sunday, the second, read in four altar-services, beginning with the Fourth after Trinity, and lastly Ephesians, read five Sundays, beginning with the Sixteenth after Trinity and ending with the Twenty-first, have for their subject various aspects of the Truth of the Church, as a divine-human instrument in the hand of the Holy Spirit,—"the house of God, which is the church of the living God, the pillar and ground of the truth"; a body, or state, in which none are "strangers and foreigners" but all are "fellow-citizens"; to employ terms grown familiar of late, a world-wide spiritual corporation, in trust with the most precious possessions and interests of man, under the presidency and controlling management of the Third Person in the Godhead Himself.

All who have remarked the large proportion of the Services after Trinity dominated by this Church-Truth, can hardly fail to realize how much prayerful thought is due to what St. Paul in Ephesians describes as the "hope" of the "calling wherewith we are called" by Christ, and "the riches of the glory of His inheritance in the saints," and the surpassing greatness of 'is "power to usward who believe," and which he finally sums up in the one rich phrase, "the church which is his body, the fulness of him which filleth all in all." In the next chapter it is termed "an habitation of God through the Spirit," and in the third characterized in the comprehensive and eloquent words, "the breadth and length and depth and height," or "the love of Christ which passeth knowledge"; for to His Apostle, the richness and fulness of the destiny of mankind as redeemed, restored, transfigured and glorified in the risen Son of Man means all these things.

It will not be difficult to realize why Protestantism, being a tremendous moral and spiritual reaction against the idea and fact of the Church as presented in the Middle Ages, should in the first place foster a general spirit of religious independency; and in the second place incline Christians to look upon their divine

11

election to privilege in Christ in the individual way
and also in the *other-world aspect* only, neither of
which ways was in truth the way of St. Paul.   Many
might easily learn to hate the word "predestination."

Now as Vinet, one of the most profound and original of Protestants, has said, "Protestantism is not
religion; it is the principle of liberty and individuality
applied to religious things, but *nothing else*."   Right
in itself and within due limits, it is in its essence
negative.   We must have truths and institutions
which are divine and positive, and if Acts and Romans
and Ephesians teach anything, they teach that the
Church, created and guided by the ever-present
personal Spirit, is one of the most divine and precious
of realities.

Why not make it a point sometimes in this season
of the Holy Spirit to picture that greatest figure in
the Book of the Acts,—next to the Holy Ghost Himself,—the "apostle of catholicity," St. Paul, as he
expresses it, *longing* to reach the chief city of the world?
Wonderfully converted by Christ to make known
His "unsearchable riches" to the nations, his was
the hand to cast the purifying, saving salt of the truth
concerning Christ into the world-fountains of thought,
of culture, and of power, and what fountain was there
like Rome?   A candle set on a candlestick, the Lord
had said, gave light to all around; a city set on an
hill could not be hid.   What candlestick so tall, what
city so conspicuous in all the world as Rome on its
seven hills?

Why not portray him writing a letter to the Roman
Church to which, never having yet seen it, he longs to
"impart some spiritual gift" that it "may be estab-

lished." Composed of Jews who had *before hoped*
in a Messiah, and Gentiles who were now "sealed with
the holy Spirit of promise," it was to him a type and
prophecy of the universal redeemed humanity that
should enjoy "the exceeding riches" of Christ "in
the ages to come." In the final chapter of the Acts,
behold him at length settled in the imperial city.
Though a prisoner he may every day throw the salt,
and let the light of his divine message shine. And
there, with signs of Roman power and influence around
him, more than ever impressed by the thought of a
universal Church, the centre of a universal Christian
civilization, "a great family of men made partakers
of the divine existence and action," he writes another
epistle,—comparable to the one to the Romans themselves,—addressed, it would appear, not to Ephesians
only, but also to the Christians in other important
cities of Asia Minor near them, and setting forth the
self-same truth of "glory in the Church by Christ
Jesus throughout all ages, world without end."

It is, then, when writing to Christians *in* Rome,
or *from* Rome to Asiatic Christians, that the Apostle
of catholicity has this great truth,—expressed in his
own inspired language, now by the "fellowship, or
the economy, of the mystery," and again by "the
breadth and length and depth and height" of divine
love,—constantly in his thoughts. It is "the power
of God unto salvation unto every one that believeth."
What the elder Church had been to the one race of
Israel the Church of Christ shall be to all nations.
The emphasis is always on this new and wonderful
event in human history. His function is "to make
all men see" it, and to realize the eternal divine *pur-*

pose lying back of it. There is not space here, nor
are we here concerned, to point out the differences
between his letter to the Romans and his letter to the
Ephesians. Enough for our object to remark that
while the place which these together occupy in this
Season's services suggests a thoughtful examination
of both Epistles in their entirety, the two main features
of interest are the Spirit-Truth in both, and His clearly
intimated Personal relation to redemption as Universal.
And inseparably bound up with these, and again and
again enunciated, is the truth of divine predestination.

That the last assertion is correct appears, in so far
as Romans are concerned, when the Epistles for the
Fourth and Eighth Sundays are studied, *in connection
with their context*, in the eighth chapter. In this
magnificent eighth chapter of thirty-nine verses, full
of the exalting resurrection truth, and of our adoption
in the Spirit; of hope not only for mankind but for
the whole creation of which it is a part, and of the
Spirit's intercession within us when "we know not
how to pray as we ought,"—the chapter in which the
argument of the inspired treatise as a whole *culmi-
nates*, and which ends with one of the Apostle's sublime passages which are rather paeans than perora-
tions,—the Holy Spirit is named nineteen times, *i. e.*,
once in every two verses, while the climax is in the verses
beginning, "And we know that to them that love
God all things work together for good, even to *them
that are called according to his purpose*" (vv. 28–30).

With Ephesians it is substantially the same. The
climax comes (chap. 3 : 18),—on the Sixteenth Sunday,—in the glowing words, "to apprehend with all
the saints what is the breadth and length and depth

and height, and to know the love of Christ which passeth knowledge." What passed knowledge then, and passes the knowledge and imagination of thousands of good intelligent Christians in this twentieth century, is that the religion of our Lord Jesus Christ is a religion intended for and adapted to all nations, and all sorts and conditions of men. And once more close by in the context, we come upon verses speaking exultantly of "the mystery," *i. e.*, the revelation, of the election of the nations, "according to the eternal purpose" which God "purposed in Christ Jesus our Lord, in whom we have boldness and access in confidence through our faith in him."

Here also close by is the truth of the ever-present, loving, Spirit of universality and unity. In this short Epistle, about one third as long as Romans, the Holy Ghost is named twelve times, twice in this third chapter, once in immediate connection with the truth of predestination to spiritual privilege in a Church which is catholic. It is when strengthened with might through Christ's *Spirit* in the inner man that Christians will "be strong to apprehend" the generous, —the world-wide,—application of the Gospel truth and life to men. The graces and virtues of Christians mentioned,—*fruits* of the Spirit,—are such as not only become saints thus favoured and honoured of God, but also tend to "build up the *body* of Christ," till *all* shall "attain unto the unity of the faith and of the knowledge of the Son of God." And just so is it in the last five chapters of Romans, ushered in by one of the Apostle's significant and powerful "therefores": "I beseech you therefore, brethren, by the mercies of God, to present your bodies a living sacrifice."

Dr. Trumbull's book, "Our Misunderstood Bible," should contain a chapter entitled "Our Misunderstood Apostle to the Nations of the West." St. Peter, we remember, writes (2d Pet. 3 : 15, 16) of his "beloved brother Paul" saying some things hard to be understood, which the "ignorant and unstedfast wrest unto their own destruction." He little realized how many saintly men and women, by no means "ignorant or unstedfast," would in later ages misapprehend some of St. Paul's most fundamental and precious teachings. There is not a more vital and practical element in the Church's divine Message,—nor a more winning one,—than the truth of election rightly apprehended. If in those early days when it was a secret newly "made known," and alike to the Jews and the other Nations, unprepared for such a universal fellowship in the risen Christ, it seemed too good to be true, and by reason of human weakness and prejudice too difficult of realization to be true,—and there was need of one whose letters were weighty and powerful, though his bodily presence might be weak, to make all men know that behind the marvellous new "dispensation" was a "purpose of God" which was *not* new, but rather "from before the foundation of the world,"—must it not be confessed that the Church needs at least to be reminded of this fact in our own day? Are there not many in this twentieth century to whom the thought of a universal Christianity seems too good to be true, and a universal brotherhood, of the nations or of individuals, too difficult to bring about? The catholic and genuine doctrine of election is one which men require often to have brought home to them. Thousands there are who require and would love to be taught, that it is no iron chain of logic like that of Augustine and Calvin, binding some prisoners of hope, as it were, and others prisoners of despair, but the golden chain Christ would by His Spirit throw around the neck of His Bride the universal Church, to draw her each day nearer to Him "in boldness and access with confidence, by faith in him." In every good impulse, every least drawing toward Him, to be detected in themselves, however seldom, these thousands should be taught to recognize the glint of that century-old chain of loving divine "purpose." We all need to form a habit of looking out for and discerning the shining of it in others. Home missionaries and foreign, and workers in prisons and reformatories, discovering faint signs of the Spirit's presence, may take courage and say, "these are of God, who having 'reconciled all things to himself in Christ,' will 'have all men to be saved.'"

One of the most important practical bearings of the real truth of election remains to be touched upon, namely, its bearing on Missions. It has been admirably well said, that

"The idea of election has had a very false turn given to it, partly because it has been separated from another idea with which in the Bible it is most closely associated, the idea of a universal purpose to which the elect minister. No thought can be more prominent in the Old Testament than the thought that some men out of multitudes have been chosen by God to be in a special relation of intimacy with Him. * * * But this election to special knowledge of God, and special spiritual opportunity, carries with it a corresponding responsibility. It is no piece of favoritism on God's part. The greater our opportunity the more is required of us."—(Bishop Gore, Epistle to the Ephesians, page 69.)

Have we realized this principle, have we lived up to it ourselves, have we inculcated it as we ought? It applies alike to nations and individuals. As truly as Abraham, or Jacob, or the people of Israel were chosen of God to be the bearers of Messiah to the world, so truly is the English-speaking race, and each individual Christian belonging to it, "chosen" to give Christ to the world of to-day. The only question for us each and all, is how best we can do it. He who said one day, "I am the light of the world," said another day to His disciples, "Ye are the light of the world." He said, "The Spirit shall testify of me," and another time, "Ye shall be witnesses unto me— unto the uttermost part of the earth." How much this ought to mean to a people living in touch with the uttermost parts of the earth, and "allowed of God to be put in trust with the Gospel" in its purity!

Two things, then, ought to be written on every Christian's heart. Election is to present privilege; and it is "no piece of favoritism." That to which he is foreordained of God is "to be conformed to the image of his Son," and for Christ Himself the voice that came, "This is my beloved Son," was a call to service and suffering for a lost race. Each golden link in the chain divinely thrown around him,— knowledge, talent, position, wealth, a sensitive con- science even, and the will and strength to believe, examined closely will be found marked with legends like, "noblesse oblige,"—"Ye are the light of the world,—Ye shall be my witnesses." In no con- ceivable sense can "Sauve qui peut," or "Devil take the hindmost," be mottoes for the escutcheon of the Christian soldier. It is chiefly in labouring and giving to save others, that we save ourselves in Christ. We "assure our hearts before God," and make our own "calling and election sure" more than all in the act of calling others "into the kingdom of the Son of his love."

The self-same Spirit who had urged St. Paul on to ancient Troy, and thence beckoned him over the Ægean Sea into Greece by the vision of the man of Macedonia, and filled him later with the desire to visit Rome, gave him while in Rome a vision of yet wider import. Impressed naturally by the near view of Rome's imperial majesty and power, beginning however to decline, he is enabled by the Spirit to foresee a time when Christ's kingdom spreading out upon the lines of this now decaying empire shall fill all in all, beholds the breadth and length and depth and height of that new universal empire of the King of kings, which to-day we call Christianity. The very soldier who guards him, whose helmet and shield and sword and sandals suggest the spiritual equipment of the soldier of Christ, suggests also, by his disciplined obedience and soldierly bearing, the dignity and energy of Rome, but also the greater authority of Him who deserves and claims our eternal obedience.

It is a vision of *spiritual* power; like that of Zechariah, when "the Lord returned to Jerusalem with mercies," saying: "My cities through prosperity shall yet be spread abroad." The seven lamps, seen each with its pipe of olive oil, represent the Spirit's inner life, and the word of the Lord unto Zerubbabel is, "Not by might, nor by power, but by my Spirit, saith the Lord of hosts." To the careful student of the Epistle to the Romans, which Coleridge called "the profoundest book in existence," and which is none the less essentially practical,—Godet remarks, "the probability is that every great spiritual revival in the Church will be connected as cause and effect with a deeper understanding of this book,"—to the student of Ephesians also, it will be plain that St. Paul's thought is throughout like the thought of Zechariah.

The thought of St. Augustine about four centuries later was the same. "The City of God," perhaps the most elaborate and in some respects the most significant work which came from his pen, is a great apologetic treatise in vindication of Christianity and the Christian Church, conceived as rising in the form of a new civilization on the crumbling ruins of the Roman Empire; and it is true to St. Paul's conception. The whole armour of the Church is with Augustine St. Paul's "whole armour of God," not temporal but spiritual; truth, righteousness, the readiness and boldness of the gospel of peace, the sword of the Spirit, prayer in the Spirit.

If only the Latin Church had remained true to the Pauline and Augustinian ideal; had not developed it into that of "an omnipotent hierarchy set over nations and kingdoms to pluck up and to break down and to destroy, and to overthrow and to build and to plant!" (Bishop Robertson, "Regnum Dei," page 222.)

It is a truth to be preached about,—why not in the Spirit's Season especially?—that we need to return, and that it is not always easy to return, to the spiritual ideal and method of spreading the Kingdom, and of working or "running" the Church. It has not been the temptation of Rome alone to look to *might* and *power*, and forget *God's Spirit*. Good, pious, Protestant Catholics themselves need sometimes to be reminded that the "wires" of earthly policy can never take the place of the "golden pipes" and the "golden oil" of the divine Paraclete. The lesson is manifold. Priests, vestrymen, people, we are prone to make generous use of worldly methods and devices; depend upon fine architecture and fine music, wealth, social influence, and much machinery, rather than upon the word and prayer; trust to tact, management, statesmanlike policy, if not to politics and the secular power, instead of recollecting God's "eternal purpose in Christ," and invoking the personal Spirit. It appears at times as though like certain Christians St. Paul found at Ephesus (Acts 19 : 2) we had not "so much as heard whether there be any Holy Ghost." Again Zechariah and the golden pipes come to mind. "And he (the angel) answered me and said, Knowest thou not what these be? And I said, No, my lord. Then said he, These are the two sons of oil, that stand by the Lord of the whole earth."

CHRISTIAN NURTURE

Suffer little children, and forbid them not, to come unto me, for of such is the kingdom of heaven. And he laid his hands on them.—Matt. 19 : 14, 15.

Repent and be baptized. * * * The promise [of the Spirit] is unto you and to your children.—Acts 2 : 38, 39.

One part of the blessing of Abraham, to which we are heirs,

was to have his children visibly and sacramentally united with him in the covenant of redemption. By what enactment of Christ was this precious part of the blessing of Abraham taken away from us, his Gentile children?—Craik.

Young children are the fittest subjects of the new birth, because the nurture thereby secured to them will be much more effectual to its purpose, the formation of a Christ-like character, than the same nurture applied to the adult subject.—*Ibid.*

In the morning sow thy seed and in the evening withhold not thine hand.—Ec. 11: 6.

Train up a child in the way he should go: and when he is old he will not depart from it.—Prov. 22 : 6.

Ye fathers, provoke not your children to wrath; but bring them up in the nurture and admonition of the Lord.—Eph. 6 : 4.

I know him [Abraham] that he will command his children and his household after him, and they shall keep the way of the Lord.—Gen. 18 : 19.

He went down with them and came to Nazareth, and was subject unto them. * * * And Jesus increased in wisdom and stature and in favour with God and man.—Luke 2 : 51, 52.

Conversion is that gradual and ceaseless change of the renewed soul by which all the powers and affections of man are transformed into the image of Christ.—Craik.

The essence of conversion,—not to be confounded with regeneration,—is a true movement of the will, turning solidly from self and the world. It is a fatal mistake to suppose that conversion must be exactly alike in all. It wears different aspects in different men, according to their temperament, and their circumstances. With some it comes almost unperceived, like the moment when the sun begins to appear above the horizon. With others it comes through agonizing struggles, and on a sudden. But in the most sudden cases there has been a long, secret preparation; and in the most quiet there is a definite point at which the turning begins to be truly voluntary.—Mason.

Unquestionably, regeneration, which makes us children of God, is a higher benefit than conversion, which makes us begin to be good men; yet, unless it be preceded, or accompanied, or followed, by conversion, it will avail a man nothing, or rather increase his condemnation.—*Ibid.*

There is not a more glorious operation of the Spirit, or one for which we shall with greater love and gratitude worship and glorify Him hereafter,—there is none more suitable for consideration in this, His Season,—than His work in young hearts.   The word "suitable" falls far short of being forcible enough, in view of the confusions and inversions of thought and practice in regard to the treatment of the young involved in the modern popular theology.   The first Whitsunday sermon ever preached, and the first preached on the Holy Spirit, contained a word of vital importance concerning the children.   We can be sure that Jewish ears had been attent to hear that word: "The promise,"—that is to say, the gift of the Holy Ghost,—"is unto you, and to your children."   Bitter and relentless were the Jews in their opposition to the infant Church, and it has been rightly said that excitement and clamour would have arisen, and those inclined to be baptized into the Messiah's name been terribly shocked, if "for the first time in the economy of redemption the children of believers had been excluded from the kingdom of grace." Not a whisper of opposition appears to have been heard; for as in the ancient Church parents and children had been as one in the covenant of redemption,—the sacrament of initiation, Circumcision, being administered on the eighth day after birth,—so they perceived it was to be in the new, wider, and more richly endowed Church of Christ.   He would "sprinkle many nations," and the children would be accepted and made clean, and be "children of God."   This was evidently the way at the baptism in the home of Cornelius the centurion;

nor was any other idea suggested until, in the twelfth century, "one Peter de Bruis, a crazy fanatic, held that those who died in infancy could not be saved, and therefore ought not to be baptized."

This theme finds a place the more naturally in this Season of the Christian Year, because it is a period of seed-sowing, of growth, and of ripening fruits; and the Scripture implies that the economy of nature in the germination of seeds, and in the nourishment, growth, and fructification of plants, corresponds to the true and normal Church life.

How can the farmer, who knows as much practically, and as little theoretically, as any of us about the secret operation of the Spirit in the soil and in the seed,— knows how to trust and wait, and when the time comes to *cultivate*, knows that the tiny seed duly cared for will develop into a fruitful plant or a wide-spreading, century-lasting tree,—allow himself to be misled into thinking that there is no divine life in the soul of the lad by his side, until he shall have been converted as by a sudden stroke from heaven? How can the farmer's wife, who plants her garden seeds, and tends them, and makes her good bread with wonder-working leaven, fail to recognize the leaven and the life of the Spirit in her child's heart, and accept the unreasoning, unscriptural and upsetting theories of conversion, which make it to be "the beginning and almost the consummation of spiritual life—the first access of the Holy Ghost to the soul, changing at once all its perceptions, thoughts, feelings, and desires"? This, the popular offspring of modern dissent, has perplexed the minds of the young and confounded many an honest and intelligent adult. It has led thousands to look upon practical Christianity as an unreality, and hindered them from professing the belief which is truly theirs.

The Lord by His Spirit calls the whole man, and demands the allegiance and the service of soul and body alike to Himself; and this never results, nor can result, instantly. Our "hydra-headed wilfulness" does not "lose his seat all at once." Shakspeare's delightful portrayal of the sudden change in young King Henry V has a solely poetical interest. Though an archbishop says it, it is not quite true that

> "Consideration like an angel came,
>   And whipped the offending Adam out of him;
>   Leaving his body as a paradise,
>   To envelop and contain celestial spirits:"

for history declares that the stories of his youthful extravagance and dissoluteness are unfounded and improbable. If in our blessed Lord Himself the human will, though sinless, was "made perfect," still more will it be the case with wills enfeebled and corrupted by sin. By faith as a continuing power, and repentance as a continuing discipline, we come at last by the Spirit's good help to be made over again forever.

The Prayer Book is true throughout to this conception, even while praying for the new, complete, and strong *heart;* that we may "*give up ourselves* to fulfil God's holy commandments"; that "our flesh being subdued to the Spirit, we may evermore obey thy godly motions in righteousness and true holiness."

As to the secret, gradual, development of the new will in the souls of Christ's children, no one has better appreciated this truth, and the Spirit's method, so like His method in nature, than John Keble. Nor did

Keble ever pen a more exquisite poem than that for the Fourth Sunday in Lent:

> "When Nature tries her finest touch,
>   Weaving her vernal wreath,
>   Mark ye, how close she veils her round,
>   Not to be traced by sight or sound,
>   Nor soil'd by ruder breath.

> "Who ever saw the earliest rose
>   First open her sweet breast?
>   Or, when the summer sun goes down,
>   The first soft star in evening's crown
>   Light up her gleaming crest?

> "But there's a sweeter flower than e'er
>   Blushed on the rosy spray,—
>   A brighter star, a richer bloom
>   Than e'er did western heaven illume
>   At close of summer day.

> "'Tis Love, the last best gift of Heaven;
>   Love gentle, holy, pure;
>   But, tenderer than a dove's soft eye,
>   The searching sun, the open sky,
>   She never could endure.

> "Even human Love will shrink from sight
>   Here in the coarse rude earth;
>   How then should rash intruding glance
>   Break in upon her sacred trance,
>   Who boasts a heavenly birth?

> "So still and secret is her growth,
>   Ever the truest heart,
>   Where deepest strikes her kindly root
>   For hope or joy, for flower or fruit,
>   Least knows its happy part.

> "God only, and good angels, look
>   Behind the blissful screen.
>   *   *   *   *   *

"The gracious Dove, that brought from **Heaven**
  The earnest of our bliss,
Of many a chosen witness telling,
On many a happy vision dwelling,
  Sings not a note of this."

Two facts; first, a general ignoring of the immensely important truth of a universal preliminary gift of life, treated of in a previous section,—the truth that as parents give to their children a sinful nature, so every child of man has been *born* under the covenant of grace in Christ Jesus;—and secondly, the confusion, in the popular Protestant teaching of regeneration, which is wholly the Spirit's action, and which goes sometimes long before, with conversion, which is in part man's act, and should follow as a result, have wrought enormous loss to Christ and His Church, and to mankind. Thousands have imagined that because their heart and will were not yet turned wholly to God, the Spirit could not yet in any sense or degree have been given to them, and so have become disheartened or wholly indifferent. They have said, "we have not yet been 'effectually called,' and what have we to do with it?" They have waited for God, while in fact He had been waiting for them,—from their child-days,—to use the grace that they had.

We Church people have not employed the term "conversion" as freely as we might and should have done; in part, doubtless, by reason of this same unhappy confusion of thought. Even when free from it in our own minds, it has been difficult for us not to be affected by the atmosphere of the error. Though Luther wrote beautifully of the attitude of the baptized child's soul toward God, resembling its gaze turned sweetly up to the mother's face, and Dr. Bushnell of Connecticut published an epoch-making book, in Protestant circles, on Christian Nurture,—while Dr. Craik of Kentucky connected thoughts similar to Bushnell's with the truth of the Holy Spirit as held by our Church,—it has not been easy to avoid sharing the prevailing cold indifference, and to act in accordance with believing, encouraging, words like the following:

"The effect of a true Christian culture will be to induce the children to offer themselves a living sacrifice to God, renewing in their own persons their vows of allegiance, and receiving anew, with new succours of heavenly grace, the assurance of the 'forgiveness of all their sins,' and of God's fatherly love and 'gracious goodness towards them.'

"Christian nurture is always successful. I have never known the child who had been taught the elements of Christian knowledge who was not religious,—who did not show a tender susceptibility to the influences of religion."

But we are "labourers together with God" in this husbandry in the Spirit. In this field which is the wide, wide world of human hearts, there is everywhere life in the soil, and plenty of "good seed"; we can see it coming up. But we, priests and people, parents, sponsors, and teachers, have to share the responsibility and the labour. Are we doing it? We are partners with Christ and the Spirit. Material and capital are unlimited. Do we think to be "silent partners," inactive even when our own souls and the souls of those near and dear to us are concerned?

The lilies and roses which adorn our altars at Easter or on Whitsunday, or when the bishop comes, can speak to us of many wonderful truths besides the love of the divine Spirit in creating their fragrant beauty, and besides Christ's and our own resurrection, and the power of the Holy Ghost to ennoble and sweeten human life, now and forever. Their way of turning toward the sun may suggest that unconscious, scarcely voluntary turning of young hearts toward God, which so often takes parents and teachers, if not the candidates for confirmation themselves, by surprise.

And whereas the lovely, eloquent flowers presently fade and die, the soul's life and joy are everlasting. Precisely at the point where the parallel between nature and grace fails us, the glory of humanity restored and transfigured in Christ shines out. How finely George Herbert laid hold of this, picturing the contrast between the Sweet Day which, cool, calm, bright,— bridal of earth and sky,—will die to-night, and the earth will weep over it; the sweet Rose, which,—its root being always in its grave,—must also die; the Sweet Spring which, full of sweet days and roses, must also die; and the good, thoroughly changed *man* of Christ!

> "Only a sweet and virtuous soul,
>   Like seasoned timber never gives,
>   But tho' the whole world turns to coal,
>   Then chiefly lives."

CHRISTIANITY A CATHOLIC RELIGION

The Church which is his body, the fulness of him that filleth all in all.—Eph. 1 : 22, 23.

The purpose so long kept secret and now revealed, is to gather together all nations and classes of men into the one Church of

God, one organized body, one brotherhood in which all men are to find their salvation, and through which is to be realized an even wider purpose for the whole universe. In this doctrine of the catholic church St. Paul finds the expression of all the length and breadth and height and depth of the divine love.—Gore.

The presence of our Lord in this Dispensation is a presence in the Person of His Vicar. The title "Vicar of our Lord," as applied to the Holy Ghost, we draw, indeed, from Tertullian, but it is justified by Christ's own words on the night of His betrayal, "the Holy Ghost whom the Father will send in my name. If I depart I will send him unto you." The presence and indwelling of the Spirit in the Church constantly brings about the presence and indwelling of Christ. * * * It is thus that our Lord inhabits the Church in the fulness of His mediatorial power.—Downer.

Roman Catholics hold many doctrines which I believe to be true and catholic; but what is meant by Roman Catholicism is that part of the belief of Roman Catholics which is not catholic and is not true.—Salmon.

If we have rightly interpreted our Saviour's words in regard to the relation between the inward and spiritual kingdom of Christ and the visible Church of Christ as its nurse and home, then the personal reign of Christ in which His Kingdom consists, will from His resurrection and exaltation to the Father be realized in the guidance of His followers, collectively, and individually, by the Holy Spirit. In the Church of New Testament times this is abundantly verified in both respects.—Robertson.

The Creed represents the Catholic judgment.—Gore.

The name Catholic as used of the Body of Christ would need to receive some special attention in this season, were it only on account of the intimate relation which its content has to the Holy Spirit and His Mission. He was sent to be the Guide and Friend, the Life and Soul of the Church. It is the Church of a universal Saviour, and is "His body, the fulness of him that filleth all in all." The God of our Lord Jesus Christ, the Father of glory, has "put all things under his feet," given "him to be the head over all things" to this Church. It can only be a universal Church, and the Spirit is its indwelling life and power.

"Catholic" stands for these things of Christ. It does not appear on the pages of the New Testament, but language like the above from Ephesians, conveying the idea of universality, does appear on many a page. The Acts of the Apostles, and their inspired writings, are full of the truth for which the Greek word stands, and the word is adopted almost as soon as the Spirit takes up the mighty work to which He is appointed of the Father.

It is a noble term every way. To say that a painter or sculptor, a poet or novelist, is a person of catholic feeling or taste, is high praise. Madame de Stael was a genuine French woman, but it has been said that her ear was attent to catch each sound that came her way from the great thinkers of her time throughout Europe. In other words, she was catholic-minded. Charles Lamb wrote: "With these exceptions I can read almost anything: I bless my stars for a taste so catholic, so unexcluding"; and Lecky refers to "the catholic and humane principles of Stoicism."

The etymological derivation and connections of the word are noble. It is first cousin to *whole* and *whole-some*, to *hale*, *heal*, and *holy*. In the General Confession we acknowledge that "there is no health [wholth] in us." In Morning and Evening Prayer we ask God to make known His "saving health unto all nations."

To one trained in a portion of the Church holding "the Faith as confessed in the purest ages and by the

purest Churches, who opens the Scriptures to all her
children, and submits all she does and teaches to that
test," the word Catholic cannot but have a rich significance. If he has stood under the dome of the
baptistery in Pisa, and, sounding one clear note,
heard coming back to him as from a full choir the
so-called "over-tones" of it, he will realize what I
mean by the "harmonics" of this word. It connotes
all the combined and harmonious elements of Christian
Truth, and Worship, and Life, in the One Body of
Christ, as informed by the Spirit of Christ; not merely
the pattern of sound words, such as St. Paul had given
to his son Timothy to hold, "in faith and love which
is in Christ Jesus"; but the entire good thing committed
unto the Church to guard, "through the Holy Ghost
which dwelleth in us." (2d Tim. 1 : 13, 14.)

It is a word which by all its historic Christian associations pleads with us, as it were, to reclaim it from
later associations that have tended to lower it in the
minds of a large portion of Christendom. Dr. Waterman, in the Preface to his volume on the "Post-Apostolic
Age," says:

"I have had in mind (also) a certain Ladies' Historical Club
well known to me, made up of women, intelligent and studious,
who inform themselves with honest ambition and hard work in
the history of England and America, but feel no shame that they
know almost nothing of the history of the Church, and that what
they do know they generally know wrong. They think, for
instance, of the Catholic Church as a corrupt outgrowth from
original Christianity, with a 'Pope' at the head of it, and of the
early bishops of Rome as 'Popes,' which last is exactly as un-
historical as it would be to call Queen Elizabeth, Empress of
India."

"Protestants who know nothing of theology," says Dr.
Salmon, "are apt freely to concede the appellation 'Catholic,'

having no other idea connected with it than that it is the name of a sect; but those who know better feel that it is a degradation of a noble word to limit it in such a way. And in truth, if it is possible to convey insult by a title, what is really insulting is that one section of Christians should appropriate to themselves the title 'Catholic' as their exclusive right, and thus by implication deny it to others."

He adds other words equally plain and forcible: "To speak honestly, of all the sects into which Christendom is divided none appears to me less entitled to the name Catholic than the Roman. Firmilian long ago thus addressed a former bishop of Rome (and this great bishop Firmilian must be regarded as expressing the sentiments, not only of the Eastern Church of the third century, but also of St. Cyprian, to whose translation, no doubt, we owe our knowledge of his letter): 'How great is the sin of which you have incurred the guilt in cutting yourself off from so many flocks! For, do not deceive yourself, it is yourself you have cut off: since he is the real schismatic who makes himself an apostate from the communion of ecclesiastical unity. While you think that you can cut off all from your communion, it is yourself that you cut off from communion with all.' At the present day the bishop of Rome has broken communion with more than half of Christendom, merely because it will not yield him an obedience to which he has no just right." ("Infallibility of the Church," pages VI, XI.)

Words like these serve to emphasize,—if, indeed, it requires emphasizing,—the great need there is of a clearer understanding on the part of Prayer Book worshippers, as to what we mean, or ought to mean, saying: "I believe in the Holy Catholic Church, the Communion of Saints." To shed further light upon the subject I venture to quote Canon Mason, in "The Faith of the Gospel," at considerable length.

"The reason why the Church is called Catholic is frequently misconceived. It is supposed that the title refers to her local extension. So in the Te Deum it is roughly rendered 'the Holy

Church throughout all the world.' The Greek word "katholiké" means the Church whose character is one of universality. The fixing of the word to its more outward sense seems to be due to Latin writers, not well acquainted with the Greek language, and naturally prone to think more of outward organization than of ideal characteristics. St. Cyril of Jerusalem says, 'The Church is so called in part because it teaches universally, and with no omissions, the entire body of doctrines which men ought to know.' * * * The very reason why the Church is thus spread abroad lies in her intrinsic character. It is her nature to penetrate everywhere and to embrace all. Resolutely refusing to be cramped and petrified and stereotyped, by reason of the free Spirit which animates her, she is capable of adapting herself to all circumstances. Our religion,—no longer like that of the Jews, given under a form suitable to one race only,—is equally at home among all nations and in all climates, in all times, under all forms of government, amidst all varieties of social and intellectual culture. In fact, like Christ Himself, the Catholic Church is in sympathy with everything that is truly human, and cannot acquiesce in anything that is less large than humanity, being, indeed, co-extensive with the new humanity inaugurated by Christ. Her mission is to lay hold upon every soul,—not to force it into some narrow and uniform mould, but to train and develop it into showing forth those features of the life of Christ for which it was predestined." ("Faith of the Gospel," pages 230, 231.)

Five times in the Services we come upon expressions which suggest a consciousness of the Church's catholicity: "To rule and govern thy holy Church universal"; "Who hast purchased to thyself an universal Church"; " to inspire continually the universal Church with the spirit of truth, unity, and concord"; "hast purchased to thyself an universal Church."

The word "catholic," rightly understood and applied, carries us back to an age when the Church taught, not "cunningly devised fables," or mere "traditions of men," but the pure Word of God. It recalls a time when in answer to united prayer, the Holy Spirit as a Spirit of truth and of unity, revealed the right interpretation of the Word through the consciousness of the Spirit-bearing Body, as whole and undivided, when, assembled in Councils truly representative, it was still possible for Christ's people to say: "It seemed good to the Holy Ghost, and to us."

A period it was, when, as in Chalcedon, in 451, in words that carried spiritual authority and conviction with them for the entire waiting and expectant body of believers "throughout all the world," a solemn affirmation could be made like the following:

"We confess, with the Holy Fathers, one and the same Lord Jesus Christ, and with one accord we announce Him, perfect in the Godhead, perfect in the Manhood, truly God, and truly Man, the self-same, of a Reasonable Soul and Body; co-essential with the Father as touching the Godhead, and co-essential with us as touching the Manhood, in all things like unto us, Sin only excepted; begotten of the Father as touching the Godhead before all ages, but in the last days for us and our salvation, the Self-same, born of Mary the Virgin Mother of God as to manhood. One and the same Christ, Son, Lord, Only-begotten, recognized in two Natures without confusion, change, division or separation, the difference of Natures being by no means removed by reason of the union, but on the contrary, the property of each Nature preserved and continuing in one Person and one hypostasis; not as it were divided and parted into two Persons, but one and the same Son, Only-begotten, God the Word, Lord Jesus Christ, even as we have been taught by the Prophets from the beginning and by Christ Himself, and as the Fathers have handed down to us."

This, the most complete statement of the belief of the early Church about the Person of our Lord, is substantially the same as that contained in the Nicene Creed. It has been the Faith of Christendom ever since. It is of this Creed that Dr. Fulton thus expressed himself twenty years ago,—and how much his words mean to us now, in a day when probably a greater number of Christian people throughout the world are earnestly desiring and praying for Church unity than at any other time for a thousand years!

"Those who explicitly hold the Apostles' Creed, without denying any part of the Nicene Creed,—which is the precise position of most Christian lay-people,—do implicitly hold the Nicene doctrine, and to-day, in spite of all divisions, the Church of Rome, the Anglican Churches, the Oriental Churches, and all the greater Protestant denominations, such as the Lutherans, the Presbyterians, and the Methodists, maintain the Nicene Creed itself. Nay, more, even bodies of Christians who imagine that their liberty would be endangered by a formal admission of written creeds, do in fact hold the faith of universal Christendom as it is summarily contained in the Apostles' Creed, and they hold it in the very sense in which it is more precisely expressed in the Nicene Creed. In other words, notwithstanding all existing divisions, universal Christendom, virtually with one accord, still maintains the Christian Faith, as it was set forth at Nicæa, Constantinople, Ephesus and Chalcedon.

"So far as we are concerned," he elsewhere affirms, "our Church stands firmly by the Church of the first centuries. Her Christianity is the Christianity of Chalcedon, not one jot less, and not a single jot more." And again he writes: "Christianity has never been improved by adding to the Faith as thus defined. Every unauthorized definition has served only to expose it to new forms of assault. In the present times there is good need that the Christian faith should be discriminated from unauthorized additions."

It is the Prayer Book, and the testimony of the Spirit in it, with which we are concerned here. Its catholic character is revealed by the breadth, the comparative simplicity, and the fulness with which the spiritual needs of men are met by "the chief elements of the Gospel," as Dr. Mason terms them. There is no turning aside from the declaration of these chief elements, the divine Fatherhood, the whole Truth of the Chalcedonian definition as regards the One Christ, the fallen condition of man, and the rich gift of the Spirit. It is *not one jot less*. In more than one place, and notably in the Te Deum,—as old as the Nicene Creed,—in the words, "Thou didst humble thyself to be born of a Virgin," there is plain witness to the truth told in the first chapter of St. Luke. It is *not a single jot more*. Like the Bible, it is not "theological." Theology has been justly called the Queen of Sciences; yet nothing of the structure theologians have erected,—gold, silver, precious stones, or wood, hay and stubble,—strictly speaking, has become part of these sacred Offices of Praise and Prayer.

"Other foundation can no man lay," than the one broad foundation-stone laid in the New Testament and in the catholic Creeds, even Jesus Christ. Men ask in our day for a broad Christianity. We cannot have a broad Christianity, except it be like the broad ocean, also deep. Men say the "Fatherhood of God and the Brotherhood of Man,—these are the great things." They are, indeed, two mighty factors of the one true religion, two catholic verities. But the fruition of God's Fatherhood, and the actual realization of human brotherhood, will come only through the life and work of that One Christ, Son and Lord, who is co-essential with the Father as touching the Godhood, and co-essential with us as touching Manhood.

It is in sharing that same Humanity of the very Son of God, that the Church can be a universal Church, "in sympathy with everything that is human," can with the Spirit's aid transform and uplift the world. Everything human belongs to the Church, all science and knowledge, all art and literature, whatsoever things in our present life "are lovely and of good report," on account of, and through living union with, the pure humanity of the Christ of God. Because of His glorified Manhood in heaven, the place which He is there preparing for us will be a place suited to a glorified human society such as eye hath not seen, and no heart of poet or prophet hath conceived.

The things to be believed in order to be a Christian, are not, as many people in our day are apt to think, many, but few. So it was in the day when the eunuch asked, "What doth hinder me to be baptized?" and received the answer, "If thou believest with all thine heart, thou mayest;" in fact, all ancient manuscripts do not contain these words, nor the following: "I believe that Jesus is the Son of God." It would appear that all which was requisite was a desire to be baptized in the triune Name.

None other than a simple Faith would have been adapted to a Church intended for all men, in all ages, and in all lands; and we are fully prepared to believe the record of the early writers, that the Nicene fathers were reluctant to express the truth of the Apostles' Creed in a more precise dogmatic form, and that no single phrase or word was added, which was not found necessary to give distinct denial to some more or less subtle and dangerous heresy. The Church's mission was, as Canon Mason said, "to lay hold upon every soul." It was a Church for all sorts and conditions of men, and any other than a brief, scriptural statement of the common belief would have been judged a serious, if not fatal, mistake. It was a Church for children,— represented Him who had taken the children in His arms and said, "of such is the kingdom of heaven." It was long ago said that "the Bible is a stream in which the lamb can wade and the elephant can swim," and it was evidently the Spirit's and the Church's will, that the same should be true of the Creed as a term of communion for the Lord's people throughout all the world.

Is it not Christ's and the Spirit's will to-day? Too great weight can scarcely be given to the Lord's indignation at the Pharisees, and all influenced by pharisaic teaching, to hinder the children, or such as were children mentally, from coming unto Him. Wise or simple, children or adults, we are all, He taught, to enter through the children's door. When He said, "Whoso shall receive one such little child in my name, receiveth me," and then added, "Whoso shall offend one of *these little ones which believe in me*, it were better for him that a millstone were hanged about his neck, and that he were drowned in the depth of the sea," it would appear that He must have turned from the child He had set in the midst of them, to point toward those common people who "heard him gladly," and whom the Pharisees despised.

Were the Chalcedonian Fathers thinking of this,— thinking of the sin of offending God's little ones of every age and class throughout the world,—thinking of the mighty angels who alike watch over little children and all who are children in understanding and in faith,—

thinking that to offend these is to offend Christ, and "grieve" the Spirit who stands in such relation to these same little ones in the Church,—when they put forth, in substance, the following?

"It is declared to be a high crime and misdemeanor, punishable with deposition and excommunication, to demand of any man, as a condition of Christian Communion, that he should receive or believe anything not contained in the Symbol of the Faith."

Precisely this crime and misdemeanor it is, of which many Christian communions have been guilty, and the Roman Communion possibly most of all. The tendency to require belief in points unnecessary, if not actually contrary to the letter or spirit of divine revelation, is as old as it is hurtful to souls. The Pharisees hedged the law with rules of their own invention, partly in order, if possible, to ensure the keeping of it, partly also in order to magnify their own office as theological teachers and rulers of the people. Out of this mistaken idea, and motive of self-exaltation, grew the perversion of the Roman Mass as being a sacrifice of the "Victim," Christ, actually offered ever anew by the priest, and the system of Confession and Absolution as taught and practiced in the Middle Ages. The invasions of barbarians, warlike and rude, and unquestionably dangerous to Christianity, of course presented a temptation to adopt these unscriptural and uncatholic methods.

The methods, and the principle underlying them, have lived on. One may read to-day in the "Catholic's Pocket Manual," these words of introduction to the Holy Rosary, with its Indulgences and Plenary

Indulgences, and remarks on the requisite priestly blessing of the rosaries:

"In its present form it was instituted by St. Dominic, the founder of the Order of Friars Preachers, in order to stem the flood of the Albigensian heresy, then spreading far and wide throughout Europe. He framed this admirable form of prayer in obedience to a revelation received from the blessed Virgin, to whom he had recourse for this purpose about the year 1206, and to him is due the spread of a devotion which for many centuries has produced the most marvellous results in the Christian world."

The period of Church history here mentioned was one prolific in expedients of a like sort, without the slightest foundation in the Word of God, or in the teaching and practice of the early Church, and among their "marvellous results" have been the great reaction against Roman authority and teaching in the sixteenth century, and the yet more formidable losses which Rome has suffered in these later times in Italy, France, Spain, South Germany, England, and America. These losses, as given in recent, carefully compiled statements, are enormous. The Rev. Pearcy Dearmer, in his little book entitled "Re-union and Rome," says:

"Far more people left the Roman Communion in the nineteenth century than in the sixteenth. * * * It seems not too much to say that Roman Catholic countries are disappearing from the map of the world. If the above estimate be at all correct, and the present rate of shrinkage be maintained, the whole Roman Church will have disappeared in less than two centuries."

In a most true sense this prospect is awful to contemplate. For while, as protestant and true Catholics, we cannot go the full length with Pius X, speaking in his first Encyclical of the present "most afflicted condition of mankind," which "did exceedingly affright us," and which "may be, as it were, a foretaste and a beginning of the evils that are to be looked for in the last days," we have reason to regard this condition as indeed terrible.   Mr. Dearmer affirms that this tremendous defection from Rome means abandonment of religion altogether.   These millions who have left or are leaving Rome, that is, repudiating the claim of the Papacy, "having been brought up to believe that the choice is 'Rome or nothing,' and that there is no real Christianity except that of Rome, have largely revolted against Christianity altogether."

But our concern here is not with the uncatholic nature of the Papacy itself and large portions of the Roman teachings and services in particular; nor with the present fearful reaction against them, and against the Christian religion in consequence of them.   It is rather with the general tendency to add as conditions of communion things "not contained in the symbol of the Faith" in the Church's early days.   "How is it, brethren?" wrote St. Paul to the Corinthians, "when ye come together, every one of you hath a psalm, hath a doctrine, hath a tongue, hath a revelation, hath an interpretation.   Let all things be done unto edifying."

The Church in her Prayer Book approaches us as sinners, who need to receive the new heart, and be reconciled to God in Christ, bids us read: "Behold, I was shapen in wickedness, and in sin hath my mother conceived me;" bids us pray: "Make me a clean heart, O God, and renew a right spirit within me."   On the other hand, she presents for our acceptance,—ought we not to say, the Spirit presents?—no carefully defined doctrine of depravity, and no theory of the correct method of conversion to God. Reading our Lord's story of the Rich Man and Lazarus, and of the Great Gulf Fixed, and more than one of His solemn warnings concerning a Judgment to come, she calls upon us to subscribe to no formulated teaching in regard to eternal punishment, as a condition of communion. She reads the Ten Commandments in our ears, also long passages from the Old Testament Law,— "the schoolmaster to bring us unto Christ,"—but with these passages many others exhibiting our freedom in Christ. Love it is which fulfils the law. It is "a royal law, a law of liberty." Rightly speaking, the law is "not made for a righteous man," but rather for liars and murderers, and the like (1st Tim. 1 : 9). Refreshing is the Gospel reminder, midway in Lent, that in Christ we are not "children of the bond-woman, but of the free."

The historic Church reads to her children how God predestinated those whom He had foreknown, to be conformed to the image of His Son, and all things work together for their good; has predestinated us unto the adoption of children by Jesus Christ unto Himself, and would have us believe it with grateful hearts; but no doctrine of election, Augustinian or any other, is to be found in her Prayer Book. This Augustinian teaching it is of which Dr. Fulton writes:

"If you ask some of the most virulent enemies of Christianity what makes their hatred so embittered, I believe you will find that it is this and another doctrine of a similar sort which have made Christianity not only incredible to their intellect, but repul-

13

sive to their sense of justice.   It is then something of a relief to
be assured that neither the Augustinian nor the modern doctrine
of predestination is any part of Christianity" (Chalcedonian
Decree, page 109).

The Prayer Book contains no formulated statement
regarding the Trinity. It simply bids us sing what
Christians have sung for fifteen centuries, how the
holy Church throughout all the world doth acknowledge the Father of an infinite Majesty, His adorable
true and only Son, and the Holy Ghost, the Comforter.
It moves us to sing how the King of Glory, Christ,
the everlasting Son of the Father, when He took upon
Him to deliver man, humbled Himself to be born of a
Virgin, and, having overcome the sharpness of death,
did open the Kingdom of Heaven to all believers;
calls upon us in the Eucharistic Service to give thanks
to Father, Son, and Holy Ghost "for the redemption
of the world by the death and passion of our Saviour
Christ, both God and man;" contains passages from
the Gospels and Epistles which exhibit our Lord making that which in the Consecration it terms "a full,
perfect, and sufficient sacrifice, oblation, and satisfaction for the sins of the whole world;" and yet presents
to us no *theory* of the Atonement whatever. Inviting
us to

> "Draw nigh and take the Body of the Lord,
>   And drink the holy Blood for us out-poured,"

and invoking the Holy Spirit upon God's gifts and
creatures of bread and wine, that "we may be partakers of Christ's most blessed Body and Blood,"
the Church offers no definite statement concerning
the manner of His sacred Presence, to be apprehended

and received as a condition of entrance to "the banquet of that most heavenly food."

The Table of Lessons in the Prayer Book, together with the Gospels and Epistles incorporated in the Eucharistic Services, provides that church-going people shall be richly nourished with the divine Word; it is read in our ears that the Holy Scriptures are "able to make men wise unto salvation," that "every scripture given by inspiration of God is profitable for doctrine, for reproof, for correction, for instruction in righteousness, that the man of God may be perfect, throughly furnished unto all good works"; and that "holy men spake as they were moved by the Holy Ghost"; yet no definition of the nature of that inspiration is offered for our acceptance. According to Dr. Fulton, none was put forth in the Church of the Nicene Age, and his conclusion is that "no theory on the subject either is or ought to be any part of Christianity; and that objections to Christianity which are founded, explicitly or implicitly, on any such theory, are utterly irrelevant" (page 101).

As regards the scientific theory of evolution which by many is supposed to be irreconcilable with the Christian Faith, and which has had a disturbing effect on not a few Christian minds, Dr. Fulton makes the following remark: "A conflict between science and sectarianism is always possible; a conflict between science and genuine Catholic Christianity is not possible, because the Nicene Creed makes no affirmation of any kind, with which any discovery of physical science has been, or ever can be inconsistent" (page 91).

It is after discussing at length the various doctrines added to the ancient Faith of Christendom, and the difficulties, real or imaginary, created by them, that the same learned writer thus concludes:

"I know not how the thoughts which I have put before you may strike your minds; but to not a few troubled minds in these times it may come almost as a light from heaven, dispelling many a gloomy shade of doubt and difficulty, to learn that no past, present or possible discovery, whether of science or criticism, can cast one particle of doubt upon the Christian Faith as that Faith has been set forth by the only competent authority, that is, by the voice of Universal Christendom. * * * May I not ask you to admit that the Chalcedonian Decree, so far as we have yet considered it, was no tyrannical encroachment on the lawful freedom of the individual Christian, but stands vindicated in this nineteenth century as a truly constitutional and catholic law of light and liberty?" (page 101).

Bishop Webb, in a sermon on the Anglican Principle essentially Historical, writes:

"In this great principle of Historical Continuity in the Faith we find that we have a great principle of rest. In these days there is a general feeling of restlessness; * * * * Wherever you have looked during these last two or three years,—to America, to Africa, to India, to the Continent of Europe, to our own islands, —everywhere you observe a general restlessness." He points to the principle of our Church wherein we have a Faith once delivered to the saints—which we heartily believe, to which we testify, and which we are sure our children will live and die for and, please God, "keep" by the power of the Holy Spirit until Christ comes again. "Here," he says, "is a principle of restfulness for the human mind; it gives us the motto 'Semper eadem,'— 'always the same,'—like the unchanging Christ, who is the same yesterday, to-day, and forever."

But this unchanging Christ, the Bishop goes on to say, "is not a rigid and immovable Christ, but a Christ who "has sympathy with the spirit of the age, and can speak to the nineteenth century in tones that will reach its heart, a living Christ and the great Centre from which the living Body moves."

As living and moving in the Universal Spirit, professing a simple, personal, and yet corporate, Faith in a divine-human Lord, the Church of the ages contains a principle of adaptation and of liberty, of breadth and comprehensiveness. In it is the rest of *life*, not of stagnation. It has a genuine missionary power. It has a message for the world.

It may be worth our while to look a little deeper, and ask why the millions are restless, and why the historic Faith offers a cure. I believe the answer lies, in great part, in the fact that its simplicity is that of *pure dogma;* in other words, of divine revelation, and not of mere human doctrine. Received through men, indeed, it is ultimately of God; and because of God, therefore instinct with His life and power. Rightly understood, there is no philosophy, no science, and no true art without dogma; that is to say, without certain demonstrated or generally approved principles at the foundation of it.

This fact ought to be more generally recognized than it is; especially as bearing on religion. A religion without dogma is no religion. Certain it is that such a religion will have no power to compel the human will, and to influence conduct. To have acknowledged a truth or a principle of belief and action, and then lost it, will always mean, for a being endowed as man is endowed, a serious loss in motive power. To come directly to my point, it must create the restlessness with which Bishop Webb declares that multitudes in our day are affected. And must it not be confessed that this absence of "will to believe" is largely owing to the abuse of man's power to believe, on the part of great sections of the Christian Church itself? Man-

made creeds, traditions of men, cunningly devised
fables, even sincerely and earnestly thought-out doctrines, added to the Faith once for all delivered to the
saints to keep by the power of the Spirit,—these all
have the effect to weaken the very faculty to believe
at all.

We need to reflect more carefully, and with keener
sympathy, upon this prevailing condition of soul-
impotence. Shakespear in the character of Hamlet;
Turgenieff, in his analysis of Rudin; and Sienkiewicz,
in the hero of his story, "Without Dogma," throw a
strong side-light upon the condition,—part mental,
part spiritual,—which I am endeavoring to charac-
terize. Whereas "the will is the man," in all these
three characters we find presented a case where reason
overbalances the will. We have, as Professor William
L. Phelps has said, "a melancholy, but fascinating,
and highly instructive, spectacle of futile impulses,
vain longings, and idle day-dreams." In the third
instance, "Without Dogma," the very title reveals
the lack of conviction that ultimately destroys the
hero. He has absolutely "no driving power"; as he
expresses it, *he does not know.*

The particular study here is, no doubt, that of a
sort of mind extremely common among the upper
classes of Poles and Russians. But is not the disease
more widely spread than that? In our present-day
magazine and other literature, and in the religious
attitude even of many who at times present themselves
before God, do we not discover signs of a lack of conviction, and of power to "bring things to pass" for
God? It is not that we ought to be and desire others
to be, "dogmatic," in the common, disagreeable, sense

of the term; and from this secondary and lower meaning attached too naturally, alas, to some words of high
lineage and noble significance,—*enthusiast*, *bigot*, *fanatic* even,—every man of deep convictions and earnest
purposes has reason to pray to be delivered. All
these words conveyed originally the thought of a zeal
fervent and sincere, being the result of divinely revealed
truth. Having this higher meaning of our word in
view, and believing that none can be well-established,
ardent, and active Christians without dogma, my
contention is, that the present neurasthenic, if not
invertebrate, state of multitudes around us is largely
due to the reaction against unauthorized, sometimes
audacious, additions to the Church's Faith. It is not
merely that corrupt and overloaded systems of belief
have broken down and lost their power to influence the
will and conduct, but that the will to believe and to act
has itself been impaired, and we behold entire communities, if not entire races, affected with this loss of power.

Professor Barrett Wendell tells us that Dr. Holmes'
poem of the wonderful "One-hoss Shay" was composed
as a sly satire upon the collapse of New England
orthodoxy; and from the fact that it was built by the
Deacon and used by the Parson, built in "such a
logical way," broke down "close by the meet'n' house
on the hill," and "at half-past nine by the meet'n'
house clock," it is easy to believe him. It is easy to
believe, too, that the underlying thought was a serious
and sympathetic one. Like many another humorist,
Dr. Holmes possessed a large vein of thoughtful sympathy, and in none of his published letters is this more
conspicuous than in his replies to friends who have
brought to him their religious doubts and perplexities.

My own thought,—as will already be apparent,—
is that precisely as the parson had received a shock
almost as overwhelming as that of the poor old chaise,
lying "in a heap or mound," so the hearts of men,
individually and, in large bodies, receive a terrible,
often permanently paralyzing, disturbance, when
religious systems go to pieces, in which they have
trusted as though they were nothing less, and nothing
more, than Christianity itself.   They *get up and stare
around*, not for a half hour, but for the remainder of
their lives.   Their children inherit alike their problem
and their anemic condition.   A long while staring
around, and inquiring, "What then is Christianity?"
they become, some of them restless in mind and spirit,
and very many more, alas, indifferent, joining, for the
rest of their days, the great company which the Psalmist represents asking, "Who will show us any good?"

Such deep and lasting soul-injury do those uncatholic
structures of religious thought and doctrine work, which
either on the one hand, as in the night, take away our
Lord out of faith's sight; or, on the other hand, so to
say, bury Him again under the theological inventions of
centuries.

Whether Roman inventions or Protestant, their
effect is of the same kind.   The reader has foreseen
my conclusion, that a Church inheriting, through the
Spirit, the simple catholic faith of the early days,
cannot do otherwise than protest against the one and
the other.   True it is that some non-episcopal Churches
have "in many ways a special affinity with our own
Communion."   Together with us they protest against
the exclusive claims and the erroneous teachings and
practices of the mother of all the sects of the West,

Rome. Great numbers of our own people, bishops, priests, and laymen, have come out of these non-episcopal bodies; and have not ceased to love and care for them. They know how considerable a measure of catholic and evangelical truth those communions "stand for," and that a mighty missionary force is in them, as a whole. Speaking for myself and for others, I would say, that we cannot entirely accept the poet's implication, from the Unitarian point of view,—if indeed he meant it so,—that "Orthodoxy" is now like

> "The poor old chaise, in a heap or mound,
> As if it had been to the mill and ground."

We look back thankfully to "the rock" whence we were hewn, and to "the hole of the pit" whence we were digged, conscious that much of the good which it may be is in us,—granite or marble, silver or gold, from Puritan quarries or Quaker mines, is of the Spirit of God. A goodly part of Dr. Smyth's plea, in "Passing Protestantism and Coming Catholicism," we accept. Protestantism is not entirely responsible for its own existence and for the present condition of disunion. It has achieved "splendid successes." It has its "triumphal arch." Of late years it has been "breaking up, rather than making Creeds."

We are gratefully appreciative of certain expressions in the Report of the Special Committee of the Lambeth Conference on Reunion and Intercommunion, concerning Presbyterian and other Non-Episcopal Churches.

"To many Presbyterians," the Bishops say, "we owe a deep debt of gratitude for their contributions to sacred learning. We are equally indebted to them for many examples of holiness of

life. With regard to their Churches, although their characteristics vary in different countries, they have in many ways a
special affinity for our own Communion. Wherever they have
held closely to their traditions and professed standards of faith
and government, as formulated at Westminster, they satisfy
the first three of the four conditions of an approach to reunion
laid down by the Lambeth Conference of 1888. Even as regards
the fourth, though they have not retained "the historic episcopate," it belongs to their principles to insist upon definite ordination as necessary for admission into their ministry. * * *
Many leading Presbyterian divines maintain the transmission of
Orders by a regular succession through the presbyterate."

It will be through the wider "triumphal arch" of
the Faith as broadly presented in the historic Creeds
and in our Book of Common Prayer and Belief, that
the separated Christian Communities will one day
pass in to kneel at Christ's feet again, an Undivided
Church. Dr. Smyth himself is glad to tell us that
Protestantism is no longer much occupied in devising
new formulas of faith,—speaks of the common belief
in the Apostles' Creed, of "a greater Christianity at
the door," of a "Holy Church throughout all the
world," which "the first Christian professors saw,
and which Protestantism has lost awhile." He com-
pares its various ecclesiastical confessions to "feudal
castles on the Rhine, strongly built, with moat and
tower, and their dungeons for heretics down below";
refers to denominational independency cherished and
continued as "a sin against the Holy Ghost."

"Looking broadly at the facts of life," writes this eminent
Congregationalist, "we must admit the relaxation of authority
in our churches. Religion among us has lost authority in the
family life. * * * Religion is withdrawing from the
churches. In almost any community people who are not in

their habits of mind irreligious, nor without faith in their hearts, belong to no church, confess no creed, and rarely attend public worship. He writes of a 'literature, mystical, quietistic, and spiritual, but neither churchly nor very distinctly Christian, springing up outside the churches and beyond their creeds; of religious nebulousness; of many as unattracted by Protestantism and repelled by Romanism, who, having disembarked from the faith which once held them, seem to have been left adrift in uncertainty by our Christianity; and the night comes on."

All this will mean but little to the man or woman whose Church-feeling is mere sentiment or personal enjoyment. To all who love the Church as the creation of the Holy Spirit, and bearing His message concerning Christ to mankind everywhere, it will be a different matter.

Woe unto us, theologians and teachers, who, desiring to be and to be "called masters," hinder those who otherwise would come in from entering the household and kingdom of our Lord, by our additions to the simple, broad Faith of the Apostolic days. Woe unto us, Roman or Protestant, High Church or Low, called Catholic or called Evangelical, who teach for doctrines the commandments and the interpretations of Augustine or of Loyola, of Anselm or Calvin or Luther, of Wesley or Edwards, in a way to make *The Way* which is Christ difficult to His little ones. Little ones in respect to age, or little ones as regards mental and spiritual power to feel after and find Him who is Himself the Way, the Truth, and the Life, He would take them all in the arms of His love. His Spirit is here in power, to draw all men and all children unto Him; but of little use is it for the Spirit to say, "Come," if the Bride says, "Wait; come only when you can receive this or that 'doxy,' obey such and such rules of practice, mediæval or modern, imposed as terms of membership and communion."

There are many ways in which it is possible to grieve the Spirit, and surely not the least culpable of them is this of binding burdens of doctrine upon men's shoulders which render it difficult for them to pass in through the Church door.

The Spirit of Universality and of Unity has for more than three hundred years been overruling for good the evils of a disunited Christendom; and it is above all to Him that we need and ought to turn, when, the hour having plainly come for better things, Christians are asking themselves what can and should be done to hasten their arrival. As to the question,—next to a burning one, and to many of us something like a dilemma,—shall the Church's name be changed, and if so, when? the Holy Spirit's counsel should be often and fervently invoked. The more truly catholic-minded a Churchman is, the more seriously, it would seem, he must weigh the arguments on both sides, and always "in the Spirit." The name "Protestant" expresses the historical and permanent attitude of the entire Anglican Communion toward the Roman Church. To be sure, Dr. Smyth characterizes Protestantism as passing, says its triumphal arch is about finished, and that the names of its victories on the side of Bible truth and liberty are about all inscribed on its walls; but will our parting with that name be comprehended by Christians generally, and in the Episcopal Church itself?

"Catholicism is coming," writes Dr. Smyth. And if this means that many are ready and looking for it, we who in God's providence are in trust with "the

Christian Faith as professed in the purest ages and by the purest Churches," are bound by every right and wise expedient to prove that we are. Protestantism being only three or four centuries old, and our Church and Prayer Book being what they are, many of us are keenly sensible that the present title-page of the latter does not tell, or imply, the whole truth about both. No change, however, ought to be made hastily or without some measure of preparatory education.

It is perhaps the country parson, or intelligent Sunday-school or Bible Class teacher, who is most frequently moved to desire the change. It is said that our missionaries in foreign lands wish for it. What of clergy in the home fields? Do not these and their earnest co-workers come in specially close contact with people, old and young, who have been hardened against, or rendered simply indifferent to all religion by the perplexing, if not distorted and torturing doctrinal teachings of one or another, it may be one after the other, of the hundred and fifty or more Protestant bodies? The clergyman who has lived in a college town, and year by year come in touch with young men having "the will to believe," yet refusing to believe in Christianity as it has so far been presented to them, sorely feels the difficulty I have referred to. Our Church is to these youths, soon to become men of influence in the land, just what it is to the plain folk who warm their hands, and chill each other's hearts in religious discussion, around the stove in the corner-store,—simply another protestant denomination, accentuating another individual "doctrine" or "interpretation."

The country Churchman, priest or laic, who knows the simplicity and health-bringing catholicity of the Church's message, and has a love for souls, will ask: "If Rome has, in the matter of living faith, slain its thousands,—Mr. Dearmer says, its seventeen millions in English-speaking countries, in the last century,—how many thousands is a disunited, creed-manufacturing, creed-breaking Protestantism slaying?"

"Protestant" as a distinctive part of our title is, and will long continue to be, associated in the minds of men everywhere with the independency which Dr. Smyth terms "a sin against the Holy Ghost," and with forms of religion which he declares "are losing their hold upon multitudes on all sides."

The name "Episcopal," emphasizing episcopacy as though it were the chief element in our communion, peculiar to it as another new section of the Church,—whereas the Church Universal has been from the beginning episcopal, and the historic Faith is more of the essence of the Gospel than are Holy Orders,—tends in like manner to disguise her Scriptural *wholeness*. Around the corner from the modest chapel, which it may be is ten years old, there stands on the main street of the town a fine large edifice fifty years old, also named "Episcopal." Nobody besides the Rector and one or two of his communicants is aware that the hymn,

"Welcome, happy morning,"

with which the last Easter Service began, and the Easter Eucharist itself, originated the one twelve and the other fourteen or more centuries before Wesleyan

episcopacy saw the light.   Only for these few persons
can the words of that hymn,

"Age to age shall say,"

possess their rich and stirring import.

It is not for their antiquity, in itself considered, that
the missionary thinks so highly of these features.   He
is convinced that, in our Lord's phrase, "the old is
better."   Abreast with the twentieth century in his
ideas and feelings generally, and in his interest for
humanity, he knows in his heart that the Worship
and Faith of the Church embody the *message* for the
twentieth century in this new free land of the West,
that in them men hear the voice of the Spirit, and those
simple, living verities, which our age needs.

Not the love of antiquity, but the love of humanity
was the motive of De Pressensé's words:

> "Aspiration toward the Church of the future is becoming
> more general, more ardent; but for all who admit the divine
> origin of Christianity the Church of the future has its type and
> its ideal in that great past which goes back, not three, but
> eighteen centuries.   To cultivate a growing knowledge of this,
> in order to attain to a growing conformity to it, is the task of
> the Church of to-day."

Hardly anything can be clearer than that a change
in the Church's name will be fruitful of good in the
degree that it is made with a distinct understanding
and warm sympathy on the part of her people.   It will
be desirable to cultivate beforehand in them the growing knowledge of the Church's past of which De Pressensé wrote, by means of sermons and Sunday-school
and Bible Class instruction.   The women who now
busy their minds with books bearing on Missions,

14

while their fingers work for the cause, would become yet more ardent in Auxiliary activity, if the reading were extended to take in something of early Church history. The story of our English tongue is an every-day "speaking pageant" of the experience of our more and more world-dominating race. It has also its own testimony to bear as to the Church's long life, as the bright women in the Club to which Dr. Waterman referred would perceive by a glance at certain familiar Saxonized Greek words in the larger dictionaries. The Gospel was first proclaimed in Greek. As Bishop Westcott has said:

"Most if not all the Churches of the West were Greek religious colonies. Their Scriptures, and it would appear their Liturgy, was Greek. The Rome of those days was so much a Greek city that the poorer part of the population was largely of Greek descent." The word *Church* appears, according to Worcester, to have "been derived from the Greek, through the Anglo-Saxon. The Goths, as stated by Dr. Trench, were first converted to Christianity by Greek missionaries from Constantinople, who imparted to them the word κυριακη or κυριακον, church, and the Goths lent the word to other German tribes, including the Anglo-Saxons."

Bible is another word of the same kind, and so is *evangel*, and these three words in themselves corroborate the report that Christianity was early at home in Britain. But *bishop* and *priest* and *deacon* are likewise terms derived from the Greek through the Anglo-Saxon, and these corroborate the record of history that the ancient Church of England was episcopal.

A word from our bishops now and then, in a pastoral letter or sermon, and even in a confirmation address, might greatly help on this good work of education.

The Bishop of London, speaking at the recent English Church Pageant at Fulham Palace, said:

"I believe immensely in teaching through the eye. * * * I do hope and believe that the pageant will do something to remove the astounding ignorance of so many Church people about their own Church, and to make us all prouder of the inheritance of our fathers."

Our conscience and sense of responsibility to the Spirit, and to our brother men, need arousing as truly as our just pride. An editorial in a leading London newspaper said of the Pageant:

"It is to be presumed that those who place it before our eyes are not doing so in a mere antiquarian spirit. Rather they are saying, 'This is the living institution which carries its vigor and its witness forward in ourselves. This is the old historic Church of England, of which we now are the representatives.'" (Littell, "The Historians and the English Reformation," pages 284, 285.)

How much these expressions, and the Pageant referred to, mean to us in a time when Christians of nearly every name are drawing each year closer together, and Church Unity and Missions are in the air; especially when consideration is given to Dr. Fulton's declaration, "I believe that Christian Unity will never be restored in this world on any other than the Chalcedonian basis of unswerving fidelity to the Catholic Faith, and unlimited liberty in all other particulars!"

The Rev. Mr. Littell, in the volume above referred to, presents abundant and conclusive testimony of every sort to the continuity of the English Church,— and therefore of our own,—from the early days of Christianity, in Creed, and Doctrine, and Orders, in Possessions, in every way; as against inaccurate and often worse than careless writers on both sides the Atlantic. That the Church of England never was a part of the Church of Rome; that she holds the same Creeds, has the same Sacraments, and the same Ministry, is essentially the same Church as before the Reformation, and no new Church was then set up, few can doubt after reading that work.

Now the Services of the Book of Common Prayer, we have seen, make the same truth evident in their own way, proving, as do hundreds of historical and legal documents, that what the Reformers of the sixteenth century did was not to create a new Faith, or a new Church, but to repudiate certain mediæval accretions of doctrine, and to reform the Church of many abuses. Inasmuch as few of our people are students either of Church History or etymology, a Prayer Book provided with dates, and references to the ancient Sacramentaries, and other similar matter, if practicable, would be most useful. Placed in the margins of pages, or in tables like those found at present before Morning and Evening Prayer, these aids would surely be resorted to gratefully by superintendents and teachers, and many others. In a few years large numbers of our worshippers would become aware of the meaning of the words, "I believe in the Holy Catholic Church," whose minds are far from being clear about it now. Misled during the week by the school historians, and by Macaulay, and Froude, and Hallam, by Arnold, and even Green, it would be possible on Sunday to set young and old straight as to whether the English Church was in any sense or degree whatever the *creation* either of Henry VIII or the English Parliament of the sixteenth century.

The saying, "that the force of a word is exactly proportionate to the number of ideas which it connotes," is certainly true as applied to the venerable word of which we have been speaking. It connotes the entire wealth of divine truths and institutions with which Christ's Spirit has enriched us,—and to which no Church in Christendom has a better claim. To employ it frequently in a familiar and natural way would have a more educational and illuminating effect than to make a place for it in our title. It would cast new light upon the old Faith, and be a much-needed lantern to the feet of inquirers in our day. *Catholic* stands for wholeness. Our age needs to be guided to the entire truth of the Apostolic and Nicene period, "not one jot more, and not one jot less." As Dr. Fulton said:

"We often hear men say, 'Give us the Christianity of Christ!' It is a just demand. It represents a lawful and laudable resentment at the endless additions to the Christianity of Christ, by which the Gospel has been obscured and Christ Himself has been hidden behind a mass of human inventions. By all means let us have the Christianity of Christ, and nothing else than that. But by all means let us have the whole of it! Let us have all that the Apostles remembered and the Evangelists recorded; and then let us have the deep meaning of it all, the fulness of the truth of it, which the Holy Spirit revealed to them." ("Chalcedonian Decree," page 65.)

It is in the Trinity Season, when to the Epistles belong the dominating thought and motive of the Services,—that we have shown to us this same "deep meaning of it all," the "fulness of the truth of the Christianity of Christ." In other words, these Sundays of the long Pentecostal period contain the distinctively "strong meat" of the Gospel, belonging "to them that are of perfect age," not "milk" for such as are babes (Heb. 5 : 12–14); the "things" of Christ which He said the disciples were "not able to bear" before His departure, but which the Spirit would teach them. In these more advanced truths consist the vital and dominant elements of the Gospel to which the Bishops in Chalcedon bore their testimony, and which the consciousness of Christendom has accepted as the witness of the Spirit in the Church. "This is the Faith of the Fathers," the cry went up when the record of the great Council was read. "This is the Faith of the Apostles. This we all believe."

THE HOLY MINISTRY

Our sufficiency is of God; who also hath made us able ministers of the new testament.—2d Cor. 3 : 5, 6.

His grace which was bestowed upon me was not in vain.—1st Cor. 15 : 10.

I therefore, the prisoner of the Lord.—Eph. 4 : 1.

I bow my knees unto the Father * * * that Christ may dwell in your hearts by faith.—Eph. 3 : 14, 17.

I thank my God—that ye are enriched by him in all utterance.—1st Cor. 1 : 4, 5.

Praying for me, that utterance may be given unto me.—Eph. 6 : 18, 19.

Let men be careful how, in their human speculations they depart from the simplicity of the sacred Scriptures, and trifle with the holy and exalted ministry which God has appointed; lest on the one hand they degrade it, as many do, into a sacrificing priesthood, like that of an effete paganism or that of an abrogated Judaism; and lest on the other hand they degrade, as many others do, into a mere man-made committeeship of a mere human society that Divinely-constituted ministry in the Church of God which is the "gift" of the Holy Ghost.—Bishop Vail.

We may not even appear to think lightly of the historic Episcopate which is supported by the practically unanimous judgment of nearly fifteen centuries, and has been amply justified by its results.—Bishop Westcott.

The world is suffering upon every hand for lack of preachers who can go forth into it with the learning, the devotion, the fire of the men who conquered the philosophy of Greece, and the old lore of Egypt, and won to the Gospel the wide practical knowledge of the world-mastering Rome; men who can now so preach the truths of God's word and the Divine life of the Son of Man to the mind and the thought of this age, that eternity shall become again to the hearts of those who hear even more real than time, and the spirit and teaching of Christ be felt as more wise than all the earth-bounded sciences of man.—Dr. Garrison.

He should be full of the Holy Ghost as a preacher. Otherwise he may not have that special form of power which, under God, reaches the heart of the impenitent, creates a deep longing for God, inspires fear and hope, and at last faith in Christ as the Saviour of men. A man may be a great saint. His life may be lived on the heights; he may be intensely earnest; may desire to seek and save the lost; may have the natural gift of eloquence; but beside and above all these there must be the direct gift of the Spirit for the special object of convincing men and drawing them to the Lord.—Dr. Dale.

In an age when many who profess and call themselves Christians apparently have no conception that there is any direct influence of the Spirit in the making of a minister of Christ, and think of the ministry as only a profession which the people authorize, or which a man may take up or may lay down at his pleasure, it is a much-needed testimony to Scriptural truth which the Prayer Book bears. It speaks of the Ministry as an official gift of the Holy Spirit now, as it was in the Apostles' days. So far as the Trinity Season is concerned, let it be observed that the six passages from the Epistles,—from First and Second Corinthians and Ephesians,—found in six Sunday Services, being those of the Eleventh, Twelfth, Sixteenth, Seventeenth, Eighteenth, and Twenty-third Sundays, they clearly mark the sacred Ministry as one of the Trinity Season themes and subjects of prayer.

As to the ministry being Apostolic, it is to be understood at the outset and always, the whole body of the Church is apostolic. No proof is forthcoming that the commission given by Christ on the evening of His Resurrection was addressed to "the eleven" to the exclusion of "them that were with them"; or that the Pentecostal Spirit fell only on the Twelve, to be dispensed to the rest. Within the Church of the New Covenant all are priests. None are secular. Priests and people, we are all "kings and priests unto God," we are all "a royal priesthood, a peculiar people." Therefore are all, ministers or laymen, consecrated in our baptism,—some of us believe, in our confirmation more particularly, to be in our several stations, and according to our individual opportunities, mediators "unto God" on behalf of others, and responsible to Him for the spiritual well-being of those around us.

On the other hand, as Canon Mason expresses it, "Ordination," that is, "promotion in the hierarchy of which we are all members, carries with it an intensified power of priesthood." And this order is "essential," not a mere convenience. The Church was from the beginning, and is always, an organism in the Spirit.

Some one has asked, "Can we think of anything that is done in the Church without the Creator-Spirit?" Indeed when we speak of religious institutions as founded, have they not rather been created, and grown? Our Lord Himself, in the Spirit, created the Apostolate, and the manner in which it developed afterward into an ordered ministry was, as has been already observed, a way of life. When the sun rises, the plant is there. Enough for us that within the life-time of those who learned from the Apostles it was recognized that no Church could be complete without the Episcopate, and the other two orders of Priests and Deacons; and that only Bishops might ordain.

Enough for us that this Apostolical Ministry, spreading widely in the world, and hence compared by our Lord to a net (Matt. 13 : 47), and also comparable to the human spine, vertebrate, linked together, flexuous and flexible, a wonderful bond of unity, communicating life and nerve-force to every part of the body, became a universal, historic, ministry. "It is evident unto all men reading Holy Scripture and ancient Authors, that the infant Church was born of the Spirit practically thus equipped, and that "from the Apostles' time there have been these Orders of Ministers in it." (Preface to the Ordinal.) It is, however, also evident that this same three-ordered Ministry would have exercised its various spiritual functions more freely and beneficially, and stand out more clearly to-day before Christendom as a divine institution, nobly planned and full of grace and power, had not the Papal system crippled and paralyzed the Episcopate, cutting off its flow of healthful energy.

When Luther deplored the loss to German Chris-

tians of what we call the historic Episcopate, and
Calvin made a distinct effort to recover it for Switzer-
land, when John Wesley protested against separation
from the Church of England, it was because they
knew what the Episcopate had been to the Church
Catholic from the beginning, and believed it to be
essential to the continuity, integrity, and vigour of her
life throughout the ages, and in all lands. It is only
just to quote here the assertion in Palmer's Treatise
on the Church, that neither Luther nor Zwingli were
Separatists, and that Calvin "expressly defends the
obligation of human traditions, amongst the rest
approves of the constitution of the primitive Church—
arch-bishops, bishops * * * arch-deacons, sub-
deacons * * * in fact the whole hierarchy. This
system he regarded as scarcely in any respect dis-
sonant from the word of God."   (Vol. II, page 51.)

How rich then is our heritage, and how solemn our
responsibility in regard to it! Inheritors of the Truth
in its wholeness, and of divine institutions unimpaired,
and still invested with saving power,—not least among
these the gift of the Spirit in Holy Orders,—we owe
it not merely to ourselves, but to the world for which
the Son of God died, and to which we are "sent,"
above all to the personal Spirit Himself, to guard,
cherish and transmit them pure and entire.

Speaking of those who deny the perpetuity of the
Pentecostal Gift, Dr. Downer asks,

"What then shall become of the vast heathen world, if the
power given to the Church to evangelize it has been withdrawn,"
* * * "where is the power that is to accompany the written
or spoken word, when the ambassador for Christ stands forth
in His Name to utter his testimony? Where is the sacred link

that must join the outward sign with the inward grace, that must give all their sweetness and all their efficacy to the sacraments of God's love?" * * * "It is not so. The living Spirit is with us still—to perform the labor, to do the difficult task, to speak the difficult word."

The four Ember (Quatember) Weeks,—and the Trinity and September ones especially,—ought to lie near the hearts of parents and sponsors, of Sunday-school and all Christian teachers.

For who may say how far back in the individual mind and soul preparation for the priestly and pastoral life can, and therefore should, begin? While the Church's Ministry did not at the beginning, nor does it to-day, as some have imagined, derive its authority from below by delegation, the man upon whom the sacred authority and duty devolve does come from below; from the people, out of the pew, out of the school. The family worship and life, parental example and influence, the prayers and the tactful words of teachers, the Church's fellowship and social atmosphere, with his own youthful praying and thinking, have under the Spirit made him what he is. Hannah of olden time has not been the only mother who has prayed and promised to God, as the sacred record reads. "For this child I prayed; and the Lord hath given me my petition which I asked of him; therefore also I have lent—granted—him to the Lord; as long as he liveth he is granted to the Lord." One now living and in Holy Orders, with whom I am acquainted, was, in times of doubt as to his fitness and sufficient readiness to receive the holy charge, kept constant to his purpose partly by the knowledge that his dear mother had consecrated him to the Church's sacred ministry, hypothetically, before he was born.

Criticisms of the Church's clergy as regards devotion and a consecrated spirit, or wisdom, or tact, or any sort of spiritual and mental furnishing, reflect in no small measure, if not quite as much, upon the character of the homes and social circles, the Sunday-schools and other schools, out of which they have come.

PRAYER, WORD, AND SACRAMENT

Ask, and it shall be given unto you.—Matt. 7 : 7.

The engrafted word which is able to save your souls.—James 1 : 21.

Baptism doth also now save us.—1st Pet. 3 : 21.

Whoso eateth my flesh, and drinketh my blood, hath eternal life.—John 6 : 54.

Desire the sincere milk of the word, that ye may grow thereby. —1st Pet. 2 : 2.

Strong meat belongeth to them that are of full age.—Heb. 5 : 14.

That which we have heard, which we have seen with our eyes, which we have looked upon, and our hands have handled, of the word of life.—1st John 1 : 1.

I dare say I am speaking to many Non-conformists who honestly believe, or have been brought up to believe, that an outward and visible sign, like Baptism or Confirmation or Holy Communion, gets between the soul and God. Yes, it does, if a mother's kiss gets between the mother and the child—if the mother's kiss gets between the love of the mother and the child, so as to stop it; it does if the rope on the ice-slope which connects me with my guide gets between me and my guide. And

therefore I do ask those honest, earnest people who have been
divorced and driven from the old home to which they all once
belonged,—for it is within the last three hundred years that all
the non-conforming bodies in England have taken their rise,—
to ask themselves this question: "Has there not been misunderstanding? Is it really Jesus who said, 'Go into all the world
and baptize them in the name of the Father, and of the Son, and
of the Holy Ghost?' Then baptism cannot be only a form,
because Jesus was no formalist. Is it really true that in the
New Testament, in the Acts of the Apostles, it is said, 'Then
laid they their hands upon them, and they received the Holy
Ghost, for as yet He had fallen upon none of them'? Then it
cannot be wrong to think that the laying on of hands is the
outward and visible sign of the falling of the Holy Ghost, because
it is in the Bible. Have I been misunderstanding the Holy
Communion? If Jesus Christ took bread and said, 'This is
my Body,' and took wine and said, 'This is my Blood,' then it
is not the Church that founded the doctrine of the Holy Communion. Jesus Christ would never have used that language
unless He meant that in some very special way we became in the
Holy Communion partakers of the Divine Nature. He must
have meant in some special way to convince me of His love and
give me of His Spirit." Therefore, I ask those who have, perhaps, been kept for years from the old home and the old Sacraments, to think over why they should not have the ring put upon
their fingers as the prodigal did; why they should not have the
robe; why they should not have the feast which has been prepared, and accept the love of the Trinity in the ordained way.—
Bishop Ingram.

Our religion is a catholic, many-sided religion,
because we are human, and many-sided ourselves,
made of the dust, although as Tennyson sang,

"Thou wilt not leave us in the dust."

Christ was human, is human now in heaven, and by
the Spirit He comes, and touches, influences, dwells
in us, through these many sides. Christ, we are told

by the disciple who had leaned on His breast and received His life in the first Eucharist, was seen and heard and handled; and by his Spirit He is heard, handled and seen now, in the sense that the visible Church is called, and therefore is, His Body. To listen to the Word is to listen to Christ, and to touch and receive the holy things He has appointed to represent Him in this the Spirit's era is to touch Him. This is the truth of the Incarnation as it affects us now. Whether the ministers of the Lord, the Spirit, preach or baptize, lay on hands, or offer the memorial of Jesus' death and glorious resurrection, He is with them even to the end of the world, in the Spirit.

Of prayer it has been said, that "all Christian prayer in the Lord's name is founded upon the eucharistic Communion and Sacrifice"; and conversely this Communion is itself that greatest of all prayers, in which, offered with our lips and with our hands, and blessed by the Spirit, we ask and receive most richly.

Putting together what St. Peter and St. James respectively say regarding Baptism and the Word, we learn that both are means of grace. The Word itself has a saving power and is in a way sacramental. According to the Scriptures, in the Word as truly as in the Eucharist, Christians receive and feed upon Christ through the Spirit. It is "milk." It is "strong meat," just as His "flesh is meat *indeed*, and His blood drink *indeed*." It was the Spirit who created us human, and of the dust, of the earth earthy, and who in every little child born now unites the opposite elements, spirit and flesh, and it is He who makes all the different means of grace work together for our nourishment and growth in the new life in Christ.

And it is a wise Christian obedience that uses them all, and seeks to learn and appreciate their value for body and soul as redeemed through the life and death of a divine-human Saviour. It learns to admire and love them as different avenues by which the Father, in His Son and by His loving Spirit, imparts the life which shall be forever spiritual, yet wholly human.

By these various means the mighty work of reconciliation and restoration is carried on. These all are the voice, the hands, the everlasting arms, the very kiss, of God. What the Bishop of London says above of Sacraments as figured by the mother's kiss applies really to the whole method and manner of Christ's holy Incarnation,—His flesh-becoming,—as applied to our entire humanity, body, soul and spirit, forever. In the Word itself the true believer feels as it were the Father's, the Son's, and the Spirit's embrace of "love divine, all love excelling." Beside the "ring" in the most evangelical and comforting of all parables, that of the prodigal son, the touching words, "He fell on his neck and kissed him," are not there for nothing. In Baptism, in Confirmation, in the Communion, and just as truly in the Absolution, in all earnest prayer in the Spirit, and in many a sermon, thought out, delivered and *listened to* in the Spirit, one may feel the ring going on, and feel God's kiss on the lips, in forgiving, reconciling love. It is as when friends "make up" in the every-day earthly life. Eye and tongue, hand and lips, all have their part in it.

Thus Word and Prayer and Sacrament are all as one in the Spirit, and considering Who the Spirit is, and what we are, we should expect it. God's holy Word is a "word of grace," a "word of salvation," a word "quick and powerful." We need to go to school to it, *learn the language* of God to our human soul and spirit, not trusting merely to what Shakespeare calls love's *"feeling* disputation," *i. e.*, demonstration.

Mortimer says to his Welsh wife, Glendower's daughter, whose heart he knows, without knowing yet her mountain language: "I understand thy looks; * * * I understand thy kisses, and thou mine, and that's a feeling disputation, but I will never be a truant, love, till I have learned thy language." Applying the principle, thus poetically and humanly illustrated, to our earthly-heavenly relationship to the Father in the Church of His dear Son, mediated by that Third Person Whom Bishop Andrewes termed "the Love-Knot of the Trinity," we shall desire and pray never to play truant and shirk our task, till we comprehend with all saints what God would in holy Scripture *tell* us of Himself and our deep need of Him.

Returning to the side of "feeling disputation," is it not a fact that we can hardly over-estimate what it is graciously intended to be to us, in connection with the enlightening and quickening Word? Not as children merely, but as grown men and women, we often feel a want of being taken as it were into the arms of God. There are times when on account of certain physical or mental conditions, or a sad yielding to some besetting fault, it is hard to pray, or even to think of God and thirst after Him, as at other times we can. Well is it for us then to realize what the Holy Communion is meant to be to our weakness, our coldness, our very skepticism, namely, God's comforting, life-giving embrace.

And what, finally, of our own side in this heavenly

transaction,—our own return of thankful affection and confidence? Can we think of the Prodigal Son as not returning his father's kiss, of the Shunammite's child waxing warm and opening his eyes, at the touch and embrace of Elisha, yet making no sign of loving gratitude? "Kiss the Son," it reads in the Easter Morning Psalm, "lest he be angry, and so ye perish from the right way." Let the man who thinks this a harsh word take sober second thought. Let him reflect on what the Eucharist means to God Himself as our opportunity to render grateful adoration. In the gift of His dear Son, He has done immensely more than to run and meet us. He has gone the whole way, to bring us home. By the Incarnation and Atonement, and the present work of the Spirit founded upon them, God has through the centuries been, so to say, stretching Himself upon our humanity, mouth to mouth, eyes to eyes, hands to hands, in a life-giving contact; and every Communion is, in part, an open, personal acknowledgment from our side that this is the real truth about it.

The things, then, that Christ and the Spirit have joined together, let no man put asunder even in his thoughts. The very thought would appear to be a tare sown by our Enemy. *Divide et impera* is one of his watchwords in the spiritual warfare against us. He would separate and set against each other not individual Christians and Churches merely, but divine and saving truths; exalt one by lowering the other; induce us to make much of this one and leave that one in the corner.

The Prayer Book is true to our soul's highest interests in joining to the Eucharistic Service, not only Epistles and Gospels, the Litany, and other prayers, but Lessons also, and sermons. It is true to the Spirit in this, which is to very many of us but one sign and fruit of sanctified common sense; since the richer the Holy Communion is as a possible means of grace, the greater must be the necessity for solemn and searching words, read or spoken immediately before it. Spiritual sermons and addresses at the time tend to deepen our sense of spiritual need at the time. They cause a hunger for that which the Holy Communion can impart. It has been well said that Christianity is a *reasonable religion*, addressed to the intelligence as well as to the affections of God's creatures. Dr. Garrison says:

"Preaching is the Divine Word coming forth, winged by the Spirit, from the heart of a true man of God, and as such has always been, and was ordained to be, a vital element in the Church's great commission, and in the work which was given her to do. * * * Especially fatal will it be to the Church of our time, should the tendency, now rife in many minds, to thrust preaching into a corner, prevail among the body of our clergy, and they grow to feel, as some already say, that 'anything will do for a sermon if only the service be performed.'" * * *

HOLY COMMUNION

My Father giveth you the true bread out of heaven.— John 6 : 32.

I am the bread of life. —John 6: 35.

My flesh is meat indeed and my blood is drink indeed.— John 6 : 55.

He took bread, and when he had blessed, he brake it.—Mark 14 : 22.

He took bread, and when he had given thanks (εὐχαριστήσας) he brake it, and gave to them, saying, This is my body which is given for you: this do in remembrance of me.—Luke 22 : 19.

Else if thou bless in spirit, how shall he that filleth the place of layman say the Amen at thy giving of thanks (εὐχασιστίᾳ), seeing he knoweth not what thou sayest.—1st Cor. 14 : 16.

The Holy Spirit whom the Father will send in my name, he shall teach you all things, and bring to your remembrance all that I said unto you.—John 14 : 26.

Side by side with the human *doing* ('this do') there is a Divine *doing*. In the religion of spirit and life a ceremony of pure commemoration cannot exist; every rite celebrated according to its spirit must contain a grace, a Divine gift, and here it must be the most intimate union with the Lord Himself. * * * How could He who said: "Where two or three are gathered together in my name, I am in the midst of them," fail to communicate Himself spiritually to His own in a feast which so sensibly represents the indissoluble union formed by redemption between Him and them? I say, spiritually; but the word implies the whole fulness of His person; for His person is indivisible If the fulness of the Godhead dwells in Christ *bodily* (Col. 2 : 9), His spiritual body cannot be separated from His Spirit.—Godet.

This idea is just the same in all Christian Churches whether the sacrament is taken with more or less submission to the mystery, with more or less accommodation to what is intelligible. It always remains a holy weighty ceremony, which presents itself in the actual world in the place of what one may call the possible or the impossible—in the place of what man can neither attain nor do without.—Goethe.

In all the primitive liturgies which we have in their original Greek, the pervading thought and life of the whole service was its dependence on the presence and operation of the Holy Ghost; in all its parts and for all who were engaged in it or to be benefited by it, its vitality and efficacy came from the personal ministration of the Divine Spirit. Its blessings were conveyed,

15

its ministers empowered, its "gifts" offered and sanctified, its recipients prepared, its communion made living, wholly by the act and bestowal of the Holy Ghost.—Dr. Garrison.

Rome and the Churches that paid obedience to her, alone wandered from the unity of Christendom in this particular. After the schism of East and West, forgetting the older tradition, growing ignorant of the Fathers, under the guidance of a materialized notion of the Eucharistic Presence, Rome slowly evolved a new and unprimitive theory of consecration, which dominated the thought of the West until the Reformation.—Dr. Gummey.

Living in the dispensation of the Holy Spirit, and recognizing Him as the Lord, and Giver of Life, and the source of all sanctification and effectual operation in the fulfilment of the Divine Will on earth, it was natural that in the freshness of its unsullied faith the early Church should attribute to His operation the sanctification of the memorial offerings of the Eucharist to the effectual participation in the precious gifts denoted by them; and that to this end it should invoke the Holy Spirit in words of solemn prayer. This it certainly did. This the Eastern Church has continually done. This, by the singular grace and providence of God, the American Use,—derived by tradition from these venerable sources through the agency of the Scottish Church influenced by the fleeting vision of the light which shone in the first gleams of the English Reformation,— has been enabled to express in most fitting and exalting form; to God's great glory and our own ineffable benediction.—Prof. William J. Seabury.

A miserable individualism in our thoughts of holy communion has taken the place of the rich and moving thought which in ancient days was so prominent, that through fellowship in the perfect sacrifice of the Son of Man we ourselves become that sacrifice. That is to say, we can only plead His passion if we are prepared to enter into unity of spirit and life with Him who offered and presents it. And the unity of spirit and life means a sacrificial manner of living. And the way in which the sacrificial manner of living is to show itself is in real brotherliness. * * * The intimate association, at the beginning, of the holy sacrament of Christ's body and blood with the fraternal meal, which at first preceded it and afterwards followed it at a later hour, of course kept intensely alive its social meaning. It was the sacrament of fraternity. "Because the bread is one, we, the many, are one body," wrote St. Paul.—Bishop Gore.

The Lord's Supper or Holy Communion, the only Service personally instituted by our Lord and containing the few liturgical words prescribed by Him, beside the Our Father, forms together with the Lord's Day upon which it has been from the beginning performed, a monumental evidence of the truth of our religion. Sunday and this service, united, furnish in themselves a convincing proof of the substance of St. Paul's message, Jesus and the Resurrection; that the Lord is risen indeed, and our faith is not vain. In a way they can be likened to the pile of stones ordered to be taken from Jordan's stream and placed on its bank for an enduring sign of Israel's merciful deliverance at the hand of God. When our children ask, What mean ye by this Eucharist? we should know how to answer them.

Throughout the first four Christian centuries this service was generally known by this name, and it is not difficult to see the reason for it. Used by St. Luke in telling the story of the first Lord's Supper, used also by St. Paul,—whose travelling companion St. Luke was,—when apparently referring to the Communion, "Eucharist" signifies "thanksgiving-blessing." It means sacred elements blessed in joyful and grateful remembrance of a Saviour who, crucified for our sake, is now alive for evermore, and in whose life we live.

Thankful joy was associated with the Paschal Bread and Cup themselves. These, like the shew bread, and the bread and wine and slain lambs of the other solemn feasts, Messianic feasts, conveyed the thought of dependence upon God for life and redemption, of supping with God, yes, feeding upon the very Divine Life.

There was gladness in the thought of the promised presence of the glorified Jesus with His people. He had said He would be in the midst of them, where two or three only were gathered together in His name. He promised in the upper room, "I will come to you," and surely in the Eucharist itself more than in any other service would the expectation be fulfilled.

The old name "mysteries" survives in our Prayer Book service: "He hath instituted and ordained holy mysteries as pledges of his love, and for a continual remembrance of his death." Now as we have noted already, mysteries in New Testament language are divine secrets at least half-told, manifestations of God's power and goodness; and next to the "great mystery of godliness," the Son of God, who was *manifested* in the flesh, has been preached among the nations, and is now believed on in the world far and wide, will certainly be this His personal manifestation, spiritually, to His people, in a service ordained by Himself for the confirming of their faith.

"He who takes from us our mystery," wrote Professor John Duncan of Edinburgh, "takes from us our sacrament." If that Presbyterian divine, eminent for learning, for keen insight as a philosopher, and for simple and childlike piety, could say this of the Communion; if Goethe could write: "In the Lord's Supper earthly lips are to receive a divine reality embodied, and under the form of an earthly nourishment to partake of a heavenly"; and if, as Palmer informs us, in the Reformation period Oglethorpe and Ridley, Poynet, Bucer, and Melanchthon, all like the Prayer Book and the Homilies maintained a certain reality of Presence of our Lord in the holy Service, we need none of us shrink from the conception.

Whoever apprehends the Holy Spirit's relation to Christ's Things will be rather drawn to the conception than shrink from it. In this as much as in any other Gospel verity the Spirit truth solves difficulties of the intellect and of the spirit. "The letter killeth, but the Spirit giveth life." The form killeth until the Spirit is present in the form to give it life. We must think there never would have been any other than that one institution-service in the "upper room" but for the Event of Pentecost; and how worthy of our notice it is that the principal subject in what one may venture to call the first Communion Address ever given was the Holy Ghost!

Nothing was ever done, is ever done, in heaven or on earth without the co-operation of the Third Person. It was by the Creator-Spirit that man was made "of the dust" yet spiritual—in the divine likeness—and it is appropriate to cite here Bishop Gore's remark, that "from the days when the Christian Fathers were fighting their great battle against the false spirituality of Gnosticism it has been the sound argument of Christian theologians that the idea of sacraments;—the idea of spiritual gifts given through material means,—is of a piece with the whole method of God in the creation and redemption of mankind."

It was with the co-operation of the divine Spirit that in Him, who so often spoke of Himself as the Son of Man, a new human will,—in fact a new filial humanity,

—was first created and then developed and made perfect in a life of sonship, obedient, tempted, and suffering.
"Through the Eternal Spirit" He, as the Son of Man,
offered himself without blemish unto God" (Heb.
9 : 14). It is implied (Rom. 8 : 11) that not without Him
was Christ raised from the dead, and not without
Him surely was Christ as Man lifted to the Father's
throne transfigured and glorified.   It is of a piece with
this whole divine and saving process and work, that
with the personal Spirit's co-operation our Lord, as the
very fountain and source of the new world-filling
humanity, at once comes again, in an unseen life-giving
contact with our race.   Will there be a more distinctly vital point of contact than this holy Service of
His own appointing?   For the Christ of the Eucharist
is, in the genuinely catholic conception of it, and therefore in our venerable Service, not the dead Christ, but
the One who "is alive for evermore."   The bare,
the empty, cross on our altars teaches what the empty
sepulchre taught on the first Easter-Day.

In perfect consonance with the Spirit's essential and
living connection with our Lord's entire redeeming
work for us, and now in us,—with the fact that as
Bishop Odenheimer said in his Episcopal charge of
1865, "There is no power at all for the Church in these
days except it come from the Holy Ghost by whom
Christ is present,"—is the place that He, the Vicar
of Christ, occupies in the primitive liturgies.   He is
in truth the consecrator of every Eucharist.   In all its
parts, for all engaged in it and to be benefited by it, its
vitality and efficacy come from His personal ministration.   Whatever our idea of our blessed Saviour's
presence in it may be, whether, as Goethe said, the

sacrament is taken "with more or less submission to the mystery," it can only be a presence mediated by the gracious Spirit who loves us with a love of his own.

Now in the Service as it has come down to us the "spiritual references" are not confined to some few portions,—"Cleanse the thoughts of our hearts by the inspiration of thy Holy Spirit" in the opening Collect, the Invocation (in the American Use) "bless and sanctify, with thy Word and Holy Spirit, these thy gifts and creatures of bread and wine";—they pervade and saturate the whole service, make it pre-eminently "spiritual" and real. We can well understand Bishop Seabury's personal desire to fulfil the hope of the Scottish Church that the distinct Invocation of the Spirit would prove acceptable to the Church in America, and his earnest words in a letter to Bishop White (June 29, 1789): "The efficacy of Baptism, of Confirmation, of Orders, is ascribed to the Holy Ghost, and His energy is implored for that purpose; and why He should not be invoked in the consecration of the Eucharist, especially as all the old Liturgies are full to the point, I cannot conceive."

We can understand what Bishop John Williams is on good authority reported to have said concerning the gift of the Invocation to our own Church, through the agency of the Scottish Church, that it was a richer gift even than that of the Episcopate itself. Time was when the Latin Church herself offered substantially the same prayer for the Spirit, beseeching God to bless the sacrifice with His blessing and "suffuse it with the dew of the Holy Ghost." (Dr. Gummey, "Consecration of the Eucharist," page 117.) To invoke the Spirit thus is to make the service which commemorates the great

Act of reconciliation between God and Humanity in Christ a real present reconciliation in our own case. It brings the peace of sonship restored, His peace who said, "My peace I leave with you,—give unto you," and said it at the time of the institution, and in close connection with the promise of the Spirit.

It is almost immediately after this thanksgiving-blessing in the Spirit, that we offer ourselves to the Father with, by, and in the one oblation of His Son "once offered," a "reasonable, holy, and living sacrifice." Who but the Spirit, whose function it is to join us body and soul to our Redeemer in a living union, can give such an offering of ourselves a real value spiritually?

The Eucharist is also a Communion. It is both the sign and the means of union between man and God, and between man and man in God. Individualism in religion is never more "miserable" than when it hides from Christ's people this communion-side of the eucharistic truth, helps them to forget the petition, "that they all may be one," in the Lord's wonderful high-priestly prayer in connection with the first Eucharist, — helps us to forget also that the Consecrator of every memorial sacrifice is that Spirit of Unity and Fellowship, whose "chiefest joy it was, not to create the world of nature in all its joy and harmony, but to build the edifice of a social life in which nature was to find its crown and justification." The words are Bishop Gore's and he adds: "Just here the Spirit has found His chiefest disappointment"; quotes from the Didache (ix, 4): "As this Bread was once scattered upon the mountains, and, having been gathered together, became one, so let

Thy Church be gathered together from the ends of the earth into Thy Kingdom"; cites from Cyprian (ep. 73, 13): "By which very sacrament (of the Bread) our people is exhibited as made one; so that as many grains collected into one and ground together and mingled make one loaf, so in Christ, who is the heavenly loaf, we should hold that there is one body to which our company is joined and united"; cites from Bishop Serapion's Prayer of the Oblation, in his newly discovered liturgy: "For as this bread was scattered upon the mountains, and having been gathered together became one, so also, O Lord, gather together Thy holy Church from every race and every country and village and household, and make it a living catholic Church."

The Holy Ghost is by His personal divine energy the "leaven" of Christ's Kingdom; He is the great Bread-maker of the world, in this sense first, that as the Creator-Spirit, co-operating with the eternal Son in the toil and heat, the temptation and suffering, involved in the Incarnation, He did truly *make* the living Bread which is Christ Himself, and secondly, that in Him we all by partaking of that living source of a new and holy Humanity become verily one with it. Call this poetry, if you please; but what is a poem (*poiema* in Greek) but a *making?* God's entire creation, man included, was a poem. And without that making of a new manhood in Christ, in the fire of affliction, all Adam's descendants had been lost, because,—to use our simple, homely term,—the first batch had failed, though not at all bound to fail.

And in the present period of the Bread-making the

Bride the Church is allowed, yes, invited to have a hand. She too co-operates. The consecrating action is in part hers. It is a divine-human, corporate, action. Ours is a book of Common Prayer; and the eucharistic act is an act of the great priestly Body. The *Amens* in the Prayer Book continually proclaim that the Church is congregational. It is lamentable when the truth of lay-citizenship and lay-priesthood is let slip by our people, and not least to be deplored in this holy service of Communion. There is no *Amen* in the Prayer Book so winged and powerful, or which should mean so much to all worshippers, as their royal and priestly "Amen" at the close of the Consecration. None merits so well to be spoken or sung by all with emphasis, a prolonged, a "three-fold," a seven-fold Amen, as this one.

There is no masonry in the world equal to the universal, divine, masonry of the Holy Spirit by which He joins believers as "living stones" to the chief living Stone, Christ,—builds us up, in faith and unity of mind and heart, "a spiritual house, to offer up spiritual sacrifices acceptable to God, through Jesus Christ our Lord" (1st Pet. 2 : 5), nor is there an instrument in His hand so choice as this "our sacrifice of praise and thanksgiving," which is rendered spiritual and potent through His indwelling power, in answer to the Church's prayer. We read in Cornford's "History of the Prayer Book" that the people used in the early days to bring contributions of loaves and wine to furnish the holy Table with the elements that were to become the symbol and vehicle of a true inward feeding upon Christ, and of the new life of union with Him, and with each other in Him. It was a happy figure of their own participation in the consecrating act, and also of that Pentecostal miracle of universal fellowship and brotherhood, in the Spirit of Fellowship, which were meant never to cease, but more and more to prevail on earth. "A thorough Christian," says Bishop Westcott, "ought to have the Impossible for his ideal." Is it not the mighty Spirit, whom we invoke upon our sacrifices to make them spiritual, who can render the impossible possible, and who will, if we invoke Him earnestly enough, one day bring about that union of Christendom which many in our own time frankly speak of as an iridescent dream?

The opening Collect, with its petition that our hearts may be cleansed by the Spirit's inspiration, that we may perfectly love God, Dean Goulburn terms the noblest of all the Collects, and says it used to be part of a special service invoking the grace of the Holy Ghost, preparatory to the Communion.

FATHERHOOD, DIVINE AND HUMAN

One is your Father, which is in heaven.—Matt. 23 : 9.

No one knoweth the Son, but the Father, neither knoweth any man the Father, save the Son, and he to whomsoever the Son will reveal him. Come unto me all ye that labour and are heavy laden, and I will give you rest.—Matt. 11 : 27, 28.

When he was yet a great way off, his father saw him, and had compassion, and ran, and fell on his neck, and kissed him. And the son said, Father, I have sinned against heaven, and in thy sight, and am no more worthy to be called thy Son.—Luke 15 : 20, 21.

Father, the hour is come; glorify thy Son, that thy Son may also glorify thee.—John 17 : 1.

Truly our fellowship is with the Father.—1st John 1 : 3.

The message of Fellowship with the Father in Christ which we have to proclaim, has been in one form or other the inspiration of all great religious movements. And it comes to us now in a more intelligible shape than hitherto, enforced by fresh teachings of nature and history. It seems to me that which the Spirit is shewing to us in many ways. It is in a peculiar sense the message of our Church. It answers, as I believe, to the half-articulate desires of our countrymen at the present time. It is the inspiration of Foreign Missions.—Bishop Westcott.

Only when we make a point of looking into it do we discover how large a place the truth of God's Fatherhood holds in our Lord's teaching. It is the principal motive in the parable which Stier called the *crown and pearl* of all His parables, that of the Prodigal Son.

When asked by the disciples for a form of prayer, the form He gives begins, "Our Father." The most comforting of all the Comfortable Words He ever spoke, "Come unto me all ye that labour and are heavy laden," are more comforting even than we are apt to think, by reason of their connection with what He has just been saying about His own filial relation to God, and power to make His Fatherhood known to men. It is claimed that more sermons have been published upon that text than upon any other in the Bible, and yet in few of them, it is to be feared, has the connection spoken of been brought out. It was Christ's eternal Sonship which had made the yoke of His obedience in heaven easy from everlasting, and made it easy to Him even as the Son of Man.

This blessed sonship is the yoke for us, and if we will *come* to Him, He will transfer it from His shoulders, from His heart, to our hearts,—keeping, however, His share in it,—by imparting the spirit of sonship. Learning His meekness and lowliness, His own free and loving submission as a Son, we shall find rest unto our souls.

When after His Resurrection the Lord meets Mary Magdalene, and sends a message by her to the eleven, the message is, Tell them I "ascend to my Father and your Father."

Theological statements of Gospel truth have long been more or less, and at times deplorably, deficient respecting the Divine Fatherhood. Theories of the purpose of the Incarnation, and the meaning of the Atonement, have been so framed as to dim the vision of the Father's love. New England Unitarianism was in great measure a protest against these prevailing harsh and unscriptural conceptions. Now there is a widespread reaction. We have a prominent Presbyterian layman writing in "The Fundamentals" of the Revelation of the Fatherhood of God, saying: "Think how rational and sweet this conception of God makes obedience." Mr. Speer estimates that in the last discourse of our Lord, in St. John, he mentions the name of God four times while speaking of the Father at least forty times. He ends:

"Yes, that is the right way to put it to-day. Nowhere through the whole universe is there a real and satisfying God for us, except the God Who is discovered to us in Jesus Christ, and Who is calling to us to-day by the lips of Christ, 'My son, O my son,' and would have us call back to Him if we be true men, 'My Father, O my Father.'"

The Holy Trinity, in itself the most sublime and impenetrable of the truths made known to man, as read, so to speak, through the mind and heart of our Lord, especially in the Fourth Gospel, is seen to be most practical and touching. The sacrifice which reconciles God and man is a sacrifice made to God as a Father. Can it be otherwise, when the name Father is used by Christ no less than fifty times in His *communion address* in the upper room? This includes the six times that it occurs in His high-priestly prayer of Self-consecration, beginning, "Father, the hour is come, glorify thy Son, that thy Son also may glorify thee." As we read on, "O Father, glorify thou me with thine own self with the glory which I had with thee before the world was," and then, "Holy Father, keep through thine own name those whom thou hast given me, that they may be one as we are," "Father, I will that they may be with me where I am, that they may see my glory, * * * thou lovedst me before the foundation of the world"; and once more, "O righteous Father, the world hath not known me, but I have known thee, * * * I have declared unto them thy name"; three things become plain. First, He who thus offers Himself up in prayer to die for men must be both Man and God. Secondly, the atoning sacrifice will be made to God as a *righteous* Father, and the sins of our entire race are weighing heavily upon the filial heart of Jesus as being one with us through His birth of a human mother. Thirdly, this divine-human reconciliation will introduce us into a wonderful fellowship with the Father through His Son.

But it introduces us also, by the very language employed, into new ideas of the nature of the God-

head. The manifestation of the Third Person at
Pentecost completes the revelation,—the more completely in that for nigh two thousand years it has been
His chief business to bring home to men's hearts this
truth of the divine Fatherhood, and that of Jesus
Christ's self-offering as a Son. These have become
to millions "an old story,"—thank God and His Spirit,
—and what can be added now that is new concerning
it? This, however, can and ought to be said here, that
these things have been the truth and message of the
Prayer Book during many centuries, and have been a
blessed instrument in the Spirit's hand to draw mankind Godward.

Turning to that chief of Christian services instituted on the Thursday night in the upper room, and
counting here as Mr. Speer counted in the Fourth
Gospel, we find that while God is addressed in eucharistic prayer and praise once as Lord, and five times as
God, He is addressed as Father, including the case of
the Lord's Prayer, seventeen times, only so addressed
in the central, all-important part, the Consecration,
except once where it reads, "here we offer and present unto thee, O Lord, ourselves."

It can perhaps profit us to note also that the most
exalted, and to us exalting, of Christ's words have not
been words spoken to men, but words spoken to God
which men were allowed to over-hear. These have
revealed the Father's love for the Son, and Christ's
love as a Son, both divine and human, for the Father.
And the Spirit completes this rich revelation of love.
To employ the striking word of inspiration, the Son
glorifies the Father, and the Father will *glorify* the
Son, while the Spirit proceeding forth eternally from

the Father and, like the Son, subordinate, will *glorify* both. Through the door already opened in that upper room, as it were into heaven, we behold a mighty work going on for us men and for our salvation, in which the three divine Persons, each in His way co-operating with the Others, are engaged. We cannot but see that, infinite as each One is, there is somehow going to be to each in the end a marvellous "increase of glory," and indeed of "endless felicity,"—the felicity of love divinely manifested toward humanity, to receive also itself a rich reward through our grateful response of love and holy service. It cannot help being likewise true that the mutual love and devotion of Father, Son, and Spirit will experience an increase of felicity in connection with their redeeming work.

Now almost if not quite as wonderful, and lying very near to our humanity, is a truth of which not enough has been made by theology and Christian ethics. It is the truth, that man being created in the divine likeness corporately, *i. e.*, as a family, the earthly fatherhood is a figure,—more than that, an earthly imitation, almost a repetition on the finite scale,— of the heavenly Fatherhood. In this there lay a blessed divine purpose. The earthly fatherhood, representing the divine, was to help prepare the children of men,— also children of God,—for the fruition of the Divine, or for what St. John calls "our fellowship with the Father."

Undoubtedly our Lord's word, "Call no man your father upon the earth, for one is your Father which is in heaven" (Matt. 23 : 9) pointed primarily at the Pharisees who loved to be called Rabbi, or Master, but the word stood for authority, from the authority of a king down to that of a chief shepherd; and Christ would have us think of our heavenly Father as the source of all authority everywhere. Authority and obedience are heavenly principles. The harmony that reigns in heaven is owing to the obedience that reigns there. And subordination there does not conflict with equality; nor does it here. The family life on earth, in so far as it is Christianized, in other words, risen from sin and morally transfigured and glorified, in the Spirit, by Christ's own filial love, will always be something like a heavenly thing, simply because conformity to the heavenly principles is sure to produce harmony and joy here on earth.

A heavenly radiance much needs to be thrown in this age upon Authority, divine and human. It wants to be "glorified," particularly in "free America," which, however, is not really free, and never will be free, until authority *is* glorified. In order to glorify it, before all and for the sake of all in the home, fatherhood must be glorified. And while Christian mothers are always striving to make it honourable, teaching the children to obey the father, they cannot succeed unless fathers believe in the heavenly ideal, and glorify it themselves in and by living up to it. It will be an evil day for the home, the Church, and the nation, when no Christian fathers shall remain to exemplify it.

The truth of the saying that parents are in the place of God to their little children is only seen clearly, and the immense importance of it seen, in the light which comes to us from the Son's words regarding the Fatherhood on high. For by revering and obeying us in love the children are unconsciously prepared,

16

not merely to reverence authority in the state and in all earthly relationships, but also to "fear God and keep His commandments." The habit of respect for earthly parents leads on and up to a "spirit of holy fear" toward God. And our God, be it observed, is not easy-going and indulgent. Not only is He a righteous God; He is a "righteous Father." He loves righteousness, and He loves us too well to be a "good-natured" God.

It is one mark of the inspiration of the Epistle to the Hebrews that it holds in such even balance the New Testament truth of God's Fatherhood and the Old Testament one of His Creatorship. He is our Father Creator, our Father Judge. The book which begins by telling how God "hath spoken unto us by His Son," comes near to ending with the word, "Our God is a consuming fire." And the same two elements will always be found combined in the character of any father fit to be even for a day in the place of God to his child. Mother's love does not, nor does father's love, suffice for the right training of the child's mind and soul and spirit, without the Christian *man's* strong, at times fiery, indignation against all untruth and disobedience. Indeed it is to be doubted whether any other person, except our Father in heaven, can be so grieved and offended, so shocked and angered at sin, as a "righteous" human father will be at sins committed by his own child. In the eyes of God child-indulgence must be nearly if not quite as sinful as self-indulgence.

Children, and boys especially, need to be much with their fathers. The paternal companionship and influence are requisite to form the intellectual and moral fibre of Christian manhood,—what Tennyson in The Princess terms

"The wrestling thews that throw the world";

above all the world of moral weakness and sin.   Price Collier's words in "England and the English":

" An Englishman is more at home in his house than an American, first, because he is by all the inmates recognized as the
absolute master there, and because he spends more of his time
there;—Americans staying any time in England, whether men
or women, are impressed by the fact that it is the country of
men;"—and again, " fathers and sons, uncles and nephews, are
much more at home with one another than with us, and see
much more of one another, and have apparently more in common; in games, at shooting and fishing, the youngsters between
twenty and thirty not only mingle with but are boon companions of their elders;—that the English boy is more a man
of the world than the American boy, is due to the fact that
he spends so much of his time with his elders,"

all together furnish much food for reflection to American fathers, uncles, and godfathers.   Viewed in the aspect which concerns us here, they will mean much to men who cherish the Christian ideal of the home, and who, accepting the truth that in the earthly fatherhood we behold as in a glass darkly (in a riddle) the wonder and the glory of the Fatherhood in heaven, desire to walk worthily of the calling wherewith they are called to glorify it and make it a shining truth indeed.

It will be seen "darkly" and be a riddle, wherever our Christianity does not make it shine, the earthly mirror not being clear and clean; in other words, being like those mirrors of Corinthian brass St. Paul had in mind. Were he living on the earth now, he would surely tell us that our modern mirrors so far excel the ancient ones as almost to rob his figure of its suggestiveness, but could he say that the Christian family life in Christ in our day is an equal improvement upon the pagan family life in his day? As long as it is not, man will continue to see the divine Fatherhood obscurely and distortedly, if he discerns it at all. It is a serious matter, and at times appears to grow more serious. Woman may

> "make herself her own,
> To give or keep, to live and learn and be
> All that not harms distinctive womanhood;

she may at last

> "set herself to man,
> Like perfect music unto noble words;"

but "the statelier Eden" will not come back to us, when

> "reign the world's great bridals chaste and calm,
> When springs the crowning race of humankind,"

till Christian manhood and fatherhood shall have glorified itself. We go all the way with the many poets who have united with the Holy Scriptures to exalt woman, and bear witness to the power of her influence; applaud Tennyson's lines:

> "Happy he
> With such a mother! Faith in womankind
> Beats with his blood, and trust in all things high
> Comes easy to him, and though he trip and fall,
> He shall not blind his soul with clay;"

but do we not at the same time seem to stand equally in want of poets who shall sing of the other side of the truth, and help to throw the combined radiance of Scripture, and of enlightened reason and conscience, around the earthly fatherhood which is quite as "nobly planned" in the mind and heart of God?

THE SPIRIT AND CHRISTIAN WOMANHOOD

As one whom his mother comforteth, so will I comfort you.—Isa. 66 : 13.

I called upon God, and the Spirit of Wisdom came unto me. I loved her above health and beauty, and chose to have her instead of light, for the light that cometh from her never goeth out.—Book of Wisdom 7 : 7, 10, 11, 12.

In the Book of Wisdom, Wisdom is identified with the Holy Ghost.—Westcott.

The Jerusalem which is above is free, which is our mother.—Gal. 4 : 26.

In the Gospel according to the Hebrews the Saviour Himself says, "Just now my Mother, the Holy Spirit, took me by one of my hairs and bore me away to the great mountain Thabor."—Westcott.

We are to despise nothing which belongs to *human nature, which is the likeness and image of God.*—Kingsley.

If then man, woman, and child together image God, apart, it would seem, they must image the three divine persons. This is as much as to say, that Woman in her unfallen state was the earthly image of the Holy Spirit.—Elizabeth M. Jefferys.

What if earth
Be but the shadow of heaven and things therein
Each to each other like, more than on earth is thought?
—John Milton.

To think of her is to thank God.—Henry Esmond, of his "dear lady".

The unit of humanity as created in the divine likeness was quickly resolved into two, and then into three. Before man was born of woman, woman taken from his side was born of man, proceeding forth from him. Having been thus very part of man, in becoming ever again his companion and helpmate she has only been coming to herself, and developing in that sphere of helpful companionship which surpasses all other friendship and intimacy. In holy marriage we become one again, and the result of the union is fruitful in manifold ways for ourselves and the world. "This is the Lord's doing and it is marvellous in our eyes."

And "whoso is wise will ponder these things, and they shall understand the loving-kindness of the Lord." Whenever, wherever this union in the family has been entered into intelligently, and reverently, in the fear of God, and the holy vow and covenant surely performed and kept, not only have love and peace come,— not only has the earth according to God's holy will and purpose been replenished,—there has also been great mental and spiritual fruitfulness in the household life and outside of it. Had the marriage state been held more honorable in the Church's earlier days, and monasticism not contributed to keep it on low ground, the development of woman's mental power, and her influence for good, would be far greater than they are to-day. As it is, it would be a long story to tell what she has accomplished in literature and in education, in reform and missionary work, for the uplifting and saving of the race. What beautiful children she has borne that were not of the flesh, but of the brain and spirit,—poems and hymns, novels and essays, of high ethical order and merit; what noble movements for the elevation of mankind have originated in her soul!

Woman makes the home, and, through the home, the Church and the state. In peopling the earth, and bringing up the young in the stedfast fear and love of God, she peoples Paradise and Heaven, makes citizens for that kingdom and "citizenship" which, as the apostle said, "is in heaven" (Phil. 3 : 20). In all these things she is as truly an instrument of the Holy Ghost as the blessed Mary was in her wonderful, all-surpassing way. In the Sunday-school, in the Mission field, and wherever she has seen and accepted her calling in the gentle, obedient spirit of her who replied to the angel of the Annunciation, "Be it unto me according to thy word," often have those not given in marriage known the blessedness of fulfilling spiritually Isaiah's word: "More are the children of the desolate than the children of the married wife, saith the Lord."

Now the higher woman rises toward the intellectual and spiritual level God has evidently ordained for her, and the purer and nobler become our ideals in the home life, and the richer the fruits of woman's thought and activity in Christ, the more impossible it becomes not to think of her as in some sort the "earthly image" of the loving and gracious Spirit. "There is," as one of the Fathers said, "no sex in heaven." There, as our Lord said, "they neither marry nor are given in marriage, but are like the angels." The older we get, and therefore, God helping us, the nearer to that life "in the resurrection," the better we are fitted to realize the spiritual nature of the intercourse

and companionship with God and the angels. Nevertheless if in our thoughts we eliminate the physical
and earthly features of this present life, it becomes
difficult not to see, that the three-in-one of the home
are in some sort the image of the Three-in-One on the
Throne above. The thought has come to many,
that not only was woman intended to be a finely
tempered instrument in the Hand of the Spirit, but
also, in her purest and noblest state and condition,—
as "planned" of God,

> "To warn, to comfort, and command,"

a fitting type of the Third Person in the Trinity Himself.

We are taught that God created man in His own
likeness? Did He not create man's other half,—his
companion and support,—whom, being "perfected,"
Lowell calls "Earth's noblest Thing," also in His own
likeness? If He did so, then is there in God,—to
express it in the impersonal way,—a side, an element,
of divine perfection corresponding to what we most
admire and love in Christian womanhood. Then
too must there be in the Universe of God, and above
all in the Church of the redeemed, a sphere of action
appropriate to these particular divine and heavenly
characteristics. Our Lord never referred to the
Spirit otherwise than as "He;" "I will send Him
unto you,"—"He will guide you into all truth."
Moreover, as a Spirit of Power, and of Judgment;
who will convict the world of sin, a Fire that will con-
sume the world and cleanse the heart of man, we
must think of Him differently. Yet other scripture
truths and metaphors point to attributes which cor-

respond to what Goethe suggested, and may, with his marvellous, half-religious, intuition, have distinctly intended, by "The eternal Feminine" in the second and more serious part of Faust. It is the mother-love and solicitude, the nourishing, fostering care, the charm of which none ever appreciated more highly than did Goethe, and perhaps most of all woman's power to draw out, and bring to perfection, the best that is in man, intellectually and every way.

It is a great gift in woman, and blessed are the women who use this gift for high spiritual ends; as not all do. Now when we hear St. Paul speak of "the Church which is the mother of us all," hear St. John describe New Jerusalem as coming down out of heaven adorned as a bride for her husband, Christ, and presently tell how "the Spirit and the Bride say, Come," remember that the Holy Spirit is the Breath, the Voice, the Soul, of the Church, who in it mothers our souls,— is not our thought justified that there is not a little in the personality and sphere of the Spirit which answers to woman's attributes and duties in life? She came out of the first man to be a comfort and blessing to him and to his offspring; and from eternity the Holy Ghost proceeds forth from God to serve the Father and the Son, and to comfort and inspire us who are God's children. He is subordinate to the Father and the Son, being sent by them on His glorious Mission to the world, sent to take of the Son's things and show them to us, and to impart the spirit of sonship to mankind.

In this subordinate place and function the Spirit is, nevertheless, equal in essence with the other divine Persons. We give Him, with the Father and the Son, "all honour and glory," while the heavenly choirs sing, "Holy, Holy, Holy"; and in like manner is woman great in her sphere of obedience, equal to man, while submissive to his will. To alter slightly the words and the significance of the classic line in Romeo and Juliet:

> "Her bosom's lord sits lightly in his throne."

She is like the Spirit in that she is more dearly loved and more warmly admired, when with the Spirit she does not speak of herself. "He shall glorify me," said Christ, and this the Paraclete has been doing during nineteen centuries; and for this it is that we worship Him, and sing some of the most beautiful hymns that are sung in His honour.

If now it is true, that in the tender solicitude and the devotion of the nobly-planned and perfect woman, —as also in her proper sphere in the home and national life,—a "likeness" to the Holy Spirit is recognizable, is it not a truth well worth holding up before her? Will it not tend to inspire her with a well-nigh infinite respect for her womanhood, and with reverent affection for that state of life for which it hath pleased God to prepare her? Should it not lead her to think often of the gracious Spirit, and to invoke Him in the midst of trying and difficult tasks,—help her to realize also how far she falls, when she falls, from that circle before the Throne where the mystic lamps of the Spirit burn?

On the other hand, this truth will tend to bring closer to every heart,—and not least when we ourselves have experienced gentle ministrations in our homes,— the tender love of the Spirit Himself. If it was a shame to us to grieve our mother, what is it to grieve the Holy Spirit of God? We shall perceive how small need there has been in any age of the Christian Church to look to the mother of our Lord, or indeed to any other departed saint, for sympathy and aid in hours of trouble and sorrow. No woman's heart was ever so compassionate as the heart of Him who bore our sorrows, and was tempted like as we are, or, again, the heart of this Other Comforter, whom He has sent to us, and who is with us and in us to stay, till time and trouble shall end.

SEED, FRUIT, GRACE, AND THE NEW HUMANITY IN CHRIST

Is the seed yet in the barn?—Haggai 2 : 19.

And to thy seed, which is Christ.—Gal. 3 : 16.

Begotten again, not of corruptible seed, but of incorruptible, through the word of God, which liveth and abideth.— 1st Pet. 1 : 23.

He that soweth unto the Spirit shall of the Spirit reap eternal life.—Gal. 6 : 8.

Ye who would be justified by the law are fallen away from grace.—Gal. 5 : 4.

Grow in grace.—2d Pet. 3 : 18.

By grace are ye saved through faith; and that not of yourselves: it is the gift of God.—Eph. 2 : 8.

Ye all are one man in Christ Jesus, and if ye are Christ's, then are ye Abraham's seed, heirs according to the promise.— Gal. 3 : 28, 29.

Without Christ the Christian people have no existence. He is the source of their life,—to *allow themselves* to be circumcised, was *then and there* to be shut out from Christ.—Bishop Lightfoot.

Injustice was inadvertently done to the strength of the argument in Chapter IV, when the service for the Thirteenth Sunday was there said to contain no distinct reference to the Holy Spirit. For the passage from Galatians beginning, "To Abraham and his seed were the promises made," stands in the closest and most vital relation possible with the words of the next verse but one before: "that upon the Gentiles might come the blessing of Abraham in Christ Jesus; that we might receive the promise of the Spirit through faith." The great leading thought of Galatians, that the faith which works by our filial love in Christ, and which the Spirit *creates* in us, making each one of us "a new creation" in the risen and glorified Son of Man, is inseparably bound up with the whole striking portion regarding our Lord and Saviour as Seed.

But this same truth is the truth of all three Sundays, the Thirteenth, Fourteenth, and Fifteenth. Whether the Spirit is actually named or not, and whether the blessed new life in mankind is spoken of as seed, or fruit of the Spirit, or the new creature (creation) by which, as a *rule* (a canon,—a carpenter's or surveyor's line) "as many as" shall *walk* receive their great Apostle's blessing of peace as a new and wider Israel of God, it always signifies the one thing. And so it is with the word "grace," which occurs in the same fourth chapter with the injunctions to "walk in the Spirit" and "be led by the Spirit." Grace in the portion "Ye are severed from Christ, ye who would be justified by the law; ye are fallen away from grace"; what avails in Christ is "faith working through love;" would that they who unsettle you by talking of circumcision "would even cut themselves off;" stands for just what freedom, and seed and the new creation do, namely, that new humanity which our glorified Lord now *is*, and which the Blessed Spirit brings to us. As Bishop Lightfoot said, "without Christ the Christian people have no existence." For what some one has said, We must lose Christ as man to regain Him as *God*, does not cover the whole truth of the matter. We lost Him as the visible, self-limited, and humbled Christ, that we might by His ever present powerful Spirit have Him again in us, a source of inner moral and spiritual power, the Second Adam, reproducing Himself in countless millions of the children of men. Some one else has said, that to paint like Raphael one must be Raphael. Now Christ in us by His Spirit is, so to say, Raphael in us. He is Himself the soul and the genius of the new humanity. If we do not see and feel this yet, we shall see and feel it one day, and shall love and adore Him for it through all eternity.

The early part of the Trinity Season, and the latter part too, is a seed-sowing season, a time when the phrase "Thy seed, which is Christ" and the words later on, suggestive of a world-filling Christ-life, "There can be neither Jew nor Greek, there can be neither bond nor free: ye all are one man in Christ," will have a rich significance for us. And so with the word in Romans 9:8, "The children of the promise are reckoned for a seed," that in Isaiah 65:23, "They are the seed of the blessed of the Lord," but especially the words in Psalm 126:6, 7, "Though he goeth on his way weeping, bearing forth the seed, he shall come again bringing his sheaves with him."

The Spirit is Himself the great Sower of precious seed in the world of Nature and the world of Grace alike. The farmers, and the spiritual husbandmen, all the good people in Christian homes and schools and Sunday Schools who in any sense obey the injunction, "in the morning sow thy seed, and in the evening withhold not thine hand," are sowing in the Spirit. And what cheers us most to remember, is that "he that soweth *unto* the Spirit shall of the Spirit reap eternal life" (Gal. 6 : 8). He is the Life-giver, and that which He sows spiritually, whether in Word or Sacrament, by whatever means, or without means, is the Christ-life. Godet, speaking of the Apostle's phrase, which he terms "strange," and is almost a paradox,— "the *law* of the Spirit of *life*," asks, But is it possible to sever these two relations? If the Spirit produces spiritual life in the believer's heart, is it not because He is the breath of the living and glorified Christ? He takes of that which belongs to Jesus, John 16 : 15, and communicates it to us."

Now that which characterizes a seed is, that it contains the principle of life. There is the smallest possible weight and bulk to it. The farmer "goeth forth bearing" a small bag of seed on his shoulder, whose fruit in a few weeks will require strong arms many, with horses and wagons too, to bring it into the barn. In fact, since that which he sows is not quickened except it die, when we eliminate mentally the part which does die, the really "precious" content of the bag carried out weighed *nothing*. It was *visible* only to God who had created it, and sustained it in life, and enabled it to multiply almost infinitely. To me it seems that this fact is richly suggestive in the spiritual way, and not least as bearing on the greatest and most precious of all divine verities which concern us, the heavenly seed which is Christ, the last Adam, who has become a life-giving spirit for our redeemed race. "The second man is of heaven," and he is *forever man*, and throughout the ages His Spirit will communicate this divine-humanity, *spiritual substance* or *essence*, to us who have thrown our hearts open to it by faith.

Now then keeping this truth, of the Christ-life a seed, in mind,—which, since all life, though plain fact, is as yet unfathomable to our intellect, is scarcely more unfathomable than a grain of wheat, or the "flower in the crannied wall,"—let us think of the other very different term "grace," and the lesson St. Paul teaches concerning it. This lesson is that all those who, undergoing circumcision, would become righteous before God in living faithful to the Jewish law, mutilate themselves and spiritually cut themselves off from the New Testament privileges in Christ. They are no longer in the Spirit, no longer by faith wait in hope, as Christians do, for the righteousness which will come by faith. It will be not a formal and imputed righteousness only but also a real personal righteousness, because faith, in the Spirit, *worketh through love*. This is freedom, because the Son makes us free. It is a true, inward, life, because whoso hath the Son hath life. Do we not read in 1st Thes. 1 : 3 of the work of faith, and labour of love, and patience of hope in our Lord Jesus Christ? Does not St. James say a Christian can declare, "I by my works will shew thee my faith"?

"Ye are severed from Christ," writes the Apostle:

ye are fallen away from this sphere of grace in the Spirit. He does not mean that they are fallen from God's favour, as though they had committed this or that grievous sin. It is something different, and far more dangerous to the soul. They have banished themselves,—are like Hagar and her son; not "out in the cold" as we express it, but out in the heat and dryness and barrenness of a desert where nothing will grow. One must remain in Christ to grow, for Christ is life. His Spirit is life. It is a sphere in which we pray for and fully expect the *increase* of faith and hope and love;—and it can scarcely be a mere coincidence that this increase is the subject of the Collect for the Fourteenth Sunday.

How distinctly the identity comes out between Christ as a Seed and Christ as Grace, where the word *wait* is heard: "We through the Spirit by faith wait for the hope of righteousness"! It is in connection with the Christ life in the Spirit that in Romans 8 : 25 it is said, "If we hope for that which we see not, then do we with patience wait for it." Is it not this way with the farmers? St. James, who evidently loved the outdoor life and watched farmers at their work, wrote (5 : 7), "Behold, the husbandman waiteth for the precious fruit of the earth, being patient over it, until it receive the early and the latter rain." Farmers need to be, and generally are, patient, because they have to deal with seed, and life. They sow, and wait, cultivate and wait, pray for rain, some of them, and wait. The Holy Spirit sows the Christ-seed in the hearts of men and children and cultivates it and waits with a loving, divine, patience.

It seems to me that, quite apart from any question

of the Jewish law, there is great need to tell men in our day, in every day, what a wonderful thing of inward life and growth the new humanity is, in God's eternal Son and in His Pentecostal Spirit; tell them often what it means to fall away from grace, and earnestly beg them not to do it, but to stay by Christ and in Christ, our only "hope of glory," of liberty, of moral fruitfulness, of spiritual comfort and joy. Who of us all is not liable every day to fall out of Christ and His grace, and in this way be lost, as men fall out of a ship that is bearing them safely over deep waters? We fall out of grace when we make efforts to be good, and please God or man, without prayer and the other divine helps, and again when praying and striving we do not wait for the spiritual life in us to grow, and bear fruit, wait patiently though eagerly for our entire redemption from the power of sin and evil habit.

As parents and teachers, as priests and ministers of Christ, soul-shepherds and farmers and vine-dressers, bound to interpret by our own teaching and life the Spirit's patient method of culture, we fall away from the truth and method of grace, when we do not wait patiently for the growth and development of the free, *natural*, Christ-life in others, most of all when we preach morality, or Old Testament righteousness,— preach the Church in an outward and formal way, saying "the Church bids us do thus and so," instead of preaching Christ in the Church, the very Soul and Life of righteousness. Nothing in the Church "is anything apart from Christ" and our race's new "existence" in Him,—the new creation. We need all to think often upon what the Spirit by His Apostle saith to the Churches, "As many as shall walk by this canon

17

(κανόνι), peace be upon them and upon the Israel of God," and "The *grace* of our Lord Jesus Christ be with your spirit, brethren.   Amen."

CONFESSION AND ABSOLUTION

Whoso confesseth and forsaketh (his sins) shall have mercy.—Ps. 18 : 13.

If we confess our sins, God is faithful and just to forgive us our sins.—1st John 1 : 9.

That repentance and remission of sins should be preached in his name among all nations.—Luke 24 : 47.

He breathed on them, and saith unto them, Receive ye the Holy Ghost: Whose soever sins ye remit, they are remitted unto them; and whose soever sins ye retain, they are retained.—John 20 : 22.

Confess your faults one to another, and pray one for another, that ye may be healed.—James 5 : 16.

There is no evidence from either allusions in the fathers, or the testimony of historians, that the primitive Church had any conception of private confession and individual priestly absolution as an element of Christian life or discipline for all its members.   *   *   *   In the Reformation time the whole matter was transferred to the daily services, and in presenting it there the position of the Church of England is declared with definite and unmistakable clearness.—Dr. Garrison.

In itself, so far as the movement of grace is concerned, the Absolution is the same, whether public or private.   The difference lies in the method of preparing to receive it.   If souls are able to grasp it for themselves as firmly, it is as valid and full when uttered in a general formula to a thousand together as when uttered to them one by one.   It is to be feared that the public Absolutions are as a rule more listlessly received than the private.

The Church vindicates for her children the liberty with which Christ has set us free. * * * If conscience tells them that a full and explicit confession before God alone, joined with the general confession in the public service, would be more beneficial to their advance in holiness than private confession, no man may compel them to the latter. If conscience tells them that a private confession would be beneficial, no man may dare to forbid it them. Upon the doctrinal question, indeed, the English Church leaves no doubt whatever: but the practical question is left to be decided by each soul separately.—Dr. Mason.

Nothing can appear plainer than that the Church, which Christ appointed to be the Spirit-bearing Body to our race, He willed also to be a Forgiveness-bearing Body. Only God can send the Spirit, God only can forgive sin, but He has given to the Son as Son of Man the right and the power to do both, and the Son after His mighty resurrection passed both privileges, in a way, to the Church as His Bride, and as also being in a very real sense divine-human, in Him. John 20:22 makes this clear. The gift of the Spirit, and the gift of power to remit sins are received together, in one moment, one act, one *breath*, "Receive ye the Holy Ghost" and "receive," He seems to add, "this authority to forgive in my Name, and in virtue of my Deed of Sacrifice and my Victory in *your* name."

It appears also by a careful study of passages bearing on the event, that both gifts were conferred not merely on the twelve, or rather ten, but on the congregation of believers. It is good to know and to think of this often. All confirmed, if not all baptized, people share the benefit and the responsibility of these two great privileges. It gives a rich significance to St. James' injunction, "Confess your faults one to another and pray one for another." But it means

most of all to a Churchman,—or can and ought to
mean it,—in connection with the solemn transaction
which takes place almost in the first moments of our
service, on Sundays or on weekdays, at the Eucharist
or at Morning or Evening Prayer.

The purpose in making this heavenly-earthly transaction the theme of one of these sections is distinctly
practical. According to this Church's view of Confession and Absolution, which many of us are convinced
is the catholic one,—the view of the early Church,—
this open, congregational act, in which the Church as a
whole acts for Christ, in the Spirit, as "a royal priesthood," in prayer, and faith, and mutual sympathy,
dispensing, in Christ's name, and through her sacred
appointed ministry, the gift of pardon which her Lord
alone obtained for her, is indeed solemn and most real.

There is surely a great need of presenting the subject
clearly and definitely. Whether one calls the action
sacramental or not, whether or not one believes the
general and open way which our own Church without
doubt prefers and would commend to us, it is plain
that the great majority of her children do believe in
and choose it, and it is a matter of serious importance
that they should be assisted to "grasp it as firmly"
as *possible* "for themselves," that it *may* be "full and
valid" to them. Many will cease to receive the benefit
"listlessly" when taught what the benefit is. The
absolution is no mere statement of God's will to forgive,
but a gift of forgiveness, where there is repentance and a
firm intention to forsake sin. If those of our people
who would rather confess to God than to man, whether
to a mother or a sister, a wife, an intimate friend, or a
priest, were but taught and urged to do it thoroughly

and sincerely,—keeping nothing back, naming to God, before Communion, or before an afternoon service of prayer, secret faults or besetting sins, as particularly as they would tell a priest or a dear friend,—our General Confession would have a solemn reality, and the Absolution bring a blessing which now it is to be feared they often do not.

Our people need to be instructed before all to invoke, upon their preparation and upon their confession, the same convicting and enlightening Spirit whom our Lord "breathed on" His Church in the hour when He made it a Church carrying, as it were, forgiveness in His name to all mankind. Many need to be told that self-examination amounts to little without the Spirit, that He must examine us and try our reins and our heart, or Confessions, and Communions also, will do us little good. They need reminding that in our Confession the things "we have not done and which we ought to have done" are those first mentioned, and are by no means the least important. We who are too well brought up and well environed to be in danger of great sins of commission, can easily displease our heavenly Father every day, if not every hour, by our sins of omission. Idle hours, idle words, idle thoughts, —education, good family, personal attraction, and wealth, used only for our own advantage,—these are things which are going to make the Intermediate State much less of a Paradise to them than thousands of Christians now imagine.

How many think that because they possess but the "one talent," that is to say, are only moderately endowed mentally, moderately well off, *not* "talented," they need feel only slightly responsible for mankind and for God's Kingdom! These are the average, every-day people, just those "common folk" of whom Lincoln said, "God must love them, because He has made so many of them." He does love and care for them; but He approves and cannot help loving them more, when they put out to interest for Him and His world, the single talent's worth of wit, of money, of social influence, of whatever capacity, He has given them. The great majority of us, citizens, soldiers, Christians, are of the one-talent sort; and God is much more than we are apt to suppose depending on us, each in our humble way and narrow round of duty to labour and contend for His Kingdom of truth, of purity and of holiness in this world: and if we indeed strive to do it, every day reporting to Him to be inspected, reproved, and improved, will there not be far less of teaching and correction necessary in that future State of waiting and of discipline, in the way to which all are going?

Thackeray, in "George the Third," quotes the verses, —"the sacred verses,"—which Dr. Johnson wrote on the death of his humble friend, Levett, "innocent, sincere,"

> "Of every friendless name the friend;"

and the last verse is,

> "His virtues walked their narrow round
> Nor made a pause nor left a void;
> And sure the Eternal Master found
> His single talent well employed."

It is not easy to imagine active vestrymen, however thoughtful and devoted, giving time to a book like this; but should there be one who is also open to a piece of friendly advice, I would counsel him to say to his rector what one of the best vestrymen I ever had once said to me: "Please preach a sermon on the one talent"—ask him too for more than one discourse on the General Confession. For, "sacrament," or plain every-day "rite," in this Confession, with the Absolution following, we enjoy one of the chief means of grace in the Comforter's hand.

CHRISTIAN ENTHUSIASM AND MUSIC

Sing ye to the Lord for he hath triumphed gloriously.—Exod. 15 : 21.

Sing us one of the songs of Sion.—Ps. 137 : 3.

O sing unto the Lord a new song, and his praise from the end of the earth.—Isa. 42 : 10.

We also joy in God, through our Lord Jesus Christ, by whom we have now received the atonement.—Rom. 5 : 11.

Be ye not foolish, but understanding what the will of the Lord is. And be not drunken with wine, wherein is riot; but be filled with the Spirit; speaking one to another in psalms and hymns and spiritual songs (odes), singing and making melody with your heart to the Lord; giving thanks always for all things in the name of our Lord Jesus Christ to God, even the Father; subjecting yourselves one to another in the fear of Christ.—Eph. 5 : 17–21 (20th Sunday after Trinity).

> When Music, heavenly maid, was young,
> While yet in early Greece she sung.—Collins.

This is the sort of wisdom which enables a man to do what our Lord expects of spiritual leaders, to "discern the time." It is a rare quality, but according to the measure of the gift of Christ to each, it is attained by spiritual thoughtfulness, single-mindedness, and prayer. There is to be, secondly, a strong and sociable enthusiasm, expressing itself in uninterrupted joy, and based upon deep draughts of the divine Spirit. Lastly, there is to be a spirit of submission, mutual accommodation and order. * * * It is probably true to say that, among other characteristics which our generation exhibits, is a lack of great enthusiasms and strong convictions and inspiring leaders. * * * Truly if rashness has slain its thousands, irresolution has slain its ten thousands. The spirit St. Paul would have us cultivate is not this cowardly miscalled wisdom, but rather the spirit of the ideal soldier, of the "happy warrior."—Bishop Gore, on Ephesians.

Seek the completest satisfaction of your nature through your highest powers, * * * not through those elements of your being by which you are bound to earth, * * * so your faculties will be quickened with a new force and you will see the glory of heaven. Deep springs of joy will be opened on every side; and you will feel with fresh sympathy the splendours of common things. You will be touched with a noble excitement, which will be, as it were, a foretaste of the rapture of saints, an excitement which when it passes away, will not leave you wearied and worn out, but conscious of a loftier life.—Bishop Westcott.

Painting, however lofty and idealized, nevertheless depends entirely on what has been seen, or may be seen, around us. * * * Architecture, though of higher dignity, as being not merely imitative but to some extent creative, did nevertheless originate in imitations of natural objects, and can never exceed the narrow limits imposed on it by its necessary localization. Like painting, it is essentially perishable. * * * But music, as it is not an imitative, but a creative art, so are its productions as imperishable as the minds which have created them. Music too speaks a universal and unchanging language. * * * Even when married to words, music is really independent of them. * * * Music of the highest class does express a sequence and development of thought, though that be not compressible into the narrower channel of articulate speech. And especially does it lend itself to the expression of *adoring* thought, that thought which sinks before the felt presence of the Deity, and which is as ineffable as the Deity itself.—Bishop Reichel, Cathedral Worship.

Music is the only fine art the practice of which is used in Scripture to give some idea of the employments of the blessed in heaven.—*Ibid.*

The words from Ephesians in the altar-service for the Twentieth Sunday after Trinity form a striking passage; not least by reason of the combination in them of widely different features as one whole. It may remind us of a small canvas upon which one of the world's master-painters has grouped many figures, representing many aspects of human life, all in artistic harmony. We seem to see Ephesian merchants buying up their opportunities to use them for personal advantage in particular commercial situations; Roman and Greek warriors kept "in step" and stimulated by martial music; St. Paul lying on his couch at midnight, disturbed and saddened by sounds of revelry and riot, without in the dark Ephesian streets, during his more than two years' stay in that great heathen city. We seem to hear bands of Passover pilgrims in the olden times, singing antiphonally the dear songs of Sion on their way up to Jerusalem; and again the early Christians, also singing "one to another," antiphonally (as Pliny too described it), their "psalms and hymns and spiritual songs." And our own imagination supplements the varied scene with French and Swiss, English and American, armies, marching to songs which stirred devotion to their respective countries.

The underlying motives of the inspired picture are Christian wisdom, earnestness, unity, and the enthusiasm that will ever result when the glorious ideals of life in Christ are entertained, and arduous duties are done, and dangers heroically encountered, by the many.

St. Paul was a wide-visioned man to whom nothing human was foreign; but with the human and the natural in him there is found ever the supernatural, gospel, element. We find it here in his truth of the Pentecostal Spirit. The joy which is healthful and real, the enthusiasm which is true and lasting, and will not like that of wine leave the manhood shrunk and weakened by and by,—all these are of one blood with the original meaning of the noble Greek word. For these are chief fruits of the Spirit's life in our hearts, while to be "enthused" means literally to be *filled with God*.

This then is one of the truths to be shown to our people in this season—which we are dealing with as the long Pentecostal Season. One of the marked characteristics of the Church's early life was a next to miraculous, joyous enthusiasm, typical of the eternal blessedness of Humanity completely redeemed; and enthusiasm and joy are ear-marks,—heart-marks,—of the Spirit's indwelling life to-day.

We read that "the disciples believed not for joy," when Christ first appeared to them in the upper room. After His Ascension, when we might have expected feelings of depression, "they returned to Jerusalem with great joy." The kingdom of heaven, it reads in Romans 14 : 17, "is not meat and drink, but righteousness and peace and joy in the Holy Ghost." There is something wanting, something wrong, about us, if we are gloomy Christians. St. Paul is in this regard our greatest exemplar, after Him who "endured the cross despising the shame, for the joy that was set before him." When he was left bound in Rome, as he said, "the Lord's prisoner," deep springs of joy and hope seem to have opened in his heart, and he became most enthusiastic.

But I am merely suggesting themes for sermons, not "sermon-stuff." All I would here say is, that Christians need to be taught that they must look upon the Spirit, look to the Spirit, as a divine well-spring of joy, and of "that noble excitement which will be as it were a foretaste of the rapture of saints." It is "feeling," but feeling founded upon powerful convictions, and a partial "experience."

What remains to be examined is the vital relation of sacred music to this life of the Spirit in our hearts. Pope wrote:

> "Some to church repair,
> Not for the doctrine, but the music there;"

nor are they *wholly* wrong, if Bishop Reichel's thought is correct, that music, "even when married to words, is really independent of them." Milton's line,

> "Such sweet compulsion doth in music lie,"

and Bishop Reichel's other remark relating to music's capacity to "lend itself to the expression of *adoring* thought,—thought which is as ineffable as the Deity itself,"—encourage me to say out more freely and fully things I have long felt to be true.

There is little need to show how large a place music holds in the Scriptures, Old Testament and New, and not merely in connection with the Psalms, and in the apocalyptic Vision of St. John. Scarcely greater necessity exists for showing the relation of music to all art, and all human activity. Kant described architecture as a sort of frozen music, and Schelling and Madame de Stael have each in their way expressed the same thought. Our use of the term "harmony" in relation to painting, sculpture, poetry, and every form of expression, in relation to character and conduct, and to family and social life and effort, is one of many indications of the kinship. So of love, and humility, and all united action. When St. Paul, after writing of psalms and hymns and spiritual songs, says presently,—and here it seems to me commentators have failed to apprehend his subtle thought,— "*submitting* yourselves one to another in the fear of God," it would seem to be impossible for a chorister, or any musical person, not to think of the absolute necessity of listening each moment to the organ and the other singers, in due mutual attention and submission, in order to attain perfect harmony and rhythm in chant and hymn.

Hymn tunes, instrumental accompaniments, and voluntaries, composed and rendered in reverent faith and love, and with the thought of due submission to God, and to each other in the fear of God, we must believe, possess a spiritual power all their own. They open the heart and mind to receive the truth about God, help to confirm resolutions to love and serve Him, and love the Christian brotherhood.

Music as truly as sacred poetry is a creation of the Spirit. Borne upon the air, at times a long distance, and from above,—produced by the air in wind instruments,—it is peculiarly fitted to remind man of the unseen, ever-present, heavenly, Paraclete. Collins' invocation, beginning,

> "O Music, sphere-descended maid,
> Friend of pleasure, wisdom's aid,"

is specially appropriate to religious musical composition. Joseph Haydn, leaning against a pillar of the old church in Vienna, and listening for the first time to his own Oratorio of The Creation, performed by a competent choir and orchestra, was overheard saying to himself: "Das kommt vom Himmel; es kommt nicht von mir." All good music comes from heaven, and sacred music more than all. It is a peculiarly heavenly creation, preaches a gospel all its own, warns, convicts, commands, invites, pardons, and receives, in a message of its own.

One reason why the truth of the Holy Spirit has been "sadly neglected" from very early times until now, is that He is unseen. Our Lord has been seen and handled, listened to speaking with a blessed human voice, which in the gospels seems at times actually to come to us, "sounding o'er land and sea." Now there are many "Voices of the Spirit," but no one has literally heard them; and Music, speaking to the very depth of our spirits a next to spiritual language, would appear to be a special and precious instrument of the Holy Ghost in convincing us of our sin and need of pardon, and convincing us of the Father's readiness to pardon for His dear Son's sake.

To realize how much Christianity has done to elevate music, one would need to hear the tom-tom of heathen worship, and then listen to The Creation or The Messiah. A young Japanese woman studying in America, being asked about the condition of musical art in Japan, answered; "O, we are doing a good deal, and are making progress, but you will understand that we cannot fully comprehend and appreciate German and English music until we have entered into your religious ideas." The reply was as suggestive as it was intelligent. Our music, even our love songs, are to a greater degree than we are apt to imagine what the religion of Christ has made them. Palestrina, and Bach, and Händel, Haydn, Mozart, Beethoven, are behind and in our entire world of musical thought. Therefore is there less excuse for weak, sentimental, and "trashy," music in American homes and churches.

And what has not music given in return, as a spiritual auxiliary to the Church? It was largely by its solemn and elevating Gregorian music,—superior to and gradually supplanting that of Ambrose,—that the Latin Church through Augustine's mission won its way to the heart of our fierce English ancestors, and the fact was as creditable to their innate feeling as it was to Gregory's skill. For centuries the Latin Church was helped on by its proficiency in holy song. English and American Christianity and civilization owe much to the Latins in this regard, and our responsibility in respect to musical composition, education of the people in music, and training of the congregation to sing in the service, is the greater on this account. There is no solemnizing and uplifting, no socializing and harmonizing influence, equal to that of united song in the House of God.

We may not be able to go all the way with Lorenzo, pouring into the ear of Jessica his feelings of dislike for

"The man that hath no music in himself,
Nor is not moved with concord of sweet sounds,"

but this we must think true, that "the motions of his spirit are dull," if not "dull as night," and the

motions of any religious body are so, and its missionary effort and progress not likely to be notable, which
does not believe in sacred song, and cultivate it. Our
rich collection of hymns, and of chant and hymn tunes,
form a considerable part of our catholic heritage; and
it is to the Spirit's creative energy that we are indebted
alike for the one and the other. To the Spirit and the
Bride we owe the Scriptures and the Creeds; the Spirit
and the Bride have given us the Lyric of the new
covenant in Christ. There is cause for gratitude,—
in the Spirit's Season especially,—that whereas the
Prayer Book itself is not rich in prayers directly
or indirectly invoking Him, the Hymnal is in this
respect remarkably rich. Beside the Whitsuntide
hymns proper, and certain beautiful Confirmation
hymns, there are many others which in whole or in
part are directly prayers to the Spirit. These, if
used now, and at other times in the Christian Year,
will go a long way to supply the lack of prayers to,
and for, the Third Person, such as abounded in the
primitive liturgies. They will do not a little to com-
pensate for the neglect of Spirit-doctrine, and of
grateful adoring meditation upon Him in these later
times, and tend to revive the Church's sense of
dependence upon Him as the other Comforter, the
Lord, and Giver of life.

When through the use of these hymn-prayers,
and as a divine response to them, all Christendom,
impressed with the Spirit-truth, shall in some sort
realize what the Holy Ghost has been, is now, and
ever shall be, to the kingdoms of Nature and of Grace
alike, can we not imagine a greater than Haydn or
Händel arising, who shall give the Church a grander,

sweeter Oratorio of The Creation;—its theme not
merely the birth of the light, "the waters' foaming
billows," and the earth "with verdure clad," or what
"the heavens are telling" of God's glory in sun and
moon and stars, with what Adam and Eve once
breathed in each other's ears about their happiness
in a state of innocence? It will have for its theme
the history of a new humanity in a yet more splendid
setting, "a new heaven and a new earth, wherein
dwelleth righteousness." It will sing of a race with
nobler possibilities than the first, through vital union
in Christ with the Godhead Itself; a Humanity
created first in the Person of our Lord, and through
the trial and suffering of His human soul perfected
primarily in Him, to be afterward created, developed,
and perfected on the widest scale in that other Body
of Christ termed in Scripture "the fulness of him that
filleth all in all."

What other form of expression, even inspired, might
in our day expand more beautifully the Apostle's
thought, in 1st Cor. 2 : 9,

"Things which eye saw not, and ear heard not,
    And which entered not into the heart of man
    Whatsoever things God prepared for them that love him;
    But unto us God revealed them through the Spirit " ?

For the dominant motive in that more heavenly
and spiritual composition will be the mighty Spirit's
part in this all glorious "Operation." It will be an
Oratorio of the New Creation in Christ's Spirit, who
together with the Father and the Son, will be magnified as harp and viol, lute and organ, tongue and
pen of man, have never magnified Him before.

THE SPIRIT AND THE LORD'S DAY

And God said, Let there be light, and there was light.   And the evening and the morning were the first day.—Gen. 1 : 2, 5.

I am the light of the world.—John 8 : 12.

The first day of the week cometh Mary Magdalene early * * and seeth the stone taken away from the sepulchre.—John 20 : 1.

Upon the first day of the week, when the disciples came together to break bread, Paul preached unto them.—Acts 20 : 7.

This is the day which the Lord hath made: we will rejoice and be glad in it.—Ps. 118 : 24.

I was in the Spirit on the Lord's day.—Rev. 1 : 10.

Ye are all the children of light, and the children of the day.— 1st Thes. 5 : 5.

> Come, let us all with one accord
> Adore and magnify the Lord,
>   And festive service pay,
>
> On this the day that God hath blest,
> The day of peace and heavenly rest
>   The Lord's own holy day,
>
> That saw primeval darkness break
> And that more glorious life awake,
>   That lasteth evermore;
>
> That saw hell's legions prostrate fall,
> And Christ, triumphant over all,
>   His own to heaven restore.
>
> This day the peace that flows from heaven
> Was unto the Apostles given,
>   When doors were closed at night;
>
> This day the Holy Spirit's flame
> Upon the Church's teachers came,
>   And filled their souls with light.—Ancient Hymn.

> The Sundays of man's life
> Threaded together on time's string,
>   Make bracelets to adorn the wife
> Of the eternal glorious King.
>   On Sunday Heaven's gate stands ope:
> Blessings are plentiful and rife;
>   More plentiful than hope.—George Herbert.

The old saying, "Keep Sunday and Sunday will keep you," would seem to need changing into "Save Sunday and Sunday will save you." As Bishop Whitaker said in the *Church Standard* six years ago: "We regard the whole drift of things concerning it with serious alarm. We believe this drift to be ominous of evil to the religious, moral, and even physical well-being of the American people." How strange that so many professing to be Christians, who have not only warm hearts and quick consciences, but intelligence besides, do not appear to have taken the alarm! They do not realize that the Lord's Day,—the day He "hath made" for Himself and us by His victory over Sin and Death,—constitutes, together with the holy service of "praise and thanksgiving" instituted by Him, one of the most substantial evidences of the truth of Christianity. Every Sunday, with its Sunday Communion, tells the world anew that Christ is risen, and that our faith is not vain.

But some who do realize this, and would gladly save Sunday for their own souls' sake, and for Christ and the world, do not know how to save it.

The manner in which Sunday has been regarded, and its authority upheld, by vast numbers of Christians in later times, may remind one of the image set up by Nebuchadnezzar, part gold, part silver, part iron, and part clay. Not that the ancient Sabbath had iron and clay in it, but that being the Spirit's institution, and as it were of silver, and anciently a cheerful feast, Puritanism by changing it into a fast day, and by making it the foundation of our more glorious New Testament day, mixed iron and clay with it. Constantine's foundation for Sunday had the iron of imperial authority in it. It gave new and wider recognition to Christianity. It gained a weekly day of rest for man and beast. It has endured like iron in this sense down to our own times. But our Sunday is all of gold. The Head of it, Christ, is gold. The Spirit descended on this first day, to make it still more emphatically a Day of Light. On this day many enjoy bright visions of heavenly truth, and golden-mouthed preachers preach the truth. Must we not attribute it to the Spirit of Wisdom, that the day when the light was created was, so to say, reserved for its peculiarly honourable position in relation to the new, universal, "dispensation" in Christ and His Spirit?

The old day, the Sabbath, part of that system of "ordinances" which the Scripture says was but the "shadow of things to come," the Body being "of Christ,"—speaks of as now taken "out of the way," being nailed to His Cross (Col. 2 : 14, 17), was nevertheless ideally, as exhibited in Exodus and, as we saw before, particularly in Deuteronomy, certainly like unto silver. It is a shining day in many a Jewish household throughout the world now. But the Lord's Sunday, as a day of rest and worship and joyful fellowship for His Church, is, as we have said, all of gold. The foundation is itself precious. We see this plainly by comparing the texts above given. In the hymn quoted (No. 26 in our Book)—judging by the almost childlike simplicity and reality of it, a very ancient production,—we find the Old Testament event of the creation of light, and the two supreme New Testament events, the Resurrection of our Lord and the Imparting of the divine Spirit to His Church, set forth as vitally connected with our Sunday. If only these two verities of the Christian Faith, of which Dr. Milligan said the one had been scarcely less ignored than the other in our time, held a larger place in our thoughts now, and were seen in their true relation to Christ's Day, no such "serious alarm" would exist in Christian minds generally as has been referred to.

Is not this the truth about the Sabbath which was of silver, and Sunday which is golden, that both are to be esteemed institutions of the Third divine Person, and possessing a vital relationship to each other? But it was the relation of the seed to the plant. And "that which thou sowest is not quickened except it die." The Seventh day Rest of the elder covenant went down as it were dead, with Christ, into the grave; and, having slept with Him, rose with Him a new, transfigured, and more glorious, institution, a more spiritual day, restful, peaceful, and joyful in a richer, fuller sense. As the three-ordered ministry in Israel, and circumcision, and the old covenant sacrifices, died that they might live again, in another three-ordered ministry of the New Testament, a new Sacrament of initiation, a better Eucharist,—the same, yet not the same,—as Jesus Himself came forth the same, yet not the same Christ, so was it with this day.

And the Lord, and Giver of the new Christ-life,

was the Life of this Day. Plainly the Pentecostal Church received it,—just as it received those other transfigured, freer, and more heavenly institutions,—as from the Holy Ghost, in whom it implicitly believed as the Vicar of Jesus Christ. What need existed then, and what need exists now, for distinctly authoritative apostolic and ecclesiastical utterances, to confirm a Christian's belief in, and keep firm his loyal affection for, this Day? The Sunday law resembles the Gospel law generally. It is a "royal law, a law of liberty," and all the more binding for the conscience and heart. It is the "law of the Spirit of life." It is that law of love, which is "the more excellent way."

To eat the sour grapes of Puritanism on the one hand, or ecclesiasticism on the other, is to have our own teeth, and what is so often worse, our children's teeth "set on edge." Many years ago a bright, handsome boy in Exeter Academy, fond of fun and "popular," was asked by his rector, "How is it that you are so boylike and gay, yet faithful to your Church and to the Communion?" The answer came, after some moments, "I think it must be because my father made Sunday the happiest day in the week to all the children."

To love our Sundays spiritually, yet humanly, is to save Sunday to ourselves and those around us. The Scripture says, He that loveth his wife,—and it might have been added, his family and God's greater family the Church,— loveth himself. And so he that loves his Sunday and makes it a day of rest, of worship, and of benefit and happiness to others, loveth himself.

What has been said of Good Friday and Easter

as being the death and rising again of the Old Testament Sabbath, George Herbert quaintly says in a different way.

> "The Rest of our creation
> Our great Redeemer did remove
>   With the same shake which, at his passion,
> Did th' earth, and all things with it, move.
>   As Samson bore the doors away,
> Christ's hands, though nail'd, wrought our salvation,
>   And did unhinge that day."

But God forbid that in this era of the Spirit the other strong man, our Enemy, should prevail to "unhinge" the transfigured Sabbath of the risen Christ; that we should, as Bishop Whitaker said,

"lose the Lord's Day as Catholic Christendom knew it for fifteen hundred years,—part with its splendid gain of a weekly day of rest for man and beast," which would be "criminal folly. * * * Apart from all strictly religious sentiment, we hold that the civil state will strike at one essential condition of its own permanent well-being if it does not guard the precious heritage. * * * God forbid too that we should not go back to first principles, and reclaim for the Lord's Day the sanctity which it received at first by reasonable worship."

And somehow the "nailed hand" is ever mightier than the mailed hand, or the militant word. Should earnest Christians be led by their very earnestness to place dependence upon Church canons and civil authority, again I beg to urge reliance on spiritual means. By "the finger of God" our Lord cast out devils to the confusion of Beelzebub, and God's Finger is the Holy Ghost. The history of Christianity proves that since Pentecost the Stronger Man has been overcoming His and our Enemy, taking from him his armour, and dividing his spoils, mainly by miracles of love and wisdom.

It is to be borne in mind too that, pray, preach, and live as we may, the Lord's Day can never be brimful of "rest and gladness," of "joy and light," until this world has become *wholly* the Lord's world. Of the perfect "rest which remaineth for the people of God" our Sunday is the reminder and promise. Let us confide in this promise with the same grateful, child-like, simplicity which breathes in the very ancient hymn I have quoted, and which ends

> "Then on this day let us adore
> Our God, and supplication pour,
>   That, when worlds pass away,
> Through Christ's dear grace our souls may rest
> In peace and joy, forever blest,
>   Till the great Judgment day."

REVERENCE AND GODLY FEAR

I will send my beloved son: it may be they will reverence him when they see him.—Luke 20 : 13.

Let us have grace, whereby we may serve God with reverence and godly fear.—Heb. 12 : 28.

And every creature which is in heaven, and on the earth, and under the earth, and such as are in the sea, and all that are in them, heard I saying, Blessing, and honour, and glory, and power, be unto Him that sitteth upon the throne, and unto the Lamb forever and ever.—Rev. 5 : 13.

"The word was made flesh and dwelt among us," but while we tell men of His hunger and thirst and pain, His human affections, His accessibility to temptation, and His nights of prayer, we must also enable them to recognize His glory—"the glory as of the only-begotten of the Father, full of grace and truth." I think I have sometimes seen in the writings even of those who would claim for themselves exceptional fidelity to the orthodox and Evangelical creed, the unambiguous proof that they have a most inadequate sense of the majesty of the Son of God. They speak of Him with a fondling affection which is inconsistent with true reverence. Their faith in His sympathy with them in their sorrows is real; but there is no such awe as must come from a deep and living sense of His moral authority. They are always lying on His breast; they never fall at His feet with wonder and fear. There is a similar failure to recognize Him as "the brightness of the Father's glory and the express image of His person," in theologians of a very different school— theologians who acknowledge in their creed the true Deity of our Lord, but who are so interested in His human develop- ment, so fascinated with the ethical perfection of His charac- ter, with His tenderness to the imfirmities of men, His merciful words to those who had grievously sinned, and the charm of His human friendships, so touched with the pathetic story of the tears which He shed over Jerusalem, and the agony which came upon Him in the garden, that they ignore the manifes- tations of that Supernatural and Divine glory which again and again broke through the clouds in which it was for a time con- cealed."—R. W. Dale.

In hardly another point is the Prayer Book more dis- tinctly true to the New Testament, and to the Church's sacred traditions, than in that of reverence; for God, and the Son of God, our Lord Jesus Christ. Popular Protestantism has not always been so reverent, and it is one of the most eminent of modern Protestant divines whom we have found calling attention to the fact. There may be many constant readers of the New Testament,—not a few Prayer Book Christians, —who need to be reminded that as we pass on from the Gospel period, if one may so speak of it, into the

Pentecostal, the Spirit's era, the time when apostles and prophets spake and wrote as enlightened by the divine Paraclete, our Lord is spoken of differently. He wears His glorious heavenly titles, as being the Ascended Lord.

Pentecost marks the turning-point. In more senses than one is it true that St. Peter, St. Stephen, and St. James, like St. Paul, know the Saviour "no more after the flesh." His name is like Himself trans- figured and glorified. "God," declared St. Peter on the first Whitsunday, "hath made that same Jesus, whom ye (of the house of Israel) have crucified, both Lord and Christ" (Acts 2 : 36). In the fifth chapter (v. 31) it is again announced: "Him hath God exalted with his right hand to be a Prince and a Saviour." Stephen while being stoned calls upon God, and cries, "Lord Jesus, receive my spirit" (7 : 59). The future Apostle to the Nations, overwhelmed by the vision of the glorified Son of Man near Damascus, asks, "Lord, what wilt thou have me to do?" (9 : 6), and St. James writes to his fellow disciples of the faith, not of Jesus, but "of the Lord Jesus Christ."

Precious to us as the record is of the time when Christ lived "in the flesh," walked and talked with men by the lake side and in the house,—relieved as in a sense we are after the scene of glory upon the holy mount, to find ourselves, as it were, again with Him as before on the plain, in the life of every day,— dear as is the thought of what is yet coming to His true followers in the future, prefigured by that familiar intercourse,—the other side of the glorious truth may not be forgotten by us. This other side is, first, that He who was well-pleased to call Himself the Son

of Man was also the adorable, true and only-begotten
Son of God in heaven, and secondly, that one of our
very best means of preparation for the blessed intercourse with Him hereafter is to meditate upon, and by
the Spirit's help realize, His *present glory*, even as man.

Profoundly suggestive to faith is the fact that
the very disciple who leaned on the Lord's breast at
supper is the one who in his late years had the vision
of Him in His glory, heard the voices of the ten thousand times ten thousand around the throne, ascribing
"blessing, and honour, and glory, and power" unto
God, and "unto the Lamb for ever and ever."

Jesus,—the same as Joshua,—a divinely-given and
beautiful name, was none the less a human one.   Other
boys in Nazareth may have borne it.   It was the name
that corresponded to His state of self-humiliation
for our sakes.   When used, as it is occasionally in
Hebrews, it is in connection with His lowliness and
patient suffering on man's behalf.   In the Acts,
and in the Epistles generally, this humble, earthly,
name, which marks His oneness with us, becomes
heavenly and great by being associated with the
name Christ (Messiah), and that other name which
was "above every name" (Phil. 2 : 9) Jehovah
(Lord) held by the Jews too sacred to be pronounced
aloud except in the temple.

"It is not for us," wrote Dr. Dale in "Fellowship with
Christ," page 137, "to prolong His humiliation, to keep
Him uncrowned, to withhold in these the days of His triumph the homage which He voluntarily surrendered during the years that He was visibly present among men."

Not to honour our blessed Redeemer by remembering reverently to employ these His present titles, in

the language of praise and prayer, in sermons, and in the daily intercourse with Christian friends, is by so much the less to honour ourselves as redeemed in Him. We are already new creatures and virtually glorified by our mystical union with the risen Lord: as the Scripture declares, sitting with God "in the heavenly places, in Christ Jesus." (Eph. 2 : 6.)

It ought not to pass unnoticed that neither in the New Testament nor in the Prayer Book is Christ spoken of as "dear," except in that He is dear to God; as when St. Paul writes to the Colossians (chap. 1 : 13) of the Father "who hath translated us into the kingdom of his dear Son." The Prayer Book,—and shall we not thank the guiding Spirit for it?—never leans to the side of sentiment and familiarity, or to the "fondling affection which is inconsistent with true reverence." It never forgets the majesty of God or the Son of God. There is reason for gratitude in the fact that few hymns in the Church's Hymnal can be faulted in this respect.

Again I say, thank the Holy Spirit! And note how near to the time of His own epiphany falls the Sunday whose Epistle (1st John 3 : 13) contains the words: "Hereby we know that He abideth in us, by the Spirit which He hath given us," and "If our heart condemn us, God is greater than our heart, and knoweth all things," while its Collect reads:

"O Lord, who never failest to help and govern those whom thou dost *bring up in thy stedfast fear* and *love;* Keep us, we beseech thee, under the protection of thy good providence, and make us to *have a perpetual fear and love of thy holy Name; through Jesus Christ, our Lord.*"

CHRISTIAN SOCIAL ETHICS

Blessed is he that considereth the poor.—Ps. 41 : 1.

Thou shalt not defraud thy neighbour, neither rob him: the wages of him that is hired shall not abide with thee all night until the morning.—Lev. 19 : 13.

Is not this the fast that I have chosen,—to undo the heavy burdens, and to let the oppressed go free, and that ye break every yoke?—Isa. 58 : 6.

He hath filled the hungry with good things.—Luke 53 : 1.

Blessed be ye poor.—Luke 6 : 20.

And all that believed were together, and had all things common; and sold their possessions and goods and parted them to all men as every man had need.—Acts 2 : 44, 45.

And the fellowship of the Holy Ghost be with you all.— 2d Cor. 13 : 14.

We have fellowship one with another.—1 John 1 : 7.

It is high time that the whole strength and influence of the community should be deliberately, patiently, used to raise the standard of life of its weaker members.—Minority Report of the (English) Labour Commission.

It has been one of my chief joys to watch the gradual acceptance of the master-thoughts of corporate obligation and corporate interdependence, till now it is (may I not say?) universally acknowledged among Englishmen that we all belong to one body, in which the least member has his proper function.—Bishop Westcott.

The organization of industry is the organization of national life.—*Ibid.*

The best modern conscience is to be reached and touched and won in no way so effectively as by a strong and consistent appeal to the principle of brotherhood.—Bishop Gore.

We have no right for their sake, or for our own, to preach contentment to the poor, or bribe them into acquiescence, until we have given them the elementary justice of an equal opportunity of living the life which God intended for them.— Peile, Bampton Lectures.

The mass of professing Christians themselves regard their religion as rather static than dynamic. They would fain be tarrying all their lives in the Interpreter's house, instead of tramping the open road with Mr. Greatheart, through difficulty and peril and extreme discomfort, but on towards the Heavenly City.—*Ibid.*

If we took the words, "Become as little Children" seriously, they would seem repellent or absurd to people who value themselves chiefly on cautious judgment, business acumen, and a proper sense of their position. * * * The starved, commonplace, spirit of us must suffer a change "into something rich and strange" before we have a right to call ourselves disciples of Jesus Christ, or profess to be forwarding his cause in the world. * * * Class distinctions, which do not seem to grow fainter with the advance of political democracy, are the great barrier to Christian work, for they seem to make impossible the sympathy and open speaking which are the condition of spiritual influence. * * * The very existence of such a dilemma proves how profound a revolution in human thought or feeling is needed before Society can be brought into accord with Christian principles.—*Ibid.*

> Our splashes upward, O gold heaper,
> > And your purple, show your path,
> But the child's sob in the silence curses deeper
> > Than the strong man in his wrath.—Mrs. Browning.

Not least important among the signs which announced the Holy Spirit's descent upon the Church were those two ethical miracles, first a new sympathy for mankind the world over, and the desire to preach the Gospel to every creature; and, secondly, a wonderful manifestation of human fellowship. The primitive Church was one family. They "had all things common; sold their possessions and goods, and parted them to all men as every man had need." It was a spiritual phenomenon, a *singular* thing. Barnabas who owned a field in the rich island of Cyprus, "sold it and brought

the money, and laid it at the Apostles' feet," and the
Collect for St. Barnabas' Day speaks of him as
"endowed with singular gifts of the Holy Ghost."
That the noble generosity of this "son of consolation,"
or of other early Christians, was singular in the sense of
being un-Jewish, cannot be affirmed.   Long chapters
in Exodus, Leviticus and Deuteronomy are largely
taken up with injunctions in regard to neighbourly
charity and kindness to the poor and to strangers.
The command to keep sacred the seventh day as a
day of rest is (in Deut. 5 : 14, 15) based chiefly on the
obligation to consider servants and "the stranger that
is within thy gates; that thy manservant and thy
maidservant may rest as well as thou.   And remember
that thou wast a servant in the land of Egypt, and that
the Lord thy God brought thee out thence through a
mighty hand and a stretched out arm."   Many of us
would be glad to hear this Deuteronomic law read in
the Chancel service rather than the Exodus one, and
if this may not be, it may be practicable otherwise, in
the way of Church decoration for instance, to remind
Christians by these words of their duty to household
servants and other wage-earning people on the Lord's
resurrection day?   That Jewish people, now comparatively homeless and churchless in the world, both
keep their ancient Sabbath, and are kind to the poor
in a manner to shame many who enjoy the richer
heritage in the true Messiah, is certainly due to those
Old Testament injunctions of humanity.

What was singular, however, and notable in the new
covenant spirit of love, was that it was a universal
love.   And it was of the essence of His religion who
said. "Love one another as I have loved you," and

who loved *all* men with the love of *sacrifice*. Ex-President Patton was right when he said that the things of social ethics are things which belong on the ground-floor in God's House. It is true that, as Uhlhorn wrote in "Christian Charity in the Ancient Church," it was "first love" with those early believers. "Youth does not reflect, it acts from the direct impulses arising from its present abundant vitality, and so it was with the charity of the period." But it was also a "wonderful work" of the Lord, the Spirit. We must regard it as a type of the free, yet wisely controlled and regulated life of love in the Spirit, which should be hereafter.

Our duty then as priests and people, teachers and learners, all possessing the Spirit for inspiration and for guidance, is to provide a large space on the ground-floor for these same social duties in Christ; to be always asking how that prophetic moral and spiritual miracle can best and soonest find its realization in the world which Christ came, not merely to save at last, but to make now, and in every possible way, happy and blest. We need to pray over it together; to call upon each other to mark the slow progress made from year to year. Great tact and patience are required; and one can learn much of both from Christ's method. His blessed mother had sung, "He hath exalted them of low degree; He hath filled the hungry with good things," and He at once began to teach saying, "Blessed be ye poor; yours is the kingdom of heaven; the poor have the Gospel preached to them." But he was too wise, and kind to them, to say just how much the "kingdom," in His own mind and purpose, included of benefit and of joy. His Apostle to the Gentiles was in like manner patient and tactful. How sorely he must have felt the want of social reform of every kind among the Nations; the degradation of the home life, the shame and pity of slavery, and other pagan abuses and miseries! Yet how discerning, discrete, and self-controlled he was, by the aid of the Spirit of Wisdom, in his method of meeting the difficulties! It was that self-same manner of sowing the "seed, which is Christ," and awaiting its springing up, and the fruit of it, to which reference has been made in a preceding section.

Should not our method of teaching and influencing be a like one? Should it not be generally a method of exhibiting principles, and inspiring new and higher motives, without going much into details or discussing single cases? The subject is naturally complicated and difficult, and appears to grow more so as time goes on. It is a question whether Professor Richard T. Ely's word, in his admirable work on "Social Aspects of Christianity," "I should say that half of the time of a theological student should be devoted to social science," does not go too far. The result might be a more frequent hearing of the disagreeable remark, "I wish our rector and the clergy in general would confine themselves to preaching the simple Gospel."

Beyond question the simple Gospel includes the truths which underlie social science; and men, and women too, if not many children besides, need reminding of these truths. Some one has said, "Predestination is believed in by the rich in one respect anyway, and that is in respect to the poor." Not a few in our day need to be told that the Scriptural predestination is "not favoritism, but election to responsibility." They may be interested to hear a sermon on the text, "Thou shalt remember the Lord thy God;

for it is He that gave thee power to get wealth," glad to be taught that they are elected to be well-off and comfortable, that they may co-operate in the work of bettering the condition of such as are not so, precisely as they have been called to faith in Christ chiefly that they may be the means of bringing others to Him.

Maybe they will listen patiently when Peile is quoted saying, "Most of the tricks and immoralities of trade are due to the increasing stress of competition," and that "It is the ordinary consumer who is largely to blame for this excessive competition through the prevailing passion for cheap bargains"; and finally, that "The responsibility of deciding how trade should be carried on lies upon the conscience and intelligence of the general public." Business men will not resent it, when the clergy, acknowledging the difficulty of the subject in general, and their own want of knowledge of details, and of leisure to study them, earnestly invoke prayerful reflection and co-operation on the part of the laity. Will not the women in our congregation,— even the least thoughtful and sympathetic of them,— listen kindly to Professor Ely's story of the lady in the church society meeting who sat silent while the others discussed the servant-girl question, and finally said, "Really I have no trouble with servants." "How is that?" all exclaimed. Finally she confessed that she made her servants a matter of prayer, and asked that she might be taught her duty to them. "Your duty!" was the surprised exclamation; but a new light began to dawn on them. Some confessed that they had asked the Lord to send them good servants, but no one else had ever asked to know her duty to them.

19

Uhlhorn, commenting on the past slow progress of Christians in working out social problems, says:

"Not till the Reformation was the source returned to, the primitive Christian notions of riches and poverty, of property and alms, of work and vocation revived, and consequently new fountains of active love unsealed. These notions, however, are very far from having been fully carried out. * * * The first duty of our age is to realize in action the evangelical and reformed ideas concerning charity and the relief of the poor, in connection with those concerning calling and work, wages and property. Beginnings, thank God, exist. Would that they may but develop with increasing power!"   (Page 398.)

Both North and South become each year more grateful to God that the evil which so weighed on the soul of Whittier has been forever removed, but other social troubles remain to distress us, and certain of his lines "On a Prayer Book" may, in view of these troubles, touch not least the Prayer Book worshipper.   First come words regarding the "sweet ritual, beautiful but dead", and holy hymns from which the life has gone out because of the absence of humanity, and then,

"O heart of mine, keep patience! Looking forth,
   As from the Mount of Vision, I behold,
 Pure, just, and free, the Church of Christ on earth,—
   The Martyr's dream, the golden age foretold!
 And found, at last, the mystic Graal I see,
   Brimmed with His blessing, pass from lip to lip
   In sacred pledge of human fellowship;
   And over all the songs of angels hear,—
   Songs of the love that casteth out all fear,—
   Songs of the Gospel of Humanity!
   Lo, in the midst, with the same look He wore,
   Healing and blessing on Gennesaret's shore,
   Stands the Consoler, soothing every pain,
 Making all burdens light, and breaking every chain."

Not in divine poetry, however, but in the divine Paraclete, will be found truest inspiration and the hope of victory. The noblest poems of Humanity ever written, and the most eloquent sermons ever preached on it, the soundest treatises on Christian Ethics yet composed, cannot change selfish and prejudiced hearts, without Christ's Spirit; Christ's own humane words and example cannot. All these are like "the clay" with which He anointed the eyes of the blind. For it was not the clay, but the accompanying power of the Spirit "given without measure" to Christ which, as we all know, did the work. So it is now with those "miracles greater than" His own miracles, which He promised His people should perform in the Spirit's era, and which we must all pray and labor to perform in the Spirit; nor are there many *greater*, and therefore more difficult, than this one of raising the "standard of life of the weaker members" of our redeemed humanity. It is just these "master-thoughts" and efforts of "corporate obligation and corporate inter-dependence," that are next to impossible, because at least nine out of ten Christians are quite blind to their existence. Therefore, while we talk and labor, that is, make and use the clay, we must invoke the Spirit, and believe in His power and good-will more than in our clay. It is His affair more than it is ours: for all fellowship and communion in heaven and on earth and the resulting community of feeling and action, is "the Communion of the Holy Ghost."

"O Most Holy Trinity, in the ever flowing abundance of Thy Love sending forth the Holy Ghost the Paraclete, to create and form Thy Church, the mystical Body of Christ; grant to us to be ever fervent in the Unity of the Spirit, that always abiding in Thy worship and service, we may grow more and more steadfast in Faith, Hope, and Charity, more and more patient and active in all good works to the honour and glory of Thy name, through Jesus Christ our Lord. Amen. ("Short Office of the Holy Ghost.")

OUT OF DOOR SPIRIT-TRUTHS

And Isaac went out to meditate in the field at the eventide.—Gen. 24 : 63.

And Moses went up unto God and the Lord called unto him out of the mountain.—Exod. 19 : 3.

They that go down to the sea in ships, these see the works of the Lord, and his wonders in the deep.—Ps. 107 : 23, 24.

The trees of the Lord are full of sap; the cedars of Lebanon, which he hath planted; where the birds make their nests.—Ps. 104 : 16, 17.

The only objects of which the mind and the heart never grow weary are rural ones.—Rousseau.

One clergyman was heard to say to another, "your sermons always take me out of doors." Now so to teach is to be a priest of nature, and of the Creator-Spirit. The service itself begins at once to take us out of doors in the Venite: "The sea is his, and he made it; and his hands prepared the dry land." The Bible does this, from Genesis to Revelation. The first tells how "God planted a garden eastward in Eden, and there he put the man whom he had formed"; the last describes New Jerusalem, with its "pure river of water of life," and "the leaves of the tree for the healing of the nations." The sixty-fifth Psalm, the one hundred and fourth Psalm, in fact the Psalms as a whole, keep us in close touch with the outdoor life.

It is the same with the Gospels. We journey to Bethlehem with Joseph and Mary, journey with the wise men; journey down into Egypt, and then to Nazareth, with the infant Christ. In His ministry our Lord is always abroad, now teaching on the mount, now going into a mountain to pray, again, standing by the lake and pointing at the little white-walled towns on the hill-side lighted up by the setting sun, or at a candle some one has lighted on the shore, and drawing from them first lessons on the duty of His Church to be every way a missionary power for Him. "So," He says,—and we can almost see His outstretched hand,— "So let your light shine before men." Tempted and victorious at the beginning in the desert, He is tempted and victorious finally in a garden under the light of the Passover moon.

In the Acts, and in St. Paul's Epistles it is much the same. We are out of doors, and ever on the go while the field of action widens. The first Whitsunday sermon ever preached, and the great service of Baptism, which resulted from it, could only have been in the open. The most notable sermon of the Apostle to the Nations was that on Mars' Hill. His three missionary journeys, and the inspired letters composed at different places, and addressed to Churches in Asia and Europe, keep the New Testament student, and attentive worshippers in the second half of the Church's Year, mentally journeying and sight-seeing.

In summer and autumn many are working, many

playing, in the open air. It is a time of travel, of sojourning by sea and lake and mountain, of garden-life and porch-life. How profitable then so to teach in Sunday School and in Church, after the outdoor fashion of the Master, as to attract men and children indoors, bringing Nature into Church to illustrate the things of Grace! The thoughts set down in these pages have been day by day "taken to walk" with the hope and prayer that they might be the truer and healthier for it. The purpose in this section is to touch upon three subjects which in a sense belong out under God's sky, or above it: the Nineteenth Psalm; the Ellipse as a figure of the perfect life, according to the law and the prophets, namely, the golden rule; and the Angels.

The Nineteenth Psalm, beside being one of the three which make up the noble Third Selection, is the first of the Christmas Day Psalms. "In the Latin Church it is appointed for use also on the festivals of the Ascension and of Trinity Sunday; so likewise it was in the Sarum Use; and in the Gregorian Use it is appointed for the Annunciation." (Wordsworth, quoted by Perowne.) It is easy, as in the case of Psalm Twenty-three, to believe that it was composed by King David himself,—that the thought came to him already when, a shepherd lad, he beheld the sun rising above the eastern mountains. There are few children, even few adults, who do not need to have pointed out to them the exquisite parallel, which the sacred writer would have men *feel*, between the law that regulates the movements of the heavenly bodies,—enables them to declare the glory of God and bear their silent yet eloquent witness to human faith concerning His majesty and power,—and the higher and more spiritual law which converts, cleanses, enlightens and regulates the soul. What would become of the world we live in, and of us, if the sun did not rise to-morrow at exactly the appointed moment, or if rising it failed for a day to send out its warmth and light, and pour forth its chemical and life-sustaining properties upon the earth's surface? On the other hand, if each man, woman, and child in the world were as faithful to God's commandments as the heavenly orbs are strict to keep in their appointed courses, and perform their tasks, what a pure and perfectly harmonious life our existence would be! Are there any even among genuine Christians, who do not at least need to be reminded of this truth? Is not the Spirit's season a time to remind them, since He, who "actuates" what the Son "regulates," and the Father "originates," and who is Himself the *law* of the celestial system, is also the *Holy* Spirit, and the law of the spirit of life in us? We know what He does for the sun and the stars in the kingdom of nature:

"Thou dost preserve the *stars* from wrong;
And the most ancient heavens, through Thee are *fresh* and *strong*."

And He does the same for us in the kingdom of grace.

The second topic lies not far removed logically or analogically from the first. One needs not to ascend mountain peaks or go down to the sea in ships to "see the works of the Lord" and His wonders. Lying in a hammock or on the grass, of a summer night, he may be impressed with them, especially if learned, even a little, in science. The planets, we are taught, move not in circles but ellipses. And the geometrical formula,—which is a formula of the mighty Spirit,—is "a curve such that the sum of the distances of any point from two given, called the *foci*, is equal to a given line." This truth of geometry and of astronomy corresponds to the Scripture truth in the rule, "Thou shalt love thy neighbour *as* thyself." Self and the neighbour are the two foci which must govern the Christian's life with the brother man. To be self-centred is selfish and unchristian; on the other hand God would not have us,—if one may coin the word,—neighbour-centred. Christ Himself implied that self-love, rightly understood, is not selfishness. My first duty is to God, and my own soul; more than this, to develop and cultivate my own noblest capacities; nor need I fear to love too much my new and better self in the Spirit. The oval is a form of the ellipse, and the eggs on the table at the morning meal may be more than a suggestion of our Lord's resurrection and our own in Him through the Spirit; even an emblem of the life we should live together throughout the day, in the home and everywhere.

The truth which we may say peeps above the horizon where the Dauphin, in King Henry V, says,

> "Self-love, my liege, is not so vile a sin
>   As self-neglecting,"

comes to fuller view in Measure for Measure, when Isabel, determined to keep her sacred self "unspotted from the world," replies to Angelo,

> "Better it were, a brother died at once,
>   Than that a sister, by redeeming him,
>   Should die forever."

God would not have us annihilate ourselves even before Him, or for Him, and strictly speaking, neither is the worship, nor the loving service of God, self-annihilation. Is it not safe to say that if Christians could but rise by the divine Spirit's help to the height of loving their neighbours as themselves, the Day of the Lord would be almost in sight?

The above given quotation from Measure for Measure is used by Professor George Harris in his work on Moral Evolution (page 141) and readers are referred to his thorough discussion of self-realization and altruism in Chapter VI.

None of the Church's services take us mentally *abroad* more effectually than the one which falls on September 29th, Saint Michael and All Angels. It emphasizes a truth in which natural science makes it each year more natural to believe. The air and the soil are now known to contain millions upon millions, and millions of millions, of living creatures. The wonders of the microscope minister to faith, as truly as do the wonders of the telescope,—that is to say, where "the will to believe" already exists. The innumerable hosts of animate beings, large and small, of different grades of strength and intelligence, all in their way made for a practical purpose,—*ministering,*—cause the existence of multitudes of angels to appear the more probable. They also enhance in our thoughts the appropriateness of that majestic Old Testament title of God, "the Lord of hosts": "Bless ye the Lord, ye his angels that excel in strength, that do his commandments, hearkening unto the voice of his word. Bless ye the Lord, all ye his hosts: ye ministers of his, that do his pleasure." Theology and angelology are intertwined in the Scriptures almost like two strands in a cord. To untwine and separate them as seen in patriarchal and later history, in our Lord's earthly life, in the life and work of the Apostles, in The Revelation, is in effect to destroy the record.

The Holy Ghost it was who as a Creator-Spirit, accomplishing the Father's will, created the angels free, as man afterwards was made free, and to His *grief* also it was that certain of them abused the noble gift, and by ambition fell. No wonder is it that this led to "war in heaven," as pride and ambition have been a cause of war on earth; or that fallen angels, jealous of man in his innocence, should seek to tempt him likewise into sin; and no wonder that the good angels, beholding a great plan of divine redemption unfolding in human history, should not merely desire, as St. Peter said—(1st Pet. 1 : 12), to "look into" it, but to have a hand in it, and that, as our Lord intimated (Mat. 18 : 10), angels of high rank and near to the heavenly throne were put in charge of Christ's "little ones," children in age, or children in understanding, and morally. The Collect which speaks of the services of angels and men being "constituted in a wonderful order," and prays that they may indeed "succour and defend us," is a Gregorian Collect, and probably composed by Gregory; since he preached a notable sermon on the wonderful order, and on the different ranks of the angels, as made evident in the Scriptures.

Dean Alford's suggestion is valuable, that "angels, having only the contrast between good and evil, without the power of conversion from sin to righteousness, when witnesses of such a turning to God would long to penetrate the knowledge of the means by which it is brought about."

The real wonder is, that men who are watched over and as it were waited upon by angels, and who being unlike them in certain aspects are so like them in others, should not merely care little to "look into" their life-problem, but even question their existence. The Bible being so full of allusions to them, it seems only natural that men should long to "penetrate" their secret. Gregory does not seem to have possessed a speculative or specially theological mind, but rather a religious and practical mind; and thoughtful, prayerful contemplation of his theme can only increase our love and gratitude to God.

This can but be one of the subjects to which we may apply Bishop Westcott's assertion, that the serious study of doctrine is the noblest exercise of reason, and Professor Curteis's thought, that only *faithless* reason is not to be trusted. Certainly we may learn humility from these mighty angels who devote themselves to guarding and ministering to Christ's little ones, and learn from them to shun that uncomfortable and dangerous fault, envy; for that Christ "took not on Him the nature of angels," but human nature, and that we to whom they minister, and in whose behalf they even wage war with wicked angels, have been made but a little lower than they, and through union with the Divine shall at last be "crowned with glory and honour," might stir envy in beings less confirmed in magnanimity and holy submission.

Good angels could tell much to make men surer of virtue being its own reward; and bad angels much of sin, and envy especially, being its own quick punishment.

CHURCH ARCHITECTURE

And thou shalt make a vail of blue, and purple and scarlet, * * * and the vail shall divide unto you between the holy place and the most holy.—Exod. 26 : 31, 33.

Your iniquities have separated between you and your God.—Isa. 59 : 2.

I am the way.—John 14 : 6.

By his own blood he entered into the holy place, having obtained eternal redemption for us.—Heb. 9 : 12.

The vail of the temple was rent in twain from the top to the bottom.—Matt. 27 : 51.

Who made there (by his one oblation of himself once for all offered) a full, perfect and sufficient sacrifice, oblation, and satisfaction for the sins of the whole world.—Communion Office.

Having therefore, brethren, boldness to enter into the holiest by the blood of Jesus, by a new and living way which he hath consecrated for us through the vail, that is to say, his flesh; and having an high priest over the house of God; let us draw near with a true heart, having full assurance of faith.—Heb. 10 : 19–22.

Ye also as living stones are built up a spiritual house, an holy priesthood, to offer up spiritual sacrifices, acceptable to God by Jesus Christ.—1st Pet. 2 : 5.

The term "frozen music," applied as we have already noted to architecture, is not without meaning; and yet the dominant thought and motive in genuine catholic and Christian architecture, namely man's drawing near to the Father through the Self-offering of His dear Son in human nature, is of all warm truths to be laid to our cold hearts the very warmest.

Writers on the subject say that, whereas architecture had its origin in religious feelings and observances, its noblest monuments among the nations of antiquity being temples to the gods, the pointed arch in particular, invented or introduced in the twelfth century, owed its diffusion and progress to the Christian religion. Moreover, they say that the idea is by many thought to have been derived from the interlacing of the branches of trees in the forest. It is not difficult to accept the suggestion, for one who has himself experienced Bryant's feeling beautifully expressed in "A Forest Hymn." Do not those influences to which he gives the name *sacred*,—influences of "the stilly twilight" and "the gray old trunks mingling their mossy boughs"; of the sound of "the invisible breath which sways all their green tops," stealing over one, and bowing

> "His spirit with the thought of boundless power,
> And inaccessible majesty,"

frequently come to the Churchman in sanctuaries which are truly churchlike? Together with these come other impressions, of which Whittier has sung, suggested by our Lord's promise to be with even the two or three gathered together in His Name:

> "In one desire
> The *blending* lines of prayer aspire;"

and again,

> "He findeth not who seeks his own,
> The soul is lost that's saved alone."

Returning to the more strictly architectural suggestions, pointed arches suggest many raised hands folded in prayer, as truly as they do boughs interlaced in the deep woods. And often the idea must have come to men, that long naves, like those in our churches, leading to a generous Chancel and the Sacrarium beyond, with its altar-table and bare cross, constantly repeat to the eyes and the heart the story of the Incarnation and the consummating Act of the Atonement followed by the Resurrection and Ascension. Christ was, and is, the Way. The open rood-screen, if there be any at all, continually reminds us that through His flesh, that is, His humanity, perfected in suffering obedience, the Way is now open. The ancient vail,— the vail of our sins,—being taken away, the divine majesty is no longer "inaccessible." We "have boldness and access with confidence by the faith of Him,"—can not only *see* through but *go* through, as it were, into the "heavenly places," and enjoy already in this life fellowship with the Father and with His Son, in the Spirit.

A perfect Church intelligently interpreted will be, like sacred music so interpreted, one of the Spirit's noblest auxiliaries to faith. It preaches eloquently saving truths which at times might otherwise not be proclaimed at all.

THE TRANSFIGURATION OF CHRIST

And Jesus taketh with him Peter and James and John, and bringeth them up into a high mountain apart by themselves: and he was transfigured before them.—Mark 9 : 2.

We wait for a Saviour, the Lord Jesus Christ, who shall fashion anew the body of our humiliation, that it may be conformed to the body of his glory.—Phil. 3 : 21.

It is sown in weakness; it is raised in power; it is sown a natural body; it is raised a spiritual body.—1st Cor. 15 : 43, 44.

When Christ, who is our life, shall be manifested, then shall ye also be manifested with him in glory.—Col. 3 : 4.

Then shall the righteous shine forth as the sun in the kingdom of their Father. He that hath ears to hear, let him hear.— Matt. 13 : 43.

Ascension was as much the natural way for Jesus as death is for us. He might ascend with the two who talked with Him. But to ascend now would be to ascend without us. Down below on the plain He sees mankind, crushed beneath the weight of sin and death. Shall He abandon them? He cannot ascend unless He carry them with Him; and in order to do this He braves the other issue (exodus) which He can only accomplish at Jerusalem.—Godet.

The Transfiguration may be regarded as designed to strengthen the hearts, first, of those who witnessed it, and then of all those to whom their witness came. But in addition to these it has ever been contemplated in the Church as a prophecy of the glory which the saints shall have in the resurrection. As was the body of Christ on the Mount so shall their bodies be.— Archbishop Trench.

While the Feast of the Transfiguration would be in place in Lent, near the Holy Week, because our Lord was strengthened by it, in the Spirit, to undergo His sufferings, and the faith of His disciples strengthened to witness them, we cannot but see, that it is still more emphatically in place in this Season. For it was the Spirit's function to give to the Son of Man already then an *earnest* of the glory that should be His after His Ascension; as it would belong to the Spirit to raise Him from the dead, and to make Him forever glorious as Man in heaven. Moreover, Christ is only "the first-fruits" of the great harvest of Humanity redeemed;

and it will be the Spirit's joy to fulfil the promise of the Scripture, and "fashion anew the body of our humiliation, that it may be conformed to the body of Christ's glory" in the great Resurrection Day.

It is plain that the Epiphany Collect does not bring out the entire truth and object of our praying, in the phrase "fruition of thy glorious Godhead"; since our Saviour's manhood, as the scene on the holy mount shows, is glorious, and the saints must have complete fruition of that. Equally true is it, that the Collect for Transfiguration Day, beautiful as it is, falls short in this point, that redeemed mankind will be privileged not merely to "behold," but also to share the King's "beauty." The Bride shall herself be clothed with the splendour that is His, through her possession of His inward life in the Spirit. Hymn 167 in our Book is one of those ancient hymns which exhibit in a simple and real way the beliefs and hopes of the early Christians. Gregory (Moral. xxxii. 6, quoted by Trench) has, "In transfiguratione quid aliud quam resurrectionis ultima gloria nunciatur?" Leo the Great has a similar passage. The Greek service-books reflect the same thought; and the first and third verses of the venerable hymn which we sing,—or may sing, if we will,—are as follows:

> "O wondrous type! O vision fair
> Of glory that the Church shall share,
> Which Christ upon the mountain shows,
> Where brighter than the sun He glows!

> "With shining face and bright array,
> Christ deigns to manifest to-day
> What glory shall be theirs above,
> Who joy in God with perfect love."

Our Lord was evidently transfigured not by an outward and reflected splendour, but by an inward one. The glory shone from within, and it was the glory of a perfect and a triumphant Manhood. Now it is most instructive to read St. Paul's reference (in Phil. 3 : 21) to the "change" that is coming to Christians, in connection with what he has said before regarding "perfection," and pressing "toward the mark"; it is illuminating to study St. Peter's description (2d Pet. 1 : 16–18) of the scene on "the holy mount" in connection with his previous words concerning escaping "the corruption that is in the world," not being "barren nor unfruitful in the knowledge of Christ," not being spiritually *nearsighted* in respect to Christian purity, and making "the calling and election sure." For so we learn the practical bearing of Christ's transformation on our transformation, and that with us too it will be from within outward. By the Spirit's help we are, as it were, to glorify ourselves. There are moments in men's lives,—who has not witnessed such?—when their countenances shine with a light distinctly spiritual, coming from within, and transfiguring their faces. These are figures of that better thing which shall come to the people of the Lord in the day of the Lord; when, as it reads in the Book of Wisdom (5 : 16), "The righteous shall receive the crown of royal dignity, and the diadem of beauty from the Lord's hand."

Ours will be a transfigured and glorified Humanity, the "spiritual body", which is but the natural body "changed." The flower is a transparent, glorified, leaf; and the Christ-life when it flowers out in us will be the self-same manhood with which we were born, renewed, changed, and made more lovable through our new birth

20

and development in Christ, in the Spirit. And hereby we know that our transfiguration is assured, by the Spirit's work actually going on in us. They are blest who, recognizing the process thus going on, can say with St. Peter, not "we shall be," but "we are, partakers,"—"I, who *am* also a partaker of the glory that shall be revealed." (1st Pet. 5 : 1.) When such is our case, we can better realize the rich, twofold, meaning of "the Voice from the excellent glory." For "this is my beloved Son in whom I am well pleased" is a voice for us, as truly as the transfiguration is for us. In fact the latter will be the consequence of the former. We shall be obedient sons, honoured and glorified, shining forth as the sun in the Father's kingdom.

Not far from three centuries ago Thomas Case in England spoke after the same fashion of the resurrection. Such glorious things were spoken by God of it as it were daring presumption to have reported or believed, if He had not said them. And they that would secure themselves an interest in the glory which shall be put upon the saints' bodies in the resurrection should labour to experience this beatifical transfiguration first in their souls, on this side of the grave.

"It is good for us to be here," Simon Peter said, and good it was, in itself and in its results. But the final transformation of humanity for which the life here, and that in Paradise, are the preparation, will be "far better." What that unending future with Christ in the Spirit shall be for mankind has not "entered into the heart" of prophet or of poet, nor has any one dreamed it. This we can say, that "God is not a man that He should lie" to us in the day dreams, or in the night dreams.

It will be a glorious new existence socially, a great, new, human brotherhood. Of this also the foundations are being laid here by the Spirit of Union and of Fellowship. We cannot be saved alone by ourselves. Whittier's word must not be forgotten:

"The soul is lost, that's saved alone,"

St. Peter's word must not, concerning seeing only "what is near," and one needs to add to this, because spiritual near-sightedness and spiritual far-sightedness have equally unfortunate results. Many plan and labour merely for the present life, being "blind" to the things beyond. Again others "see afar off," and reflect on heavenly joys, while they have neither eyes to see, nor ears to hear of, present obligations. How many make much of the Communion of Saints in Paradise, who make little of the Communion of Saints in Christ's Church Militant! To pray for and minister to the saints who are here is the more pressing duty, and faithfully performed it will bear richest fruit in Paradise and in Heaven.

In all these spheres, the Holy Spirit is personally, deeply, interested. It is His affair to bring to pass the complete transfiguration of our race, of which the scene on the Mount was the type and prophecy. As Dr. Downer has said:

"The work of the Holy Spirit entered upon a new phase at the Coming of Christ to redeem mankind. It will enter upon a still more glorious, and a final, stage at the Coming of Christ to receive His Church. For this the Spirit of Grace is preparing souls on earth and souls in Paradise. The Second Advent will be the *terminus a quo* of this stage of the Holy Spirit's work, and eternity will be the *terminus ad quem;* for we cannot conceive of a time when He will cease to perfect, to bless, to teach, and to glorify the saved. Thus, while complete in one sense, the Spirit's work will be progressive and eternal in another" (page 331).

GREGORY AND THE LATIN CHURCH

While gathering and reflecting upon the material for this volume it has been borne in upon me more and more forcibly, how great is the debt of Western Christendom as a whole to the Latin Church, and in particular to the first Gregory. It is an obligation never to be ignored. Dean Church's fine tribute to the "one old man far away" has been given in the section on Missions, but the subject merits further treatment.

It is not a debt of allegiance. The right of Rome to this allegiance, as ecclesiastical history clearly proves, was resisted from the first. But the obligation otherwise is a different matter, and is large; it ought to be an easy and pleasant duty to acknowledge it. It is in good measure an obligation to the noblest and most saintly bishop Rome has ever had, to whom more than to any man except St. Paul the West owes, under God, its Church life. A. H. Hore writes ("History of the Church Catholic," page 289):

"Augustine, in spite of the fact that he was not a great man, nor a successful missionary, for which he was too narrow-minded and unconciliatory, laid the foundation, as Bede says, '*nobly*,' of the English Church. He renewed the union which the English conquest had broken with Western Christendom. He founded the See of Canterbury and from him the Church of England derives the succession of its bishops. He laid the foundation of the political unity of England." He writes (page 338): "England never forgot its debt of gratitude to Rome, how Gregory had sent St. Augustine to found, and another Roman bishop had sent Archbishop Theodore to organize, the National Church."

In counting up the items of our indebtedness to the Latin Church in the early times,—the times of its spiritual vigor and genuine catholicity,—we go back naturally to three eminent bishops of Rome, to whom in fact we all, without thinking of it, go back every Sunday and all the days, offering prayers which they composed. The vigor and the spirituality of the pure Gospel truth were in those men; in Leo, in Gelasius, in Gregory. The Collects coming to us from their Sacramentaries, "live and move and have their being," Dean Goulburn said, "in the very atmosphere of Holy Scripture. Always in the centre of these brief petitions there's a truth, or thought,—and a fundamental one,—which is distinctly evangelical; and associated with it we find a desire, a need, which is of the atmosphere of the time when the prayer originated."

Their days were days of storm and stress such as the world has scarcely ever seen. The tribes of the North were beginning to pour down upon the decaying Roman Empire. The period was close at hand of which Dean Church wrote: "For more than three centuries it seemed as if the world and human society had been hopelessly wrecked, without prospect or hope of escape." It is true that in these Collects there is no sign of absolute hopelessness. A great spiritual beauty in them is the sense of reliance on God; but when we come continually upon phrases like these: "The chances and changes of this mortal life; The fear of our enemies; Assaults of our enemies; That thy Church may serve thee in all godly quietness; May not fear the power of any adversaries; That our hearts may surely there be fixed where true joys are to be found"; if we know the history, we almost think to hear Attila, and Genseric, and the Lombard Agilulph shouting at Rome's gates. Pestilence and earthquake added to the fear. There were heresies and schisms threatening the Church's inward life. There was the radical and widespread error which struck at the Scripture truth of man's dependence upon the mercy and grace of God for power, not only to please God, but even to believe in Him. There was the error in relation to the Son of God our Saviour, that He had not become in truth our Brother, which took away, not only His power of human sympathy with us, but that which is the very *fons et origo* in us of the new filial obedience and capacity for fellowship with Christ and the Father.

Errors like these were "adversaries" more dangerous to the Church and to mankind than Goths or Huns or Lombards, and that for which we have to thank God and the Spirit of God, is that able, valiant and saintly men were providentially raised up not merely to pray against the adversaries, in the words the Church now uses, and to teach others to pray, but to go forth themselves to meet them. Leo and Gelasius were such men, and above all Gregory. If ever there have been men who had greatness thrust upon them, these were such. Greatness was thrust upon the Latin Church almost from the beginning. Long before Roman bishops became Popes,—and neither Leo, Gelasius, nor Gregory were Popes in the historic sense of that title,—the Churches of Christ around them, by appeals to them to settle disputes and questions of authority and render assistance of every kind, made them Popes practically. Temporal power came to them by the breaking down of the empire. When secular Rome had no longer the military strength to encounter mighty conquerors like Attila, nor the address to meet them otherwise, the duty fell upon those who sat in the high places of spiritual power. Gibbon calls Gregory I "the father of his country."

Wonderfully did they meet, and did the Church as a whole meet, the manifold emergency of the hour; and the Latin Church as the most widespread and influential of all the Churches, was compelled to be ever in the front and at the head. It fell heir naturally to the prestige of the Roman name. Roman Christians, Roman bishops and clergy, would naturally possess the Roman virility to influence, to manage, and to govern. And Gregory, the greatest saint and bishop of his age, was the greatest Roman of them all as a leader of men. As Milman says ("Latin Christianity," Vol. II, page 44), "he united in himself every qualification and endowment which could command the veneration and attachment of Rome and of his age. He was of a senatorial family. * * * A pope was his ancestor in the fourth degree. To his noble descent was added considerable wealth." It would lead us much too far if we tried to name even in outline the ecclesiastical and other tasks which devolved upon him, and which he discharged with amazing energy, skill and Christian devotion. "Not from his station alone," writes Milman, "but by the acknowledgement of the admiring world, he was intellectually as well as spiritually the great model of his age."

It has been said that humility is the foundation of real greatness. Certainly our blessed Saviour saved us all by His "great humility"; and the man who perhaps more than any other saved Christianity, humanly speaking, from being wiped off the Western continent was distinguished by humility. In speaking of the conversion of the Lombards, in 599 A. D., when "in their very hour of conquest, he [Gregory] was subduing the conqueror," Milman says: "It is most singular that the influence of Gregory was obtained by means not only mild and legitimate, but purely religious."

"What then," writes Milman in another connection, "was this Christianity by which Gregory ruled the world? Not merely the speculative and dogmatic theology, but the popular, vital, active Christianity which was working in the heart of man, and the dominant motive of his actions, as far as they were affected by religion."

Gregory was a natural lover of puns, and the puns he made over the beautiful English captives in the slave market were not his first or his last. He has been faulted for it, but would that all punsters had a hundredth part of the soul-sympathy and consecration of spirit with which he contemplated those Angli from Deira, and, comparing them to angels, longed and for fourteen years cherished the purpose, to rescue them himself from the wrath to come. He had actually started for that distant mission when called back, against his will, that he might be consecrated bishop of Rome; and at the first favorable moment he inaugurated the mission of Augustine and his brother monks, which resulted in bringing the ancient and then feeble

Church of Britain in touch again with the Christianity of Europe.

It can never be said that any true member of the Body of Christ is dead, or beyond restoration to health; and the Church of Britain, originating in the sub-apostolic age, was still in parts very much alive. Driven to the North and West by the heathen invaders who occupied the remainder of the land, there were still points in Kent and elsewhere in which the old Church lived on. When Augustine came to Canterbury, did not King Ethelbert allow him the use of an ancient Christian Church, the little Church of St. Martin outside the city? Is it not "upon the ruins of a building used by Christians in Britain before the heathen Northmen had swept over the country," that the noble Canterbury Cathedral now stands? When Augustine arrived on the scene, but ten years had elapsed since the old Church had given up the contest and retired. These and other equally interesting historical facts of the kind go to prove the antiquity of our branch of the Church, and its primitive independence.

On the other hand, those old ruins under the new Christ Church, as Augustine called his cathedral, were a sign of the generally deplorable condition of Christianity in the land. The little remainder of the old British Church took refuge in Wales, as the early Christians in the Holy Land had fled to Pella. Because they were weak, and therefore afraid, or wanting in missionary love were cold-hearted toward their conquerors, as the ancient historians Gildas and Bede assert, "they never preached the faith to the Saxons or English who dwelt amongst them."

In this lack of missionary zeal and power we note the contrast between them and Gregory, and the early Latin Church upon whose character and policy he put his mark for centuries to come.   The Church and the man are thus named together, as in one breath, in the feeling that alike in his relation to our mother Church and ourselves, and to the whole Church of the West of which he was the greatest bishop, justice has not been done to Gregory as a Christian, and a worthy instrument in the Spirit's hand.   Rightly speaking, to talk of him is to talk of the most powerful member of Christ's Church Universal in its best days; and the converse is true; to speak of her in that period of relatively genuine catholicity, is to speak of him. None can realize this so well as we who Sunday after Sunday pray the prayers he prayed.   Whoever composed the article on Gregory I in the Encyclopedia Britannica (Ninth Edition), it would seem can scarcely have been one who habitually said "Amen" to those Collects, and realized the sincerity and zeal for Christ which were in him.

How sincere his love for Christ and for man was, and how far the missionary motive in him was from being either a wish to aggrandize himself or the Roman episcopate, or patriarchate, as represented by him, we might easily forget, thinking of the other Gregories who followed him, especially the Seventh. Certain historians and writers on the Prayer Book, Milman, Hore, Robertson, Goulburn, have not forgotten.   They have made the distinction, and pointed out the difference.

Gregory had a Roman mind and soul, an imperial mind.   He had a kingly personality, was in reality as much a king as ever Hildebrand was; yet a "king uncrowned," who never desired to be crowned. As Milman shows, "he became in act and influence, if not in avowed authority, a temporal sovereign." But this was "forced upon him by the purest motives, if not by absolute necessity." There was no thought of making himself more than the Patriarch of the West, and he addressed the four other Patriarchs as his equals and co-ordinate rulers of the Church. Anything else than this, he said, would be *blasphemous*, "a diabolical usurpation."

"St. Gregory, the Great," writes Hore (page 290), "by the gentleness and tenderness of his character, and by his humility and earnestness, stands out as one of the greatest of the Popes. But he was no Pope in the modern acceptation of the term, and the religion of the Rome over which he presided, and that of mediæval and modern Rome, are two almost essentially different religions." He abjured a *universal* episcopate. Having indeed a full inherent belief in the dignity and power of his position, which for two hundred years had, to be sure, been advancing its pretensions, and no doubt willing to magnify his office, he nevertheless acted in the spirit of the General Councils, and denounced anyone who claimed to be universal Bishop over the whole Church as 'the precursor of Antichrist.'"

That is to say, Gregory was truly Catholic and Christian. It has been to keep this clear before our minds that he has been referred to throughout as a bishop, and not a pope, and that the Church of which he was Patriarch and which he helped to keep pure with the catholicity of the Apostles themselves, has been mentioned as the Latin Church.

Such was the powerful missionary leader, and such the Church, that having saved Western Christianity as a whole from ruin, by the barbarian invasions, and saved the barbarians themselves by making Christians of them, went forth to accomplish a like doubly beautiful work in Britain. It required faith, Christ-like courage, and self-sacrifice to do it. Augustine and his monks, although disciplined and fortified by the Western monastic training,—a very different affair from the Eastern monastery system,—would never have had the courage or the wisdom to achieve it without the constant backing and careful direction of Gregory's masterly mind. They would have either given it up, or gone forward as they did, only to fail.

It was no easy matter to accomplish the necessary union with the ancient British Church. It was a still more formidable undertaking to win the English people to Christ. Difficult is it for us their descendants to take in the truth about them; namely, that they were harder to deal with than the Goths and the Huns, Vandals, and Lombards, who had thundered at Rome's gates and come near to making a complete wreck of Western civilization and destroying European Christianity. But so it seems to have been. Saxons, Anglo-Saxons, or English, "they were," says Hore, "of all the barbarous hordes which dismembered the Roman Empire, the most barbarous."

In a former chapter the Holy Spirit has been spoken of as the Soul of the Church, and the Spirit of Missions; we have seen that He was so thought of in the early days of Christianity. That He must have been so regarded by the great Gregory, and every missionary movement organized by him have been committed to the Spirit's guidance, seems especially likely in view of the place given to Him in the Eucharistic Services of those times. It must have been owing to Gregory's special devotion to the personal Spirit that the legend arose in later times that the Holy Ghost in the shape of a dove had often been seen hovering above him as he wrote; and the Roman Church has constantly permitted Gregory to be represented with the Holy Spirit, as a dove, floating over his head.

J. Brierley, author of "Aspects of the Spiritual," speaking in his pungent way of Religious Biography, says:

"The word 'saint' is the greatest and richest word in our vocabulary. In the darkest ages the saints shine out, exhibiting among surrounding barbarisms the overwhelming power of sheer goodness. Always in those times the warrior, the savage, bows before the saint." And he adds: "Our good Protestants need to enlarge their view here, and to rid themselves of the idea that the Christian life went underground at the close of the Apostolic age, only to re-emerge at the Reformation. It has, they ought to remember, been running all the time in a strong and glorious current." Giving a list of names, Ignatius, Polycarp, Justin Martyr, Gregory of Naziansen, St. Francis, and others, he asks: "Why do not our pastors in their pulpit teaching deal more fully with these records? There is no richer vein. Are not these lives part of the Divine revelation?"

I say "Amen" to this, and if not mistaken in my view of Gregory I would "enlarge" the list with his name, as a nobler one than that of Gregory Naziansen and meaning more to English-speaking Christians of every name. What has been said, if true, is more emphatically true when our view of Christianity is widened with the larger meaning which our Lord seems sometimes to have given to the phrase, "Kingdom of Heaven." As Dr. Archibald Robertson wrote:

"Our Saviour's teaching on the subject is closely connected with convictions and hopes which He so used as to give a new meaning to life, and open a new direction to human aspiration and effort. The Kingdom of God in His hands is a many-sided conception."

Influenced by this wider conception, I would not leave the theme, Gregory and the Latin Church of his day in its relation to Western Christianity, without inviting attention to Dean Church's intensely interesting lectures on Some Influences of Christianity upon National Character, in the book entitled "Gifts of Civilization." After speaking of the decay and fall of the old Roman civilization, and the growth out of its ruins of a new one infinitely more vigorous, the new force, or element, or aspect of the world, or assemblage of ideas, which proved able to make of society what Roman loftiness of heart, Roman sagacity, Roman patience, Roman strength was not able to make of it, and asking what that force was, he answers, as we expect him to do:

"It is as clear and certain a fact of history that the coming in of Christianity was accompanied by new moral elements in society, inextinguishable, widely operative, never destroyed, though apparently at times crushed and paralyzed, as it is certain that Christian nations have made on the whole more progress in the wise ordering of human life than was made in the most advanced civilization of the times before Christianity."

This truth in its many aspects,—aspects which we must think of as latent in St. Paul's prophetic phrase,"the length and breadth and depth and height,"—Dean Church sets before us in a wealth of argument and illustration, and a beauty of expression, which make me long to reproduce it entire on these pages. Rome had put the world under obligation by its gift of Jurisprudence, and its strong conceptions of citizenship and patriotism. Christianity appropriates these, enlarges their scope, and invests them with holier sanctions. Taking up the subject of its influence on national character, and first upon Greek character, he then shows the debt of the Latin races to Christianity.

Remarking first, that, although there has been since the fall of the Empire "so large an infusion of Teutonic blood into the populations which inherited what was then called Gaul, and the name by which they are now known is a Teutonic one, yet Latin influence has proved the prevailing and the dominant one." He shows that there was in the Italians and French "a new development and life of the affections and emotional part of our nature," evidenced in their character, and literature, and art. "The very staple of their character was altered." Passing by the unfolding of his argument in this delightful and instructive lecture, we come to what concerns us more nearly, The Influence of Christianity upon the Teutonic Races, including the English.

"No one then dreamed that these were to be the destroyers and supplanters of the ancient civilization, still less that they were the fathers of a nobler and grander world than any that history had yet known; that it was a race which was to assert its chief and lordly place in Europe, to occupy half of a new-found world, to inherit India, to fill the islands of unknown seas; to be the craftsmen, the traders, the colonists, the explorers of the world." Conquerors, heroes, statesmen, men of blood and iron,—nay great rulers and mighty kings would come from it. He talks of Shakspere and Bacon, of Leibnitz and Goethe, of English courts of justice, of English and German workshops of thought and art, English and German homes, English and German religious feeling and earnestness.

"While there was in this race of the North a foundation for this splendid new development in humanity, the Christian Church,—more particularly, the Latin Church, which had in a wonderful, almost miraculous way succeeded in place and power to the Latin Empire,—under God wrought the mighty change. A chief subject for wonder is that Christianity came not to them, as it had come to the people of the South, in the hour of their weakness and anxiety; it came in the hour of triumph. It subdued and brought to the foot of the Cross the very conquerors of the Latin Empire in the height of their success. It awakened their conscience and humbled their pride, and taught them the secrets of spiritual truth, and fear of future retribution, inspired a deeper, truer manliness, and a sincerer love of truth and reverence for all that was most noble and pure just when they had their feet on the neck of prostrate Europe."

The Dean shows that it was the Latin clergy who were the Spirit's chief instrument in achieving this astonishing result. He quotes a passage from Guizot's Lectures, which brings out not the fact merely, but a chief reason for it; namely the unity of the Church in that period. "From the fourth to the thirteenth century," says Guizot, "it is the Church which always marches in the front rank of civilization. I must call your attention to a fact which stands at the head of all others, and characterizes the Christian Church in general—a fact which, so to speak, has decided its destiny. This fact is the unity of the Church. * * * Wonderful phenomenon! * * * from the bosom of the most frightful disorder the world has ever seen has arisen the largest, purest idea, perhaps, which ever drew men together— the idea of a spiritual society."

It was the Church of Gregory, and of the Gregorian age, that accomplished, under the Spirit of Unity, the spiritual phenomenon which Guizot described so eloquently. Not our morals, our ideas, our home and national life, our literature and our art merely, but our language bear witness to the profound and wide-reaching influence of the Latin Church. It is remarkably so in regard to our religious words, these every-day words, on our tongues as much as in our Prayer Books and religious literature. These are largely of Latin derivation. They have come to us with the Church and the Prayer Book, rather than through the English Bible, which is principally Anglo-Saxon.

We speak of the *Sacrament,* and of the *Communion,* of the *saints;* stand and say, "I believe in the *Holy Catholic Church*"; utter a sentence like this: "I am *convinced* that there must have been *deep piety* in Gregory, and Leo, and Gelasius; much of *personal religion* in the Mediæval Church; there is perhaps as much, if not more, of it in the Roman Church of to-day, far as we judge it to have fallen from original catholicity."

Do we know, or look into our dictionaries to ascertain, that while *holy* and *deep* and *fallen* and *believe* are Anglo-Saxon words and *Catholic* and *Church* are Greek, not only *ascertain*, and *dictionaries*, and *original*, but *piety*, *personal*, *religion*, and *saints*, *convinced*, *communion*, and *sacrament*, are derived from the Latin. Like the Collects, the Gregorian Chants, the Creeds, and our heritage of pure catholic teaching, these familiar words have been directly or indirectly brought to us by the Church of those early days. They talk to us, if we will let them, of those times, and of our manifold indebtedness.

They enrich our religious conceptions as truly as they dignify and beautify our speech and literature. The word "Sacrament," meaning originally the oath of fidelity taken by each Roman soldier at his enlistment, stands now for the Christian's baptismal pledge of loving obedience to his Redeemer and Lord, and for the Eucharist in which he renews and confirms that pledge.

What now of the decline and fall of the Latin Church from its early spiritual ideals, and the main causes of it? One of our Lord's most significant words was, "My kingdom is not of this world, else would my servants fight." How early in its life did the most important Church of His Spirit's planting forget to live by that word! The history of the Papacy is one long story of struggle for worldly eminence and power, by means of worldly and even anti-Christian expedients.

Already in Gregory's day the thought and the desire of a world-wide empire for Rome was in the air, and in the heart of Roman bishops. It was chiefly in his superiority to this thought and motive that Gregory towered above his age, and the victory of his apparently sincere and unconscious humility was the greater, in that he was by birth and every way a typical Roman.

"The great secret of Rome's success," writes Hore, (page 337), "was its marvellous organizing power," and in this quality Gregory was exceeded by none. Hore adds, "there can be little doubt that in such unsettled and troublous times a common centre of unity, especially when the fountain-head was pure, was of the first importance to the spread of Christianity." This is true, and in that unity we must with gratitude recognize the mind and will of the Spirit. But the moment that concentration of force and influence began to be acquired and made secure through worldly means, the fountain-head ceased to be pure. Not only did the supremacy of Rome, as the same writer says, "sap the independence of National Churches," it tended to sap the spiritual vitality of the Latin Church itself. In that same wonderful power of organization, a distinctly Latin gift, there lay an immense temptation, and when "the conception of the Kingdom of God as an omnipotent Church, in the form indispensable to its practical effect, of papal absolutism, was in large measure realized in the Middle Ages," the temptation had been completely yielded to.

The Church had received then a next to vital injury. Gregory VII, a very different Gregory from the Gregory of four and a half centuries earlier, "confronted by force and statecraft, played his game with vigor and skill, and there was a gain in immediate power; but the spiritual force of the Church was immeasurably lowered." It is Bishop Archibald Robertson who speaks ("Regnum Dei," page 257). He has shown (page 101) that our Lord began a reign on earth in which He was represented by a visible society presided over by an Invisible Spirit. What His own Eye and Hand and Word had been to His people in the days of His flesh, His Pentecostal Spirit would be. This Spirit Tertullian referred to as the unseen Vicar of Christ. The only "positive" law bequeathed to this divine Society was the rite of admission to it, holy Baptism. The invisible guidance, we learn from the New Testament history, "was realized in the collective action of the Society, indwelt by the Holy Ghost."

Needless is it to point out how the intention of Christ was, so to say, thwarted, and the spiritual conception of His Church obscured, if not destroyed, when Roman bishops,—Innocent II was the first,— took to themselves the office and the very name of the Vicar of Jesus Christ. The appropriation to themselves of political, as a means of spiritual, power, for the good of the Church and the salvation of souls, was in fact spiritually fatal. It struck at the life of the Church, and of men's souls. Ever since that, the papal authority and policy, as sustained and forwarded by the Jesuits particularly, in a system which exalts submission to such an external authority to the supreme, all important place in ethics, has struck at the root of the gospel conception of filial, free obedience. We find a new legalism, as bad as the old pharisaic legalism, lifted to the very highest position spiritually by a Church which claims the homage of all mankind.

In place of a unity created and fostered by the Holy Spirit of Unity, we behold a false external unity compelled by fear; and when humanity, enlightened by the Spirit, but not always therefore perfectly guided by Him, will no longer submit, but attempts to throw off such an unreal, unspiritual unity, in the Reformation, we have, as might be expected, what Bishop Robertson terms "an irreconcilable diversity in a multitude of protesting sects."

Enough, however,—possibly more than enough,—on this darker side. Ought we not to look at Christian Churches, as well as individual Christians, as it were, through the eyes of God,—to use St. Paul's phrase, "in the very heart of Christ"? The Latin Church is still Christian, holding, with additions which we deplore, the Faith of the Ages. It is the same Latin Church which won Europe to Christ, converted our fierce English forefathers, and by the hands of Gregory and Augustine has passed on to us large portions of our catholic heritage.

In the time between *our* Gregory and Gregory VII, which we are accustomed to speak of as the dark ages, there was much of light, from the Spirit of Light. There were beautiful examples of piety, noble hymns written, and works of Christian charity done, in the power of the Spirit.

Precisely as catholic-minded, Protestants long since learned to distinguish between the Rome of these days and the Rome of fourteen centuries ago, we ought to distinguish between Ultramontanism and the faith and practice of the Latin Church as a whole to-day. Those were striking words of Bishop Potter in 1898:

"The enormous audacity which in our generation has added new dogmas to the historic creeds of Christendom, and the very novel claims of authority under which this has been done, have awakened a far wider challenge of Ultramontanism, even among its own followers, than its leaders have been willing to recognize. These cite it before the bar of history, and to that bar it must go."

In the Roman Church as we know her in our own land to-day there are,—it goes without saying,—many signs of spiritual consecration. The funeral oration of the Archbishop of St. Louis upon Archbishop Ryan of Philadelphia must have been in this aspect a revelation, and a cause of thanksgiving, to many non-Roman Christians.

"Prayer ardent opens heaven," wrote Young. Prayer, we are assured,

> "Moves the arm that moves the world,"

but to feel already a little stirring, and see heaven's gates ajar in answer to our prayers, encourages us to pray more.

There are two "subjects" of petition which there is reason to believe that many, even among those who pray fervently, pass by unheeded, namely, the conversion of the Jews and the conversion of the Roman Church to its primitive catholicity.

These two are naturally associated in the mind of one who recalls Milman's words regarding Gregory's just and humane treatment of the Jews, and his desire to win them to the true Messiah. But there is another reason for thus associating them. The Jews were as the "chosen people" a special instrument of the Spirit for the salvation of the world. The Church Universal, it has been truly said, is really identical with,—a continuation of,—the Church of the Old Testament. Not only was the Redeemer of mankind born of a Jewish mother, in Bethlehem of Judea: the first preachers of His Gospel, and founders, with Him, of His New Testament Church were children of Abraham. The Jews were divinely elected to proclaim His saving health to all nations; and had they as a people obeyed the calling, we must think the world would have been won for Messiah the Prince long ago.

The Latin Church was in a somewhat like manner divinely fitted and chosen,—maybe the more so because the Jewish people, so to speak, defaulted,—to be, under the Holy Spirit's direction, the leading and most efficient member of Christ's Body. Heir to ancient Rome's position, character, and world-wide influence, to her came the splendid opportunity, and the duty. In a way, and during a certain period, she embraced the opportunity and performed the duty bravely and well. As we have seen, she practically saved the Christianity of the West, in the sixth, seventh and eighth Christian centuries, and in large measure transmitted it to our heathen forefathers. Had she not in time also defaulted, sought grace to "fling away ambition" by which "sin fell the angels," and serve her Lord and His Vicar, the divine Spirit, with half the zeal with which she served the motive of temporal power and authority, again we can say that to-day His Name would be honoured among men, and the nations be rejoicing in His blessed reign of righteousness and peace, as is not yet the case.

But here we can but turn to the other side, suggested by those three wonderful chapters, the 'ninth, tenth, and eleventh, of Romans. We want to, and we may, apply what the Apostle there says of God's gracious intentions in relation to Israel, alike to the Jews and to our sister Church of Rome at the present time. The Apostle's heaviness and sorrow of heart on Israel's account, and his heart's desire and prayer to God for their salvation, together with his confidence that God had not cast away His ancient people, we can and ought to make our feeling and prayer as regards the Jews and our brethren of Rome. Of both we have to believe that they are "beloved for the fathers' sakes," —for the "election,"—since both Churches have been chosen instruments in the Hand of Providence. We have reason to believe that the conversion alike of the one and the other will mean "life from the dead" to multitudes in all parts of the world where Jews or Romanists are found in large numbers.

The words of Dr. Max Green, a Jewish physician of Philadelphia, regarding his own people, are as true as they are eloquent:

"Our mission and destiny are yet before us. We would long since have disappeared, if it had all belonged to the past. The world, the great Christian world, needs us. It needs our zeal for righteousness, our enthusiasm for the ideal. It needs us to help fill the earth with the knowledge of our own Scriptures, with which no nation is yet as familiar as we are. The world needs us, and our Messiah is waiting for us, to take our rightful place in His Kingdom. * * * From being a curse among the nations we shall become a blessing—a blessing to ourselves and a blessing to the world. The time will be hastened when the earth shall become filled with the knowledge of God as the waters cover the sea. The glorious Messianic age will be ushered in and God's kingdom on earth, the great human Brotherhood, under the Fatherhood and Kingship of God and His Anointed, will become an established fact."

Our chief concern here is with the Latin Church. An incalculable force resides in it to-day for the turning of mankind to Christ. Are not the old Roman organizing faculty, and sense of unity, order, and universality, with a certain Roman-soldierly courage and spirit of obedience, plainly in her still? "When thou art converted," said the Lord to Simon Peter, "strengthen the brethren"; and when Anglicans kneel to pray for the Church to which, as a missionary power, English-speaking people, as we have been seeing, owe so large a debt, let them remember that much of that missionary zeal and efficiency are in her still, that the Lord hath need of them, and that without them, transformed by the loving Spirit into a pure spiritual and evangelical power, the glorious Messianic age, and the great human Brotherhood under the Father and His Anointed,—to borrow Dr. Green's words,—will not become established facts for many a century.

The rich catholic truth of the divine Predestination of mankind as one great family in Christ, acquires a still larger significance when seen in connection with two other Scripture verities, the force of which Christians are now learning to appreciate more fully; that is, first that God in creating us in His own likeness, with free wills, necessarily limited to a certain degree the free carrying out of His own will. Already in creation the Godhead, Father, Son and Spirit, graciously humbled Itself so to do for our richer benefit in the end. God has had ever to wait for man to respond to the motions and calls of the Spirit. He may not and will not force us. Christ who said, "I am the light of the world," said also, "Ye are the light of the world," and He must wait for us to be willing to send out our light. He has said, "Ask and ye shall receive," and will therefore wait until we do ask.

It follows, secondly,—and the correct interpretation of St. Peter's words (2d Pet. 3 : 12), in respect to the coming of God's Day appears to favour it,—that by our prayers, if not by our efforts, we can hasten, and therefore can, *per contra*, delay the ripening and perfecting of His great plan for our race. While in the supreme sense it rests with Him, in a secondary and subordinate sense much depends upon us. It gives practical importance to Christian endeavour, and to supplication for blessings on individuals, on Christ's Body the Church, and on Missions. Tennyson's often quoted words,

> "For so the whole round earth is every way
> Bound by gold chains about the feet of God"

acquire broadest significance. We would underline "every way"; feel that we can help God fulfil His glorious purpose every way by praying or working, and delay Him in countless ways by our indifference and idleness.

On the other hand,—and whenever we stand on the seashore and watch the waves and the rising of the tide, and are reminded of God's omnipotence, and constancy to His great purposes of love,—we can appreciate the poetry and the comfort in the lines of Priscilla Leonard (in the *Outlook*):

> "O mighty sea! thy message
> In clanging spray is cast;
> Within God's plan of progress
> It matters not at last
> How wide the shores of evil,
> How strong the reefs of sin—
> The wave may be defeated,
> But the tide is sure to win!"

CONCLUSION

Recurring once more to Bishop Doane's words: "The subject certainly is one of large and deep importance, and it concerns every one of us in the very most essential and fundamental parts and phases of our Christian life;" I venture to "speak boldly, as (I believe) I ought to speak." The hour has come, came indeed long since, when the Spirit-Truth should be on every Christian's tongue, and in his heart; yet in how many able and valuable addresses and treatises on the religious problems of the time is mention barely made of Him! Invoked in every baptism, and on every eucharist of the American Church, He ought to be frequently invoked in sermons and instructions, and called upon in secret by those who listen. True it is that we ought to use the various earthly means and instruments; to work, to influence, to teach as did our Lord Himself; to write as forcibly as it may lie in us to write; but prayer for the Spirit's co-operation was not by Christ dispensed with or unrecognized: He taught in the Spirit, cast out devils, as He said, "by the Finger of God," which meant, by the Spirit. We have but to act and to speak as He did, the exception being this notable one, that in the Pentecostal era the Ascended Lord and His Bride the Church are in the Spirit to do *greater works* than He did while in the flesh.

Herein the wonder of Pentecost chiefly consisted, and consists; and our long Whitsuntide should bring the truth close home to the Church's faith. We need to ask ourselves whether, and where, Christians were to draw a line and say, No more "greater miracles" henceforth; the Pentecostal period is over. By Christ's and the Bride's new privilege and right the Finger of God became the Hand of God; are we using this privilege of power for all it is worth to-day? When was faith to cease being able to "move mountains"? and may not the difficulties which the majority of believers now designate insuperable, the so-called impossible achievements, or iridescent dreams,—of which Church Unity is one,—be the very mountains which faith in the Holy Ghost's guidance and power can succeed in moving? We call ourselves believers: are we believers,—are we Trinitarians,—until we believe implicitly in an ever-present and all-powerful Spirit?

No object lies nearer to His heart than Unity among Christians, and especially within the Church Catholic itself. In this volume so-called burning questions have generally been avoided, and little or nothing is said about the best method of putting their fire out, to save the Lord's "spiritual house" from harm and loss. But the great end itself has not been out of mind; and the hope has been entertained, that one good result of our study may be a clearer vision of the Comforter's power to solve such questions. Lowell in Study Windows speaks of "the universal solvent sought by the alchemists." The view from our window makes it clear that the Holy Ghost is this Universal Solvent in the Church. It is one of His most gracious operations. He unifies men and truths, through love and charity, and by opening men's eyes to see more than one side of a truth; and the two operations are seen united in the verse of the Veni Creator;

> "Thy blessed unction from above
> Is comfort, life, and fire of *love*.
> Enable with perpetual light
> The dulness of our *blinded sight!*"

.   Is it not this way in respect to parties within the Church, or to the Church and Communions dissenting from her? A passage from the Bampton Lectures of 1871 (page 425) may illustrate the point:

"There is no disinclination, on our part," writes Curteis, "to adopt from Dissenters (with the fullest acknowledgments) whatever they have of good and sound and useful. Nor has any one of the more important denominations the slightest necessity, on returning to the Church, to give up one single truth that God has taught them. * * * On the contrary, every such denomination has,—as I have attempted to show in these Lectures,—a banner and a camping ground of its own, within the broad area of the Church of England."

To old men who dream dreams, and young men who seeing visions possess the courage and vigor to aim at realizing them, it becomes every year more evident that the English-speaking race has a singular mission to the world,—to give large portions of it a Christian civilization, of which the inward life is the Spirit of the risen and ascended Lord. Now it is the Spirit Himself who can turn the vision into a reality   He alone can make "Christ for the world we sing" and "The world to Christ *we bring*" one living truth and fact.

If the argument in Chapter IV is sound, then the entire latter half of the Year of Christ is a time in which, for one thing, to present fervently and persistently this same world-obligation of our English race, and of our Church in particular, to the heart and conscience of her people. And may we not believe that one important effect of doing this would be to bring them around again to the solemn Advent time with a clearer conception of its significance as an *end* as truly as a beginning? For the end to be had always in view by each Christian, and by the Church as a Body, is the great spiritual Harvest of God. "Stir up, O Lord, the wills of thy faithful people" would thus acquire sevenfold the richness of meaning that it now has. New "Stir up" petitions would be joined with it at the next Revision. Dear as the familiar Collect for the Second Sunday in Advent is,—much as we need "patience and comfort from God's holy word" for ourselves, and strength to "embrace and hold fast" our own hope of everlasting life,—prayers of a more generous and sympathetic scope would soon add themselves, turning into a strong cry for the speedy conversion of the world those glorious Messianic promises which, long time found close under that Collect, have not had the light of their world-wide meaning in the smallest degree reflected in the Collect. Instead of being poor in prayers for Missions, and bare of invocations of the Spirit upon the various kinds of missionary and social endeavour dependent on Him, our Prayer Book would be enriched with many such, for the Advent time especially. The momentum of the Spirit-teaching and the new inward life in Him, felt in the Advent services, would at length begin, at least, to transform "Christmas" into a veritable new nativity of our blessed Lord and Saviour in His people's hearts. "The bells of the horses" in the snowy streets would, like the bells in the church towers, chime not merely "Holiness unto the Lord,"

but renewed consecration to the all-essential work
of spreading His kingdom; since for this He died and
rose, and His Spirit came; and for this especially were
we ourselves born into the world.   Epiphany also,
and Lent itself, would "sense" the mighty *thrust* of
the greatest practical truth of Christianity, that long
"strangely neglected" truth and power, of which the
latter half of Christ's Year is to remind us.